INDIGENOUS ALLIANCE MAKING

INDIGENOUS ALLIANCE MAKING

Histories of Agency in
Colonial Lowland South America

Edited by
JAMES ANDREW WHITAKER
and **MARK HARRIS**

THE UNIVERSITY OF
ARIZONA PRESS
TUCSON

The University of Arizona Press
www.uapress.arizona.edu

We respectfully acknowledge the University of Arizona is on the land and territories of Indigenous peoples. Today, Arizona is home to twenty-two federally recognized tribes, with Tucson being home to the O'odham and the Yaqui. The University strives to build sustainable relationships with sovereign Native Nations and Indigenous communities through education offerings, partnerships, and community service.

ISBN-13: 978-0-8165-5590-1 (hardcover)
ISBN-13: 978-0-8165-5502-4 (paperback)
ISBN-13: 978-0-8165-5503-1 (ebook)

Cover design by Leigh McDonald
Cover art: Me Ôk Abenkokjêkê from Instituto Kabu - Kayapó Women's Artisans Cooperative, courtesy of Artefato Gallery
Typeset by Sara Thaxton in 10.5/14 Warnock Pro with Lulo, Helvetica Neue LT Std, and Baskerville Compressed

Library of Congress Cataloging-in-Publication Data
Names: Whitaker, James Andrew editor | Harris, Mark, 1969– editor
Title: Indigenous alliance making : histories of agency in colonial lowland South America / James Andrew Whitaker and Mark Harris ; foreword by Cecilia McCallum.
Description: Tucson : University of Arizona Press, 2025. | Includes bibliographical references and index.
Identifiers: LCCN 2024059205 (print) | LCCN 2024059206 (ebook) | ISBN 9780816555901 hardcover | ISBN 9780816555024 paperback | ISBN 9780816555031 ebook
Subjects: LCSH: Indians of South America—Historiography | Indians of South America—History
Classification: LCC F2230.4 .I63 2025 (print) | LCC F2230.4 (ebook) | DDC 980.1—dc23/eng/20250416
LC record available at https://lccn.loc.gov/2024059205
LC ebook record available at https://lccn.loc.gov/2024059206

Printed in the United States of America
♾ This paper meets the requirements of ANSI/NISO Z39.48-1992 (Permanence of Paper).

Contents

Foreword

This book is the result of a three-part series of international workshops, held in 2021 and 2022 at the University of St Andrews, that brought together historians and anthropologists who write about and work with Indigenous peoples in South America to present research on the broad theme of alliances and partnerships. A key aim of the workshops was to contribute to a recent movement within the historiography of the continent that seeks to reorient perspectives in such a way as to provide a greater space for Amerindian peoples' voices to be heard. The primary topic in focus was the making and unmaking of relations. This involved historical relations among Indigenous peoples in the face of European and Latin American colonialist expansion into their territories, as well as historical relations of Indigenous peoples and polities with European invaders, colonizers, and colonialist nation-states. In addition, the different historical and anthropological studies presented in the workshop, most of which are now published as chapters in this book, aimed to counterbalance historical accounts skewed toward a Euro–Latin American perspective that effectively deletes Indigenous people's historical agency. They instead sought to highlight Indigenous peoples' effective and purposeful engagement with outsiders in South America. This engagement often takes the shape of active, conscious, and strategic participation in unfolding events and developing processes. The overall goal behind the project is to reorient the historiography of South America in such a way that the actions and voices of Indigenous people are at the center of attention instead of primarily those of the European and Latin American invaders and colonizers that ring loudest in the historical records.

I was lucky enough to be one of the anthropologists invited to discuss the original papers written for the workshops, each comprising substantive work examining archival and historical sources, as well as, in some cases, ethnographic material collected by the authors. Most of the contributing scholars are historians by training, while some are anthropologists. As such, this book is a result of exchanges between historians and anthropologists, who sought to discuss past and present modes and processes of relating between Amerindian people, colonizers, and invaders, with a focus on the oft-neglected topic of alliance and partnership. It represents the fruits of interdisciplinary collaboration and aims to stimulate a broader engagement between these fields in relation to South America.

The chapters focus on contexts wherein alliances and partnerships were formed historically (and sometimes subsequently obliterated). Methodologically, the chapters employ a double strategy. The authors go about their work using classical methods of archival investigation. By identifying evidence of Indigenous perspectives in archival sources, however scant this is in some cases, they are able to introduce these views in their texts and so counterbalance or at least modulate the dominating voices of colonizers and invaders. But the chapters also inflect historical analyses with insights drawn from reading recent ethnographies of Indigenous peoples. In some cases, they use their own ethnographic fieldwork to inform these historical analyses. Inspired by and engaging with the anthropological literature on a wide range of relevant topics, from acculturation and ethnicity, the body and epistemology, death and eschatology, predation and production, commerce and war, cosmopolitics, kinship, and relatedness and gender, the authors enrich their accounts with a broader examination and understanding of the likely social and cultural contexts within which the events and processes that emerge from their archival research unfolded.

The result is a compact collection that achieves the difficult task of offering clear and eminently readable accounts that bring to life distinct peoples, places, periods, processes, and events. These accounts focus on stories of avoidance, encounter, collaboration, or conflict, simultaneously providing insight into the complexity and multiplicity of the styles and modes of making and unmaking relatedness across Indigenous South America.

This achievement is timely. The book's chapters should not be read simply as academic exercises contributing to a limited area of specialization within history, historical anthropology, or ethnohistory. Rather, wider lessons can be learned from the discussions in its pages. I write this not simply to make the point that the predatory colonial process in all its complexity is ongoing—in fact, accelerating—and that the "lethality of whiteness," as Indigenous anthropologist Felipe Cruz (2022) puts it in his doctoral dissertation, has never been so dangerous to Indigenous people. For beyond direct and imminent threats to Indigenous rights to land, health, and livelihood in South America, and to the maintenance of cultural and ethnic distinction, there are broader dangers. What is ultimately at stake is their continued survival, as well as the survival of the planet. All of this is self-evident to any who have taken the trouble to inform themselves about the implications of the political processes operating in and on the nation-states of contemporary South America, which involve massive deforestation, ecological destruction, and biological desertification, that feed into and sustain world climate disaster. Indigenous people who speak against these processes and organize local resistance have achieved effectiveness and influence on the world stage in recent years. They have also achieved varied degrees of success in affecting the terms of debate within Latin American nations, as Aparecida Vilaça notes in the afterword to this book. Political movements have consolidated and expanded nationally, as well as beyond national frontiers, in diverse spheres and contexts. And Indigenous intellectuals—including anthropologists—have pushed debates into new territories and forced their colleagues and students to requalify and revise key terms and concepts. As this book makes clear, however, all of this has not grown out of an empty field. Nor is it a consequence of "contact" or a mere response to the impact of external historical forces on those who once were seen as "people without history" (Wolf 1982).

The chapters in this book lead us to consider that the paths forged by contemporary Indigenous leaders and intellectuals, as well as the emerging modes of relatedness among them, and between them and outsiders, must not be read—and thereby dismissed—through a trope of "modernity." Rather, they are better envisaged as innovations on conventions, as

Roy Wagner (1975) had it, as reappropriations and reinventions of former styles, and as adaptations and transformations of older forms of dealing with alterity. This is especially the case in situations where they are enacted while confronting and engaging with powerful outsiders. Among other contributions, the present book gives a solid grounding in Indigenous modes and styles of engagement with others. It does this through exploration of concrete engagements in the documented historical past, to which contemporary forms of interaction can be compared, and from which one can often surmise that these forms emerged. For this alone, it is relevant and timely.

—*Cecilia McCallum*

References

Cruz, Felipe Sotto Maior (Tuxá). 2022. "'Letalidade branca': Negacionismo, violência anti-indígena e as políticas de genocídio." PhD diss., Universidade de Brasília.

Wagner, Roy. 1975. *The Invention of Culture*. Chicago: University of Chicago Press.

Wolf, Eric R. 1982. *Europe and the People Without History*. Berkeley: University of California Press.

Acknowledgments

The chapters in this volume have developed from three international virtual workshops organized by Mark Harris and James Andrew Whitaker in 2021 and 2022 at the Centre for Amerindian, Latin American and Caribbean Studies at the University of St Andrews. We would like to thank each of the presenters—Marta Rosa Amoroso, Oiara Bonilla, Marc Brightman, Luiz Costa, Camila Loureiro Dias, Elisa Frühauf Garcia, Kris Lane, Barbara Sommer, Gary Van Valen, and Pirjo Kristiina Virtanen—and the discussants, Cecilia McCallum and Aparecida Vilaça, from these workshops. The discussions and dialogue from these events shaped the themes and orientation of this volume. The third workshop particularly helped hone and further develop the papers that are published herein.

We would like to give special thanks to Allyson Carter at the University of Arizona Press for taking this publishing journey with us and seeing it through to the end. We appreciate her interest, support, and encouragement in this project, as well as her guidance along the way. We thank Melanie Mallon for editing support with the final version of the manuscript. We would also like to thank the two anonymous reviewers whose helpful comments and suggestions improved the chapters and the clarity of the volume.

The chapters in this book are based on archival and ethnographic research. In many cases, this has involved research support through grants and fellowships. We greatly appreciate all of the sources of extramural and intramural funding that have made these research projects possible. For Marta Amoroso, this includes research support from the Coordination for the Improvement of Higher Education Personnel (CAPES) and the Brazilian National Council for Scientific and Technological Development (CNPq) in 2015–20. Camila Loureiro Dias's research was supported by the São Paulo State Research Support Foundation (FAPESP) in 2022. Elisa Frühauf Garcia received research support from the CNPq in 2021 and the Rio de Janeiro State Research Support Foundation in 2022, as well as visiting positions at the Max Planck Institute for Legal History and Legal Theory (2018) and at the Newberry Library (2019/2020). Mark Harris's research was supported by the British Academy, the John Carter Brown Library, and the São Paulo State Research Support Foundation (FAPESP). Kris Lane received research support from Tulane University, as well as a fellowship from the U.S. Fulbright Commission (2005). James Andrew Whitaker's research was supported by the American Philosophical Society, LabEx CEBA, and Tulane University, as well as a MOPGA postdoctoral fellowship (2021–22) and a visiting position at the University of Helsinki (2022).

We would also like to thank all the archivists and librarians who have made our research possible at various institutions in Australia, Europe, North America, and South America. And finally, our deepest and sincere thanks go to our many Indigenous friends in lowland South America, who have been allies and partners to us throughout the research projects that make up these chapters. To the history and memory of their ancestors, we dedicate this edited volume.

—*James Andrew Whitaker and Mark Harris*

INDIGENOUS ALLIANCE MAKING

Introduction

Allies and Partners in Anthropological and
Historical Perspectives

JAMES ANDREW WHITAKER, MARK HARRIS,
AND ELISA FRÜHAUF GARCIA

This volume explores historical relations involving alliances and partnerships between Indigenous people and outsiders in lowland South America. The chapters show how such relations have been formed and developed under a diverse array of colonial and postcolonial circumstances and conditions. In the past and present, Indigenous groups have been subjected to colonial and neocolonial fronts, which have widely ranged in form from military incursions and slaving raids to extractivist economic projects and forced missionization. These fronts have often brought loss, dispossession, and devastation for Indigenous people within an array of contexts. The chapters in this volume focus on the strategic agency of Indigenous groups within these oppressive circumstances and dilemmas.

The historiography of lowland South America has tended to focus on the agency, intentions, and goals of outsiders, who are often Europeans, North Americans, and national elites. It has too often depicted Indigenous people in positions of relative passivity and mere adaptation to outside forces. Nonetheless, in examining past and present relations between Indigenous people and outsiders, anthropologists and historians in recent years have begun to focus on the efforts of regional Indigenous groups to seek, form, and manage strategic relations (Roller 2021; Van Valen 2013; Whitaker 2025). Within this context, "strategy" involves the formulation of aims and goals that are agentively pursued within a framework of local understandings and conceptualizations. The historiography of lowland South America is turning toward a focus on such Indigenous agency, which is understood herein in relation to intentionality and efforts to take the initiative in interactions with both Indigenous and non-Indigenous others. There is a growing emphasis on how Indigenous people have sometimes taken an active role in shaping their histories and overcoming obstacles despite the unfavorable conditions and long odds of success they often faced. Importantly, however, this volume avoids taking a triumphalist approach to agency by focusing on a diverse range of contexts and a broad array of outcomes that have resulted from these Indigenous efforts to form alliances and partnerships (see Asad 2008). While we emphasize agency in historical contexts and narratives, we recognize that past and present efforts at agentive engagements with others do not always result in intended or desired outcomes. Since the cases examined herein concern Indigenous people who were already under colonial rule or on the verge of colonization, their agency was significantly impacted by profound power asymmetries.

With a focus on analyses of historical documents, we examine in this book how Indigenous societies in South America have formed various strategic relations with useful others to defend livelihoods, territories, and symbolic values, as well as to curb external threats and predation. The aim of the volume is to examine the formation and uses of these historical relations across societies within past contexts and to broaden the scope for hearing Indigenous voices within these narratives. While most of the chapters are based on research in colonial archives, we are methodologically aware of how such documents were an instrument of state power and how they played a role in the production of knowledge aimed at ruling local populations (Stoler 2002). Nevertheless, as well-articulated by Ricardo Roque and Kim Wagner (2012, 3), "colonial knowledge enables, rather than deters, the writing of history of other cultures." Within this context, it is important to remember that Indigenous people have successfully registered their voices in these archival sources and that anthropologists and historians have the appropriate theoretical and methodological tools for hearing them.

During the colonial and postcolonial eras, as Indigenous people experienced exploitation from neighboring societies and colonial invaders (Hemming 1978, 1987), new kinds of societies were being formed in lowland South America (Whitehead 1992). Within this context, Indigenous groups often strategically allied with outside entities and forces as a way of acquiring goods and curbing predation and state overreach (Sommer 2005, 2006; Whitaker 2016; see also Conklin 2010). These relations are seen in contexts ranging from missions to intimate relations and from alliance to outright conflict. Indigenous groups' aims varied from political partnerships to personal and collective transformations (Grotti 2022; Vilaça 2016; Whitaker 2025). A range of differently constituted societies emerged, some with distinct political organization and diverse forms of leadership and authority (Brightman 2020; Veber and Virtanen 2017). With an emphasis on the different contexts in which Indigenous relations with outsiders emerged, this volume contributes to historical and anthropological scholarship on Indigenous agency in sociopolitical formations in lowland South America. Overall, we seek to advance recent work on this topic and to build a comparative foundation on which future research concerning Indigenous strategies for engaging with outsiders during the colonial and postcolonial eras can be grounded.

Geographical Focus

The chapters in this volume are centered geographically on the lowlands of South America. This region encompasses what is frequently called Amazonia, generally referring to the basin of the Amazon River and often including its major tributaries and sometimes other major rivers in the region, such as the Orinoco River. The term Amazonia, however, is also often used to refer to the much broader region of lowland South America, which extends far beyond the floodplains of the Amazon and Orinoco Rivers and includes distant parts of South America, such as the Guianas and the Llanos de Mojos. For clarity, we have chosen to refer to lowland South America rather than Amazonia. Although lowland South America has sometimes been used to refer to all areas and peoples not residing in the central Andes (see Combès, Córdoba, and Villar 2020), this is not the sense in which we use this expression here. Instead, we are referring both to the Amazon basin and to other Indigenous territories on the continent with lowland and tropical geographical conditions, as well as enduring Indigenous lifeways. Although the scope of the volume extends a little beyond the geographical lowlands, as in chapter 5 by Kris Lane, the focus remains on lowland South America as understood in this sense. This regional focus is needed to bring together recent work that centers the growing historiographical focus on Indigenous agency in lowland South America.

The international scope of the chapters includes emphases on Bolivia, Brazil, Guyana, and Colombia. There is a particularly strong focus on Brazil throughout the volume. This is perhaps to be expected since Brazil is the largest and geographically most central country in South America. This focus also results, however, from the editors' strong emphasis on creating dialogue between international and interdisciplinary scholarship, which helps to highlight the range of alliances and partnerships created by Indigenous people across the region from the colonial era to the present day. The chapters take different approaches to understanding and conceptualizing such strategic relations of alliance and partnership. They variously focus on marriage, missionization, and cosmological, economic, and political contexts. This range allows for comparison and highlights contrasts between the different circumstances and across the different historical periods addressed throughout the chapters.

Historical Encounters in Lowland South America

The diversity of interactions that Indigenous people in lowland South America historically experienced with institutions and officials, including colonial agents, explorers, governments, the military, missionaries, raiders, rebels, and traders, has been described in the historical literature focused on lowland South America (Cunha 1992; Farage 1991; Garcia 2009; Hemming 1978, 1987; Langfur 2006, 2014). These relations have often been recurrent and complex. Specific historical accounts of such interactions between Indigenous groups and outsiders (primarily Europeans and their descendants) have been written for some regions of Brazil (see Davidson 1970; Harris 2010, 2018; Ibáñez-Bonillo 2019; and Menéndez 1992), the Guianas (see Burnett 2000; Espelt-Bombin 2018; Farage 1991; Rivière 1995; and Whitehead 1988), and Venezuela (see Vidal 2000), as well as intersecting zones like Roraima (Araújo 2006; Santilli 1994). Anthropologists and historians have become interested in how Indigenous groups across lowland South America understand these ongoing relations with regards to historicity (Fausto and Heckenberger 2007; Whitehead 2003) and within the context of various cosmological and ontological frameworks (Albert and Ramos 2002; High 2013).

Updating a line of inquiry from historical research on Tupinambá interactions with Europeans and other enemies (F. Fernandes 1970; see Whitehead and Harbsmeier 2008), Carlos Fausto (2012c) has examined conceptual frameworks in warfare contexts among the Parakanã in Brazil, as well as Indigenous understandings of "contact situations" involving Europeans (Fausto 2002; see also Albert and Ramos 2002). A central focus of such work has been to better understand the continuities involved in Indigenous experiences and perspectives in contrast to the transformations resulting from external influences (see also Perrone-Moisés and Sztutman 2010). Vanessa Grotti (2022), Aparecida Vilaça (2010, 2016), and Eduardo Viveiros de Castro (2011) have also described how Indigenous interactions with Europeans (particularly missionaries) during contact in Brazil were guided by understandings and goals that were different from European expectations. James Andrew Whitaker (2020b, 2025) has explored how Indigenous conceptual frameworks shaped historical interactions between Indigenous people and missionaries in Guyana and how similar frameworks are evinced in contemporary interactions with other kinds of outsiders, such as ecotourists. These are a few examples of recent work that seeks to understand how historical Indigenous relations with outsiders were conceptualized during the colonial era and beyond. Comprehending these frameworks helps clarify Indigenous strategies and goals within these contexts.

Indigenous groups' decisions and actions within these circumstances greatly varied regionally, culturally, and situationally. For example, for the Makushi in British Guiana (now Guyana), contact with Anglican missionaries was part of a larger strategy aimed at curbing slaving raids (Whitaker 2016, 2025). On the other hand, the Caribs (Kariña) in Guyana (Whitehead 1988) and the Munduruku in Brazil (Menéndez 1992) allied with colonial forces against rebellions by enslaved people of African descent, peasants, and other subaltern groups. Considering such historical contrasts, as well as significant cultural differences, it is very important not to represent Indigenous groups as being homogeneous, a portrayal often found in popular culture and unfortunately sometimes also in academic work. Riven by conflict and internal divisions, Indigenous alliances with outsiders sometimes emerged as a means of strengthening one group over its opponents (Almeida 2003; Garcia 2009). The diversity of such relations points to the semantic breadth of "alliance" and "partnership" in Indigenous South America. While such engagements often involve deep relations of cooperation, frequently constituted through marriages, pacts, and other formal and semiformal means, alliances and partnerships may at other times be more provisional or situational, as conditioned by circumstances of mutual interest or need. Such relations with non-Indigenous outsiders, which variously included missionaries, European affines, trade partners, and military allies, may differ at times from those with other Indigenous groups. Partners may become enemies, or they may hover in a liminal space between friendship and enmity (see Fausto 2012a). The motivations driving such relations may also be unclear and sometimes involve ambiguities and even misunderstandings (see Conklin 2010; and Conklin and Graham 1995). Furthermore, Indigenous alliances and partnerships may be formed between either individuals or groups, which are understood here in the broadest sense as sets of local people holding bonds of commonality often centered on kinship, language, lifestyle, and corporeal practices. These variables (particularly concerning marital customs) may condition the terms and conditions of alliances and partnerships in complex ways.

During the past and present, Indigenous people in lowland South America, such as the Makushi and Caribs, but also other traditional peoples, such as *ribeirinhos* (Adams et al. 2008; Harris 2000), have formed and continue to form these kinds of relations with outsiders for strategic purposes. The significance of such interactions is amplified in the present, as relationships are formed to promote conservation and land rights, combat climate change, reverse deforestation, fight unwanted invasions (e.g., from miners and illegal loggers), and obtain the benefits of full citizenship. These Indigenous engagements with outsiders within diverse contemporary contexts reveal ongoing "contact strategies" (Roller 2021), which continue to disrupt outdated historiographical representations depicting Indigenous people as primarily adapting to the agency of Europeans. Contemporary engagements instead reveal the agency deployed by Indigenous people in seeking, forming, and managing intentional and strategic relations with Indigenous and non-Indigenous others (Van Valen 2013; Whitaker 2024, 2025).

Naturally, the theme of alliance making in history and society owes much to Claude Lévi-Strauss, especially his research that led to *Elementary Structures of Kinship* ([1949] 1969). In some of his writings that draw on his fieldwork with the Nambikwara, Lévi-Strauss (1943a, 1943b, 1949) explores relations of warfare, exchange, and marriage across regional networks in lowland South America through marriage, godparenthood, and the "politics of the other" (*politique étrangère*). One of his core questions is how a group attends to their relations with neighboring "others" and whether these others are seen as enemies or as friends and allies. His conclusion is that these diverse relations pivot from one to the other, depending on various factors, such as the perception of the other group during exchange ceremonies and wider relations with neighboring groups. Within this context, Lévi-Strauss (1949, 151–52) contrasts the Western notion of humanity, which is seen as an ever-growing circle of people belonging to the same civilization and religion, as well as often language, with a lowland South American version, which is more of an ensemble in constant oscillation between aggression and cooperation. Indigenous notions of humanity also often avoid the separation of nature and culture that is central to Western ontologies (see Descola 2013; and Viveiros de Castro 1998). Lévi-Strauss is not overly concerned with the contingent (or nonstructural) elements of these relations. He also has little interest in those dimensions that may be initiated by the white or colonial element. As such, he does not spend much effort in addressing the questions that are positioned at the heart of this volume: What is the scale and scope of the ensemble? And who is included in it from an Indigenous point of view? There is limited engagement by Lévi-Strauss concerning how the "alliances" he describes within Indigenous societies are formed and maintained across the larger domains that extend from Indigenous groups to non-Indigenous people like himself.

Despite these limitations, Lévi-Strauss does provide some clues that can be used to address the question that has inspired this volume. In one of his intriguing and delightful early articles, he considers the social and political significance of the brother-in-law relationship across time in Indigenous societies in lowland South America. He suggests that this relationship created a "spatial promiscuity" and facilitated neighboring villages in joining up through cross-cousin marriages (Lévi-Strauss 1943b, 408). European chroniclers from the sixteenth century likened this to the Iberian tradition of *compadrazgo* (i.e., godparenthood, or *compérage* in French) because whites were often incorporated into residential groups through baptism and referred to using the local term for brother-in-law. Over time, according to Lévi-Strauss, these two institutions converged to reflect the structural position of whites in colonial society, where they became co-parents (rather than brothers-in-law per se) through baptism. Relations of affinity could thus be made with them by Indigenous people. Traces of these structural transformations among Indigenous societies are observable today, although Lévi-Strauss's limited ethnographic observations are restricted to the Nambikwara in Brazil. His explanation for the convergence also remains tentative if not hypothetical, since he suggests rather than elaborates the historical sequence of the transformations. This volume takes up the challenge of considering what impact colonization had on Indigenous understandings of making allies and enemies over time. It also considers the frameworks through which such relations were formed and maintained with both Indigenous and non-Indigenous people in lowland South America.

The theme of kinship has somewhat recently been reinvigorated in anthropology. In part, this has involved ethnological observations in lowland South America that have extended the domain of kinship relations and the production of kinship beyond the division of nature and culture (see Cormier 2003; Miller 2019; and Vilaça 2002, 2005). This theme has also received renewed impetus within the context of scholarship focusing specifically on gender relations and women's agency, which had received limited regional attention until the beginning of this century (see Lewin and Silverstein 2016; and McCallum 2001). By placing women at the center of regional interethnic dynamics, this literature has demonstrated the importance of considering gender as a central dimension in analyses of alliances and partnerships with outsiders (Barr 2007; J. A. Fernandes 2003; Garcia and Julio 2024; Sleeper-Smith 2001). This perspective has demonstrated women's agency, including especially the agency of Indigenous women, which had been largely ignored in much previous ethnographic research. It has also highlighted that most European outsiders with whom Indigenous people historically allied or partnered were identified as men. How Indigenous gender perspectives variously adapted to and shaped this dimension of interethnic contact with male outsiders is a topic that anthropologists and historians are still exploring and to which this volume seeks to engage and contribute.

As they did historically with missionaries and various colonial forces, Indigenous people in lowland South America today continue to form alliances and partnerships with businesses, consultants, ecotourists, educational institutions, governments, nongovernmental organizations (NGOs), and other national and international persons and entities as a means of furthering their own aims and goals. Resonating with many historical cases, strategic alliances with outsiders today may sometimes serve as a means of hedging against threats and various contemporary forms of predation (Whitaker 2020b). Such relations can also provide a means (sometimes involving views of outsiders as sources of things) for acquiring desiderata, which can variously include connections, goods, knowledge, money, power, and other resources depending on specific contexts (Conklin 2010; Conklin and Graham 1995, 706). For example, contemporary uses of strategic relations with outsiders to acquire goods and to curb predation can be seen within the context of ecotourism among the Makushi in Guyana (Whitaker 2024, 2025). Somewhat similar relations can also be seen within a separate context in alliances between the Munduruku, *ribeirinhos,* and their external allies in Brazil, who are actively involved in resisting dam building, defending territory, and opposing environmentally and territorially destructive projects and activities, such as unwanted logging and mining (Campbell 2015, 32; Campbell and Miller 2016; Cunha et al. 2017). Such partnerships have also been documented within different historical contexts among people in the Tapajós-Madeira region of Brazil (Harris 2010, 2018; Menéndez 1992; Sweet 1992). Contemporary alliances and partnerships with outsiders sometimes provide curbs against illegal mining, which poisons rivers and food resources; large-scale logging, which degrades landscapes and is associated with climate change by some Indigenous people; and development projects, such as hydroelectric dams, which threaten territories and ecological landscapes (see Whitaker 2020a, 2020b). These alliances sometimes provide Indigenous people with a degree of protection and empowerment against threats, although such relations can also pose risks of their own. Within the context of broader partnership relations, Indigenous people are also increasingly seeking representation and space within universities, museums, and various other cultural institutions. Through these relations, they take leadership roles in building and constructing knowledge about themselves and their communities, as well as speaking on behalf of their people to wider audiences (see Benites 2018; Ramos 2023; and Tupinambá and Valente 2022).

Central Themes and Background

Building on three virtual workshops that were held at the University of St Andrews in 2021 and 2022, the chapters in this volume examine different forms of kinship, leadership, marriage, and social, political, and military relations, as well as understandings of bodily formation and personhood, as they pertain to relations between Indigenous people and outsiders during the colonial and postcolonial eras. Originally conceived to focus primarily on Amazonia, which is the main geographical emphasis of the two social anthropologists who organized the workshops (Mark and James), the project soon expanded to include other areas of lowland South America. As we extended the discussions beyond the Amazon basin and neighboring areas, we realized the comparative potential for considering the theme of alliances and partnerships formed by Indigenous people in the past and present across our historical and ethnographic sites. The inclusion of new papers in the workshops soon broadened the geographical and thematic scope of these analyses. The chapters in this volume have developed out of these three workshops and from our efforts to examine central themes from diverse viewpoints in our work.

The workshops provided us with an opportunity to approach the histories and historiography of Indigenous groups in this region from a comparative vantage point that emphasized the unique agentive engagements and narratives evinced in the past and present. We realized early on that to engage ethically in this work would require a dual focus on the colonial contexts of the histories being considered and the agency of Indigenous people in what were often dire historical situations. Throughout all the historical periods covered in the chapters, from the sixteenth through the twentieth centuries, the relationships of alliance and partnership discussed in this volume occurred within the broader context of immersive colonial and postcolonial processes. Indigenous people often had to respond and act against a backdrop of duress and limited options. These processes gave rise to similar challenges across differences in time, place, and ethnicity. Also at stake was the shared goal of survival. The ability to ally with outsiders was essential to ensuring the survival of many Indigenous groups. Although presenting dangers and risks, such alliances and partnerships conferred advantages through increased access to essential goods, services, and broader connections. These relationships also provided various means for seeking and obtaining help in navigating colonial complexities, as well as for getting the tools needed to build projects for the future. Such collaborative engagements with outsiders, while often presenting stark asymmetries, were also fundamental in the internal conflicts of Indigenous people and sometimes in those between European colonial powers. These relations often empowered Indigenous allies by providing greater access to esoteric knowledge, goods, political inroads, technologies, and trade relations (Garcia 2014; Whitaker 2025). Nonetheless, they also sometimes restricted and encumbered Indigenous groups and often created new forms of vulnerability and asymmetrical relations, as well as frequently unwanted forms of change. These processes, in which Indigenous people were enmeshed, were considered and discussed by the participants in the workshops.

The discussions throughout the workshops led the authors and editors to focus on the concept of "Indigeneity" as a central analytical category for the volume. Although the criteria of inclusion and exclusion from this category (for example, the case of *ribeirinho* groups) have led to the concept being debated and contested at times in broader regional scholarship, we think that Indigeneity best situates the location of identity and struggle that is most foregrounded throughout the chapters. Although Indigeneity is socially and historically constructed in interethnic relationships, it continues to be the site around which many traditional peoples in the region today center their struggles for land, rights, and recognition from national and international governmental institutions. As such, this framing is taken into account in each chapter. We recognize that the adjective Indigenous, however, as well as other social predications discussed herein, is dynamic, and the perception of Indigeneity by non-Indigenous people shifts with historical and geographical contexts. This adds another layer of complexity to the development of alliances and partnerships.

From the colonial era until today, relations between Indigenous people and Europeans (including contemporary descendants of Europeans) in lowland South America vary from mutualistic to predatory and implicate divergent ontological frameworks (Descola 2013). These relations are formed within the context of diverse understandings and are spaces rife with mistranslation and differences in social expectations. In many cases, they involve the emergence of "middle grounds," revealing misunderstandings alongside shared meanings (see Conklin and Graham 1995, 695; Mentore 2017; and White 1991).[1] As such, the themes described throughout these chapters emerge within contexts of intersocietal encounter and friction (Tsing 2004).

Overall, the chapters in this volume center on topics ranging from crosscultural cooperation and antagonism between societies to divergent values and conceptualizations concerning humanity and intimate relations. They consider local contexts involving war and peace, wanted and unwanted missions, as well as reciprocal trade and denials of reciprocity. Both symmetric and asymmetric relations with outsiders are apparent. Gender and kinship are central in some chapters. Overall, the volume provides a contrastive overview of the different kinds of relations historically formed by Indigenous groups with various others in lowland South America and emphasizes how Indigenous people strategically manage their fraught relations with outsiders in the face of intense challenges in the past and present.

Engaging Indigeneity

Indigeneity and its predication (Indigenous) are major themes in this volume and point to both identity and alterity in the historical relations and engagements examined throughout the chapters. A division between Indigenous and non-Indigenous is often central to histories of colonial interaction between Europeans and Native peoples in the Americas. The social and political positioning and categorization of Indigenous people were constructed in the early modern period by European empires as instrumentations of domination. Colonial European categorizations of Indigenous societies were often based more on differences in their relations with Europeans than in actual differences in languages, cultures, or ways of life. For example, the early colonial classification of Carib and Arawak groups was mostly based on European perceptions of their respective tendencies to be bellicose (Caribs) or cooperative and friendly (Arawaks) (see Drummond 1977; and Stone 2017). Subsequent ethnological and ethnohistorical treatment of Indigenous peoples has too often homogenized such groups based on ethnicity and ethnonymity. This has sometimes led to ambiguities in scholarship regarding alliances and partnerships, which often crosscut broader group categorizations. The chapters in this volume emphasize the complexities that are revealed historically in examining such relations and the ways in which cooperative engagements were often divided across (or even within) villages, geographical areas, and ethnic groups. For example, this is highlighted in chapter 6 in relation to the complex divisions and interethnic relations formed by Makushi and Carib groups.

Across lowland South America, Indigenous people were the original inhabitants of the territories that became subject to colonial rule. Under colonial regimes, they were considered radically different from Europeans and were subjected to various forms of exploitation. Being Indigenous often entailed restrictions in rights, recognition, and dignity under such regimes. In the early period of colonization, Europeans even debated the basic humanity of Indigenous people in South America and beyond. For some Europeans, this centered on questions of whether Indigenous people had souls; some Indigenous people seem to have been contrastively more interested in whether European and Indigenous bodies were commensurable (Viveiros de Castro 1998, 475). Despite sporadic and limited efforts by European powers to restrict the abuses and enslavement of Indigenous people, such as the well-known New Laws in the Spanish Empire in 1542, such exploitation of Indigenous people continued to greater and lesser extents throughout the colonial period (van Deusen 2015, 2023). Depending on the time and place, some of these abuses were legally sanctioned while others were made possible by the white supremacy established as a result of the colonial presence.

The history of colonial abuses and exploitation is an important part of the historical and social construction of the term Indigenous. Yet, it is not the only part of its complex emergence. This term has also been strategically used and resignified by Indigenous people themselves as an

instrument of survival and assertion in colonial and postcolonial relations (Garcia 2023). Such uses of colonial categories are an important
part of how Indigenous people have exerted agency in the past and present (Monteiro 2001). Through emphasizing their Indigeneity, they have
pressed for rights and made demands under a common signifier, which
they have deconstructed and infused with fresh content. The hard-won
rights acquired by Indigenous groups under colonial rule have often been
based on this category of "Indigenous" or other similar terms, such as
"autochthonous," "Native," or sometimes "tribal." Self-identification as
Indigenous has been a strategic and often necessary means of assert-
ing collective rights and prerogatives. Nonetheless, this term is essentially used by Indigenous people in their interactions with outsiders. In
contrast, the self-understandings of Indigenous groups in the past and
present are often centered on kinship-based, geographical, commensal,
and linguistic forms of belonging (Baniwa 2006). While we use the term
Indigenous throughout this volume to indicate a common structural position shared by certain groups of people in relation to colonial subjugation, we highlight the heterogeneity of Indigenous groups in relation to
their alliances and partnerships with other Indigenous people and with
non-Indigenous people throughout their histories.

Contribution

Past anthropological and historical scholarship in lowland South America has often tended to emphasize the strategies and goals of outsiders (especially European colonists and their descendants) over those of
Indigenous people. This is particularly the case in relation to colonial
encounters between Indigenous people and Europeans. The growing historiographical emphasis in recent years on the agency of Indigenous people has emerged in tandem with a focus on how they have strategically
engaged with other groups (including both neighbors and outsiders) in
the past and present (Block 1994; Garcia 2014; Harris 2010; Hill 1996;
Roller 2021; Salomon and Schwartz 1999; Van Valen 2013; Whitaker
2024, 2025). As a result of this agentive turn, anthropologists and historians are now taking a closer look at the circumstances and contexts of
past and present encounters between Indigenous people and outsiders

in "regional systems" (Harris 2018; Vidal 2000) in lowland South America and at the different relational modalities (ranging from mastery to mutuality and from reciprocity to predation) that emerge within these encounters (Descola 2013; Fausto 2012c, 2012b; Whitaker 2025; see also Costa 2017). This entails a concomitant focus on Indigenous forms of leadership and political organization (Brightman 2020; Veber and Virtanen 2017; see also Rivière 1984). The emphasis here is centered on how local Indigenous people in this region choose to engage with other Indigenous and non-Indigenous groups within the context of encounters ranging from missionization to marriage and other intimate relations, and from commerce and trade to conflicts and warfare.

With a focus on situations involving crosscultural encounters, the chapters in this volume comparatively examine how Indigenous groups in lowland South America have formed various alliances and partnerships with neighbors and outsiders across the region. This volume goes beyond existing work in the field of ethnohistorical research by placing a comparative focus on both the political organization and the strategic intentions of a range of Indigenous groups in their ongoing engagements with others. Chapters contribute to these themes within several different contexts. Within the context of missions, the chapters move beyond narratives that reduce Indigenous encounters with missionaries to merely cultural and territorial invasions. There is a focus on how Indigenous people across the region conceptualize, appropriate, and engage with missions (see Block 1994; Capredon, Cernadas, and Opas 2023; Carvalho Júnior 2017; Castelnau-L'Estoile 2006; Grotti 2022; Van Valen 2013; Vilaça 2010, 2016; Viveiros de Castro 2011; and Whitaker 2021, 2025). Within the context of gender, kinship, and making bodies, the chapters examine how Indigenous groups engage outsiders and form relationships with them through strategic marriages, networks of kinship, and the convivial and commensal production of bodies (see McCallum 2001; Overing and Passes 2000; and Sommer 2006). In contrast to previous scholarly narratives that centered male agency (Lévi-Strauss 1949), the chapters particularly focus on relations formed by women. Within historical contexts of conflict and predation, authors in this book go beyond a focus on the agency of external forces and explore how Indigenous people have formed new groups in certain situations and created partnerships with outsiders to curb predation. Throughout these different contexts, the chapters highlight the strategies, intentions, and goals of Indigenous people in lowland South America in partnering and allying with outsiders through various relational modalities that reveal significant social and cultural dimensions. The chapters contribute to furthering and clarifying this growing field of ethnohistorical research and to reconceptualizing social, political, and ontological bases of Indigenous relations with outsiders.

This volume is positioned at the cusp of the growing historiographical turn that orients scholarly focus toward Indigenous strategic agency and intentions in past and present relations with outsiders in lowland South America. It advances scholarship on alliances and partnerships across the region while helping to consolidate new understandings concerning Indigenous goals, intentionalities, and related conceptualizations in past contexts of colonial encounter. In doing so, it uses a "regional systems" approach, which facilitates a broader analytical and empirical scale for examining the networks that configure various past and present relations among Indigenous groups in lowland South America and enslaved people of African descent, *ribeirinhos*, and an assortment of Europeans (Espelt-Bombin 2018; Harris 2018; see also Halbmayer 2017). Such an approach also highlights significant differences in the cultural values and social meanings associated with strategic allies and partners (Vidal 2000; Whitaker 2025).

The chapters in the volume have developed as a part of this historiographical turn and provide solid foundations for future research concerning Indigenous strategies and intentionalities in diverse contexts involving interactions with other Indigenous groups and outsiders in lowland South America. What emerges is a complex regional landscape that reveals the formation and reformation of alliances and partnerships along both horizontal and vertical axes. Such relations variously involve engagements with missionaries (see chapters in this volume by Loureiro Dias, Van Valen, and Whitaker), the formation of marriages (see chapter in this volume by Garcia), struggles for land rights (see chapter in this volume by Amoroso), and contexts of war and raiding (see chapters in this volume by Lane and Whitaker). These historical contexts of engagement are reflected in contemporary situations, such as interethnic and international partnerships in the Xingu (Turner and Turner 2005, 2006) and Munduruku alliances against territorial incursions (Campbell 2015,

32). With an increasing number of historical case studies in recent years highlighting Indigenous agency in regional relations with outsiders, there is a need to consolidate the different strands of research within this field and to provide a reference point for future work. That is the primary goal of this volume.

Road Map of the Chapters

The first two chapters in this book center on Indigenous engagements with others within the context of missions and present complementary approaches to examining alliances, partnerships, and Indigenous agency in relation to historical missionization. The first chapter, by Camila Loureiro Dias, examines Indigenous engagements with the Jesuit missionary Antônio Vieira during the seventeenth century in the Serra de Ibiapaba, in northeast Brazil, within the contexts of trade and Portuguese-Dutch rivalry. The author draws from Vieira's writings to describe his philosophical perspectives on Indigenous missionization and what he perceived as the normativity of consensus and agreed-on contracts in relations between the Portuguese and Indigenous societies. Within this framework, even though the missions did not always take the normative form, Indigenous people emerged with free will and with rights to choose their own allegiances and alliances. Although the chapter focuses on Vieira, it highlights early recognition of the agency with which Indigenous people in lowland South America form external relations. The second chapter, by Gary Van Valen, explores Mojo encounters with Jesuit missionaries during the late seventeenth century in what is now Bolivia. His provocative title, "These Fathers Make Us People," refers to the notion in Amazonian ethnology of bodies and humanity itself being constructed (and potentially lost) through practices and interactions with others. He uses Jesuit sources and related analyses of the Mojo language to reconstruct Mojo concepts of humanity and nonhumanity and identifies relevant predications associated with each. Echoing accounts from other areas in lowland South America, Van Valen shows how conversion became associated with transformation and a new way of being human. This emphasis on the agentive and relational production of humanity highlights the broader context of alliances and partnerships in this case and foregrounds both the significance and the ontological stakes of engagements with others for many Indigenous groups across the region.

Chapters 3 and 4 focus on Indigenous engagements with others within the contexts of gender, kinship, and making bodies. These chapters examine contrastive periods and use different approaches for considering these contexts. The third chapter, by Elisa Frühauf Garcia, focuses on Indigenous women and related cultural depictions at the national level in Brazil since the sixteenth century. With a primary focus on São Paulo and the early period of colonial society in Brazil, she analyzes the narratives and representations that variously depict Indigenous women as marginal to Brazilian colonial history, even though they were actually foundational because of the essential bonds they formed through marriage with Europeans. The chapter specifically emphasizes the agency of Indigenous women in forming historical alliances and partnerships. In the fourth chapter, Marta Amoroso examines more recent Mura relations with outsiders, in the lower Madeira region of Brazil in the late twentieth century, within the context of the self-demarcation of the Cunhã-Sapucaia Indigenous Land. This chapter shows how Mura leaders have revised and updated their alliances and partnerships with outsiders under pressing circumstances. Amoroso discusses relevant Mura concepts concerning outsiders, the conditions under which allied relations change over time, and how the production of similar bodies is connected to these relational processes.

The final two chapters center on Indigenous engagements with outsiders and others within contexts of conflict and predation, which variously range from warfare to slaving raids. In chapter 5, Kris Lane investigates Indigenous resistance and eventual defeat by Europeans in the Pacific lowlands of southwestern Colombia during the late sixteenth and seventeenth centuries. He describes how an Indigenous group called the Sindaguas, who were calumniated by the European colonists as headhunters, formed within the broader circumstances of recurrent conflict in their region. Their ethnogenesis reveals agentive dimensions in the formation of Indigenous partnerships under Spanish colonial pressure. This ended in conquest and a mass beheading in 1635. The sixth and final chapter, by James Andrew Whitaker, explores Makushi relations of alliance and partnership with European colonists, missionaries, and other Indigenous groups against the backdrop of slaving raids during the eighteenth and nineteenth centuries in Dutch and later British Guiana (present-day Guyana). Whitaker examines such relations in both symmetric and asymmetric contexts and describes how Makushi people exerted agency and strategy in forming partnerships with outsiders to curb predations aimed against them at the time. The chapter ends by reemphasizing the significance of the historiographical turn toward Indigenous agency in lowland South America.

The chapters present a variety of cases depicting relations of alliance and partnership across this important region. Coming from Bolivia, Brazil, Colombia, Guyana, and Peru, these cases evince Indigenous agency and strategy in engaging with outsiders for various purposes, from obtaining material goods to creating political connections and forming curbs against predation. The circumstances are diverse. Yet, they are largely centered on colonialism and the constraints that it posed for many Indigenous groups. The volume as a whole helps elucidate the forms that alliances and partnerships have historically taken across the region and contributes to a growing historiographical turn toward Indigenous people as historical actors and not merely passive subjects in their past and present engagements with others.

Note

1. *Compérage* may sometimes implicate such "middle grounds" in relation to alliances (see Lévi-Strauss 1943b).

References

Adams, Cristina, Rui Murrieta, Walter Neves, and Mark Harris. 2008. *Amazon Peasant Societies in a Changing Environment: Political Ecology, Invisibility and Modernity in the Rainforest.* New York: Springer.

Albert, Bruce, and Alcida Rita Ramos, eds. 2002. *Pacificando o branco: Cosmologias do contato no Norte-Amazônico.* São Paulo: UNESP.

Almeida, Maria Regina Celestino de. 2003. *Metamorfoses indígenas: Identidade e cultura nas aldeias coloniais do Rio de Janeiro.* Rio de Janeiro: Arquivo Nacional.

Araújo, Melvina. 2006. *Do corpo à alma: Missionários da Consolata e índios macuxi em Roraima.* São Paulo: FAPESP.

Asad, Talal. 2008. "Agency and Pain: An Exploration." *Culture and Religion* 1 (1): 29–60.

Barr, Juliana. 2007. *Peace Came in the Form of a Woman: Indians and Spaniards in the Texas Borderlands.* Chapel Hill: University of North Carolina Press.

Benites, Tonico. 2018. "Trajetória de antropólogo indígena e sua importância para os povos indígenas: Desafios, conquistas e perspectivas." In *A antropologia e a esfera pública no Brasil: Perspectivas e Prospectivas sobre a Associação Brasileira de Antropologia no seu 60° Aniversário*, edited by Antonio Carlos de Souza Lima, Jane Felipe Beltrão, Andréa Lobo, Sergio Castilho, Paula Lacerda, and Patricia Osorio, 537–42. Brasília: ABA Publicações.

Block, David. 1994. *Mission Culture on the Upper Amazon: Native Tradition, Jesuit Enterprise, and Secular Policy in Moxos, 1660–1880*. Lincoln: University of Nebraska Press.

Brightman, Marc. 2020. *The Imbalance of Power: Leadership, Masculinity and Wealth in the Amazon*. Oxford: Berghahn.

Burnett, D. Graham. 2000. *Masters of All They Surveyed: Exploration, Geography, and a British El Dorado*. Chicago: University of Chicago Press.

Campbell, Jeremy M. 2015. *Conjuring Property: Speculation and Environmental Futures in the Brazilian Amazon*. Seattle: University of Washington Press.

Campbell, Jeremy, and Theresa Miller. 2016. "Conjuring Property: An Interview with Jeremy Campbell." *Anthropology News* 57 (9): e141–e142.

Capredon, Élise, César Ceriani Cernadas, and Minna Opas, eds. 2023. *Indigenous Churches: Anthropology of Christianity in Lowland South America*. New York: Springer.

Carvalho Júnior, Almir Diniz de. 2017. *Índios cristãos: Poder, magia e religião na Amazônia colonial*. Curitiba, Brazil: Editora CRV.

Castelnau-L'Estoile, Charlotte de. 2006. "The Uses of Shamanism: Evangelizing Strategies and Missionary Models in Seventeenth-Century Brazil." In *The Jesuits II: Cultures, Sciences, and the Arts, 1540–1773*, edited by John W. O'Malley, Gauvin Alexander Bailey, Steven J. Harris, and T. Frank Kennedy, 616–37. Toronto: University of Toronto Press.

Combès, Isabelle, Lorena Córdoba, and Diego Villar. 2020. "Anthropology of the South American Lowlands." In *Bérose: Encyclopédie internationale des histoires de l'anthropologie*, article 2131. Paris: Bérose. https://www.berose.fr/article2131.html.

Conklin, Beth A. 2010. "For Love or Money? Indigenous Materialism and Humanitarian Agendas." In *Editing Eden: A Reconsideration of Identity, Politics, and Place in Amazonia*, edited by Frank Hutchins and Patrick C. Wilson, 127–50. Lincoln: University of Nebraska Press.

Conklin, Beth A., and Laura R. Graham. 1995. "The Shifting Middle Ground: Amazonian Indians and Eco-Politics." *American Anthropologist* 97 (4): 695–710.

Cormier, Loretta A. 2003. *Kinship with Monkeys: The Guajá Foragers of Eastern Amazonia*. New York: Columbia University Press.

Costa, Luiz. 2017. *The Owners of Kinship: Asymmetrical Relations in Indigenous Amazonia*. Chicago: University of Chicago Press.

Cunha, Manuela Carneiro da, ed. 1992. *História dos índios no Brasil*. São Paulo: FAPESP.

Cunha, Manuela Carneiro da, Ruben Caixeta, Jeremy M. Campbell, Carlos Fausto, José Antonio Kelly, Claudio Lomnitz, Carlos D. Londoño Sulkin, Caio Pompeia, and Aparecida Vilaça. 2017. "Indigenous Peoples Boxed in by Brazil's Political Crisis." *HAU: Journal of Ethnographic Theory* 7 (2): 403–26.

Davidson, David. 1970. "Rivers and Empire: The Madeira Route and the Incorporation of the Brazilian Far West, 1737–1808." PhD diss., Yale University.

Descola, Philippe. 2013. *Beyond Nature and Culture.* Chicago: University of Chicago Press.

Drummond, Lee. 1977. "On Being Carib." In *Carib-Speaking Indians: Culture, Society, and Language,* edited by Ellen B. Basso, 76–88. Tucson: University of Arizona Press.

Espelt-Bombin, Silvia. 2018. "Makers and Keepers of Networks: Amerindian Spaces, Migrations, and Exchanges in the Brazilian Amazon and French Guiana, 1600–1730." *Ethnohistory* 65 (4): 597–620.

Farage, Nádia. 1991. *As muralhas dos sertões: Os povos indígenas no rio Branco e a colonização.* São Paulo: Paz e Terra.

Fausto, Carlos. 2002. "The Bones Affair: Indigenous Knowledge Practices in Contact Situations Seen from an Amazonian Case." *Journal of the Royal Anthropological Institute* 8 (4): 669–90.

Fausto, Carlos. 2012a. "The Friend, the Enemy, and the Anthropologist: Hostility and Hospitality among the Parakanã (Amazonia, Brazil)." In "The Return to Hospitality: Strangers, Guests, and Ambiguous Encounters," special issue, *Journal of the Royal Anthropological Institute* 18 (s1): 196–209.

Fausto, Carlos. 2012b. "Too Many Owners: Mastery and Ownership in Amazonia." In *Animism in Rainforest and Tundra: Personhood, Animals, Plants and Things in Contemporary Amazonia and Siberia,* edited by Marc Brightman, Vanessa Elisa Grotti, and Olga Ulturgasheva, 29–47. Oxford: Berghahn.

Fausto, Carlos. 2012c. *Warfare and Shamanism in Amazonia.* Translated by David Rodgers. Cambridge: Cambridge University Press.

Fausto, Carlos, and Michael Heckenberger, eds. 2007. *Time and Memory in Indigenous Amazonia: Anthropological Perspectives.* Gainesville: University Press of Florida.

Fernandes, Florestan. 1970. *A função social da guerra na sociedade Tupinambá.* São Paulo: Pioneira/Edusp.

Fernandes, João Azevedo. 2003. *De cunhã a mameluca: A mulher Tupinambá e o nascimento do Brasil.* João Pessoa, Brazil: Editora Universitária/UFPB.

Garcia, Elisa Frühauf. 2009. *As diversas formas de ser índio: Políticas indígenas e políticas indigenistas no extremo sul da América portuguesa.* Rio de Janeiro: Arquivo Nacional.

Garcia, Elisa Frühauf. 2014. "Trocas, guerras e alianças na formação da sociedade colonial." In *O Brasil Colonial: 1443–1580,* edited by João Fragoso and Maria de Fátima Gouvêa, 317–55. Rio de Janeiro: Civilização Brasileira.

Garcia, Elisa Frühauf. 2023. "Quem eram os índios na Época Moderna? Identidades, direito e agêcia nos Impérios ibéricos." In *Práticas da justiça: Desigualdades sociorraciais no mundo ibérico (séculos XVI-XVIII)*, edited by Renato Franco, Silvia Patuzzi, and Marcelo Wanderley, 53–62. São Paulo: Hucitec.

Garcia, Elisa Frühauf, and Suelen Siqueira Julio. 2024. "Trajetórias indígenas." In *A Época Moderna*, edited by André de Melo Araújo, Andréa Doré, Luís Filipe Silvério Lima, Marília de Azambuja Ribeiro Machel, and Rui Luis Rodrigues, 319–44. Petrópolis: Vozes.

Grotti, Vanessa. 2022. *Nurturing the Other: First Contacts and the Making of Christian Bodies in Amazonia*. Oxford: Berghahn.

Halbmayer, Ernst. 2017. "Rethinking Culture, Area, and Comparison from the Axial Age to the Contemporary Multi-Centric World." *Zeitschrift für Ethnologie* 142 (2): 157–80.

Harris, Mark. 2000. *Life on the Amazon: An Anthropology of a Brazilian Peasant Village*. Oxford: Oxford University Press/British Academy.

Harris, Mark. 2010. *Rebellion on the Amazon: The Cabanagem, Race, and Popular Culture in the North of Brazil, 1798–1840*. Cambridge: Cambridge University Press.

Harris, Mark. 2018. "The Making of Regional Systems: The Tapajós/Madeira and Trombetas/Nhamundá Regions in the Lower Brazilian Amazon, Seventeenth and Eighteenth Centuries." *Ethnohistory* 65 (4): 621–45.

Hemming, John. 1978. *Red Gold: The Conquest of the Brazilian Indians*. London: Macmillan.

Hemming, John. 1987. *Amazon Frontier: The Defeat of the Brazilian Indians*. Cambridge, Mass.: Harvard University Press.

High, Casey. 2013. "Lost and Found: Contesting Isolation and Cultivating Contact in Amazonian Ecuador." *HAU: Journal of Ethnographic Theory* 3 (3): 195–221.

Hill, Jonathan D. 1996. *History, Power, and Identity: Ethnogenesis in the Americas, 1492–1992*. Iowa City: University of Iowa Press.

Ibáñez-Bonillo, Pablo. 2019. "The Portuguese Conquest of the Amazon: Native Networks and Riverine Frontiers (Early Seventeenth Century)." In *Rivers and Shores: "Fluviality" and the Occupation of Colonial Amazonia*, edited by Rafael Chambouleyron and Luís Costa e Sousa, 33–62. Peterborough, Ont.: Baywolf.

Langfur, Hal. 2006. *The Forbidden Lands: Colonial Identity, Frontier Violence, and the Persistence of Brazil's Eastern Indians, 1750–1830*. Stanford, Calif.: Stanford University Press.

Langfur, Hal, ed. 2014. *Native Brazil: Beyond the Convert and the Cannibal, 1500–1900*. Albuquerque: University of New Mexico Press.

Lévi-Strauss, Claude. 1943a. "Guerre et Commerce chez les Indiens de l'Amérique du Sud." In *Renaissance: Revue Trimestrielle, Extrait*, vol. 1, nos. 1–2, 122–39. New York: Ecole libre des Hautes Études.

Lévi-Strauss, Claude. 1943b. "The Social Use of Kinship Terms among Brazilian Indians." *American Anthropologist* 45 (3): 398–409.

Lévi-Strauss, Claude. 1949. "La politique étrangère d'une société primitive." *Politique étrangère* 14 (2): 139–52.

Lévi-Strauss, Claude. (1949) 1969. *The Elementary Structures of Kinship*. Boston: Beacon.

Lewin, Ellen, and Leni M. Silverstein, eds. 2016. *Mapping Feminist Anthropology in the Twenty-First Century*. New Brunswick, N.J.: Rutgers University Press.

McCallum, Cecilia. 2001. *Gender and Sociality in Amazonia: How Real People Are Made*. London: Routledge.

Menéndez, Miguel A. 1992. "A área Madeira-Tapajós: Situação de contato e relações entre colonizador e indígenas." In *História dos índios no Brasil*, edited by Manuela Carneiro da Cunha, 281–96. São Paulo: CDL/FAPESP/SMC.

Mentore, Laura. 2017. "The Virtualism of 'Capacity Building' Workshops in Indigenous Amazonia: Ethnography in the New Middle Grounds." *HAU: Journal of Ethnographic Theory* 7 (2): 279–307.

Miller, Theresa L. 2019. *Plant Kin: A Multispecies Ethnography in Indigenous Brazil*. Austin: University of Texas Press.

Monteiro, John. 2001. "Entre o etnocídio e a etnogênese: identidades indígenas coloniais." In *Tupis, tapuias e historiadores*, 53–78. Thesis for professorial chair, Universidade de Campinas.

Overing, Joanna, and Alan Passes, eds. 2000. *The Anthropology of Love and Anger: The Aesthetics of Conviviality in Native Amazonia*. New York: Routledge.

Perrone-Moisés, Beatriz, and Renato Sztutman. 2010. "Notícias de uma certa confederação Tamoio." *Mana* 16 (2): 401–33.

Ramos, Alcida. 2023. "Intelectuais indígenas abraçam a antropologia: Ela ainda será a mesma?" *Anuário Antropológico* 48 (1): 11–27.

Rivière, Peter. 1984. *Individual and Society in Guiana: A Comparative Study of Amerindian Social Organisation*. Cambridge: Cambridge University Press.

Rivière, Peter. 1995. *Absent-Minded Imperialism: Britain and the Expansion of Empire in Nineteenth-Century Brazil*. New York: Tauris Academic Studies.

Roller, Heather F. 2021. *Contact Strategies: Histories of Native Autonomy in Brazil*. Stanford, Calif.: Stanford University Press.

Roque, Ricardo, and Kim A. Wagner. 2012. Introduction to *Engaging Colonial Knowledge: Reading European Archives in World History*, edited by Ricardo Roque and Kim A. Wagner, 1–32. New York: Palgrave Macmillan.

Salomon, Frank, and Stuart B. Schwartz. 1999. *The Cambridge History of the Native Peoples of the Americas*. Vol. 3, parts 1–2, *South America*. Cambridge: Cambridge University Press.

Santilli, Paulo. 1994. *Fronteiras da república: História e política entre os Macuxi no vale do rio Branco*. São Paulo: NHII-USP/FAPESP.

Sleeper-Smith, Susan. 2001. *Indian Women and French Men: Rethinking Cultural Encounter in the Western Great Lakes*. Amherst: University of Massachusetts Press.

Sommer, Barbara A. 2005. "Colony of the Sertão: Amazonian Expeditions and the Indian Slave Trade." *Americas* 61 (3): 401–28.

Sommer, Barbara A. 2006. "Cracking Down on the Cunhamenas: Renegade Amazonian Traders under Pombaline Reform." *Journal of Latin American Studies* 38 (4): 767–91.

Stoler, Ann Laura. 2002. "Colonial Archives and the Arts of Governance." *Archival Science* 2 (1–2): 87–109.

Stone, Erin. 2017. "Chasing 'Caribs': Defining Zones of Legal Indigenous Enslavement in the Circum-Caribbean, 1493–1542." In *Slaving Zones: Cultural Identities, Ideologies, and Institutions in the Evolution of Global Slavery*, edited by Jeff Fynn-Paul and Damian Alan Pargas, 118–47. Leiden: Brill.

Sweet, David. 1992. "Native Resistance in Eighteenth-Century Amazonia: The 'Abominable Muras' in War and Peace." *Radical History Review* 53:49–80.

Tsing, Anna Lowenhaupt. 2004. *Friction: An Ethnography of Global Connection.* Princeton, N.J.: Princeton University Press.

Tupinambá, Glicéria, and Renata Curcio Valente. 2022. "O recado do manto na obra de Célia Tupinambá: Em busca de uma dialoga profunda." In *Espaço, imagem e cultura*, edited by Carla Costa Dias, Carlos Azambuja, Dinah de Oliveira, Helenise Guimarães, Renata Curcio Valente, Rogéria de Ipanema, and Teresa Bastos, 28–55. São João de Meriti, Brazil: Desalinho.

Turner, Terry, and Vanessa Fajans-Turner. 2005. "Interethnic Alliances among Indigenous and Brazilian 'Peoples of the Xingu.'" *Anthropology News* 46 (3): 27–31.

Turner, Terry, and Vanessa Fajans-Turner. 2006. "Political Innovation and Inter-Ethnic Alliance: Kayapo Resistance to the Developmentalist State." *Anthropology Today* 22 (5): 3–10.

van Deusen, Nancy E. 2015. *Global Indios: The Indigenous Struggle for Justice in Sixteenth-Century Spain.* Durham, N.C.: Duke University Press.

van Deusen, Nancy E. 2023. "Why Indigenous Slavery Continued in Spanish America after the New Laws of 1542." *Americas* 80 (3): 395–432.

Van Valen, Gary. 2013. *Indigenous Agency in the Amazon: The Mojos in Liberal and Rubber-Boom Bolivia, 1842–1932.* Tucson: University of Arizona Press.

Veber, Hanne, and Pirjo Virtanen. 2017. *Creating Dialogues: Indigenous Perceptions and Changing Forms of Leadership in Amazonia.* Boulder: University Press of Colorado.

Vidal, Silvia M. 2000. "Kuwé Duwákalumi: The Arawak Sacred Routes of Migration, Trade, and Resistance." *Ethnohistory* 47 (3–4): 635–67.

Vilaça, Aparecida. 2002. "Making Kin out of Others in Amazonia." *Journal of the Royal Anthropological Institute* 8 (2): 347–65.

Vilaça, Aparecida. 2005. "Chronically Unstable Bodies: Reflections on Amazonian Corporalities." *Journal of the Royal Anthropological Institute* 11 (3): 445–64.

Vilaça, Aparecida. 2010. *Strange Enemies: Indigenous Agency and Scenes of Encounters in Amazonia.* Durham, N.C.: Duke University Press.

Vilaça, Aparecida. 2016. *Praying and Preying: Christianity in Indigenous Amazonia.* Berkeley: University of California Press.

Viveiros de Castro, Eduardo. 1998. "Cosmological Deixis and Amerindian Perspectivism." *Journal of the Royal Anthropological Institute* 4 (3): 469–88.

Viveiros de Castro, Eduardo. 2011. *The Inconstancy of the Indian Soul: The Encounter of Catholics and Cannibals in 16th-Century Brazil.* Chicago: Prickly Paradigm.

Whitaker, James Andrew. 2016. "Amerindians in the Eighteenth Century Plantation System of the Guianas." *Tipití* 14 (3): 30–43.

Whitaker, James Andrew. 2020a. "Climatic and Ontological Change in the Anthropocene among the Makushi in Guyana." *Ethnos* 85 (5): 843–60.

Whitaker, James Andrew. 2020b. "Strategic Alliance and the Plantationocene among the Makushi in Guyana." *Social Anthropology* 28 (4): 881–96.

Whitaker, James Andrew. 2021. "Totemic Outsiders: Ontological Transformation among the Makushi." *Religion and Society* 12 (1): 70–85.

Whitaker, James Andrew. 2024. "Shamanic Alliance in the Touristic Borderzone: Strategic Hospitality and Ontology at Surama Eco-Lodge in Guyana." *Journal of Latin American and Caribbean Anthropology* 29 (1): 38–49.

Whitaker, James Andrew. 2025. *The Shamanism of Eco-Tourism: History and Ontology among the Makushi in Guyana.* Cambridge: Cambridge University Press.

White, Richard. 1991. *The Middle Ground: Indians, Empires, and Republics in the Great Lakes Region, 1650–1815.* Cambridge: Cambridge University Press.

Whitehead, Neil L. 1988. *Lords of the Tiger Spirit: A History of the Caribs in Colonial Venezuela and Guyana, 1498–1820.* Dordrecht: Foris.

Whitehead, Neil L. 1992. "Tribes Make States and States Make Tribes: Warfare and the Creation of Colonial Tribes and States in Northeastern South America." In *War in the Tribal Zone: Expanding States and Indigenous Warfare,* edited by R. Brian Ferguson and Neil L. Whitehead, 127–50. Santa Fe, N.Mex.: School for Advanced Research Press.

Whitehead, Neil L. 2003. *Histories and Historicities in Amazonia.* Lincoln: University of Nebraska Press.

Whitehead, Neil L., and Michael Harbsmeier, eds. 2008. *Hans Staden's True History: An Account of Cannibal Captivity in Brazil.* Durham, N.C.: Duke University Press.

CHAPTER 1

António Vieira Among the Indigenous People of the Serra de Ibiapaba

Sovereignty and Diplomacy

CAMILA LOUREIRO DIAS

António Vieira (1608–97) was a prominent Jesuit missionary known for his work among Indigenous peoples in Brazil. Born in Lisbon, Vieira's mission work and political negotiations significantly acted within the Portuguese empire and colonies during almost all of the seventeenth century. His writings offer crucial insights into colonial Portuguese strategies and interactions with Indigenous communities. They reflect both the challenges of missionary work and the broader geopolitical and economic motivations behind European colonization.

First published in 1736, Vieira's *Report of Serra de Ibiapaba Mission* is a curious text whose trajectory, potential recipients, and true purpose have not yet been sufficiently elucidated.[1] This text is historically important as it provides a unique perspective on the relations between the Portuguese and Indigenous communities during a period of intense colonial and religious expansion. The narrative presents a nuanced view of Vieira's mission, highlighting the resistance and agency of the Indigenous people rather than portraying them as passive recipients of conversion. The report not only documents the geopolitical context of Portuguese and Dutch rivalries but also highlights Vieira's advocacy within this context for the autonomy of Indigenous peoples, portraying them as active agents rather than passive subjects in the colonial encounter.

Through an analysis of Vieira's *Report*, this chapter explores how his missionary activities were aimed at converting the Indigenous population to Catholicism and submission to the Portuguese Crown. It emphasizes Vieira's view that this process should be conducted with the consent of the Indigenous communities and should respect their sovereignty and freedom. After briefly retracing his biography within the imperial geopolitical context, the chapter analyzes the strategies Vieira employed in his mission in Ibiapaba, the challenges he faced, and the broader implications of his mission within the context of colonial power dynamics. Having had diplomatic experience in Europe before becoming a missionary in Maranhão, Vieira seems to have viewed his experience in Ibiapaba more as a diplomatic mission than as a purely religious one. This provides a new perspective in analyzing his writings about Indigenous peoples.

To understand his ideas requires two contextual pieces of information at the outset. The first is the Portuguese-Dutch global rivalry in the spice trade. The Ibiapaba mission was one episode in the "global struggle" between the Portuguese and Dutch for control of overseas markets (Boxer 1969; Cardoso 2019). The second is the local competition between settlers and clerics for control of Indigenous labor. Located in the frontier region, the Serra de Ibiapaba mission was relevant to the Portuguese Crown for the trade in violet wood and amber, as well as for overland communication between the Brazilian coast and the frontier (known as Maranhão). Vieira therefore believed it was necessary to neutralize Dutch influence in the region. To do so, it was first essential to protect the Indigenous people from the "greed" of the local settlers.

Vieira: Cleric, Politician, and Missionary

António Vieira was no more than sixteen years old in 1624 when he witnessed troops from the Dutch West India Company landing in Salvador (Azevedo [1918] 1992). Two years later, in 1626, he reported this event in an annual letter to the general of the company, under the command of the superiors of the College of Bahia. The Dutch occupation lasted only a year. In 1630, however, the Dutch returned. They invaded Recife, in the captaincy of Pernambuco, and remained there until 1654. In 1640, they also seized Luanda, in Angola, and São Luís, in Maranhão. Luanda was taken to guarantee the supply of slaves to Recife. São Luís was seized to expand the production of sugarcane and to trade with Indigenous people in the region. The Dutch remained in São Luís for two years, until they were driven out by the local population. Meanwhile, they made alliances with the Indigenous nations of the coast and inland. They did similarly in Pernambuco.

The year 1640 also saw the restoration of Portuguese independence from Spain, and Vieira traveled to Lisbon to swear obedience to King João IV. He was soon tasked with urgent political missions and became a diplomat for the Portuguese empire. For twelve years, Vieira traveled to France, England, the Netherlands, and Rome to negotiate new procedures for the inquisition against Jews and New Christians.[2] He sought to create Dutch-style trading companies. He also tried to arrange a marriage between the heir to the Portuguese Crown and a French princess, as well as to negotiate the purchase of Pernambuco and later its handing over to the Dutch. He failed in all these negotiations, was almost expelled from the Jesuit Order, and was the target of denunciations to the Holy Office. Despite being protected by the Portuguese king, he left for Maranhão in 1652 to escape his enemies.[3] By this point, he had been given responsibility for taking over Luís Figueira's fruitless project, begun some years earlier, of establishing Jesuit mission villages along the banks of the Amazon River.

The history of the Maranhão mission dates to 1607. At that time, two priests, Francisco Pinto and Luís Figueira, tried to travel there by land from Pernambuco. After Pinto's death among the Indigenous groups of the Serra de Ibiapaba, the expedition was interrupted. Luís Figueira subsequently turned back. In 1638, he obtained a license from Philip IV granting him control of the Maranhão missions. In 1643, however, he was shipwrecked and killed by the Indigenous groups of Ilha de Joanes (Marajó). Despite efforts to continue the mission, the Jesuits had no effective presence until Vieira's arrival as superior of the mission in the beginning of 1653.

Vieira already knew what was waiting for him when he landed in São Luís. This province of the Portuguese empire was the closest geographically to Portugal. Yet it was the most distant politically. Local settlers and clerics there disputed control of Indigenous labor. Vieira tried to reconcile them but was met with resistance from both settlers and local authorities. He went back to Lisbon in 1654 to fight for a new policy concerning Indigenous people. He returned with a law that guaranteed prerogatives for the Jesuits in relation to the Indigenous people. A new governor, André Vidal de Negreiros, who had fought against the Dutch, accompanied him to ensure its implementation.

Back from Lisbon, Vieira organized various missions in Maranhão. He distributed his small army of missionaries among the existing settlements and devised a strategy to create new missions. He was personally involved in two missions, located in geopolitically strategic locations, where his previous companions (Francisco Pinto and Luís Figueira) had been killed. The first mission was among the Nheengaib in 1656. These were the inhabitants of the island of Joanes, who had resisted the Portuguese. The second was the Serra de Ibiapaba mission in 1660.

Concerning the latter, Vieira wrote the *Report of the Serra de Ibiapaba Mission* in the middle of 1661. It describes the reasons, difficulties, and results of his work in "reducing" the Indigenous people to Christianity and submission to colonial rule. Unlike other Jesuit reports, which were intended to inspire a missionary vocation and to strengthen Jesuit identity, this text consists of an unusual mixture of letters, chronicles, and travel stories (Ventura 2016, 36). It also has a strong political character, which situates it outside the norm for Jesuit writings of this type. In his narrative, Vieira does not report how he and his missionaries managed to convert the suspicious Ibiapaba people. He emphasizes, on the contrary, their resistance to receiving the faith. Without clarifying his strategy of conversion, however, he ends his report by writing of reportedly "repentant" Indigenous people who had become submissive to the priests.

Soon after his supposedly successful Ibiapaba mission, in 1661, Vieira was expelled from Maranhão by settlers and clerics who believed that his interference in the governance of Indigenous peoples harmed their own local interests. Following his expulsion, he wrote other documents addressed to the colonists. It is in these other texts, rather than in the above-mentioned *Report*, where Vieira explains his strategy of bringing the Indigenous population under Portuguese domination.

The following sections retrace Vieira's narrative of the diplomatic mission to Serra de Ibiapaba and examine some of the texts that he wrote in the context of his removal from Maranhão. The *Report* has seventeen sections, which can be divided into three major themes: (a) an explanation of the context and the geopolitical interest of the mission (1–4), (b) a description of the diplomatic activities among the Indigenous groups (i.e., the mission and its challenges) (5–13), and (c) the successful results of the enterprise (i.e., "reduced" Indigenous people, open trade, and routes) (14–17). Following the thread of the narrative, one can see what in Vieira's opinion hindered the establishment of an alliance with the Indigenous people. Subsequently, within the other texts, his diplomatic strategies become apparent. The analysis of his texts in this chapter shows that colonial agents, including missionaries like Vieira, recognized that Indigenous people are agentive and intentional political actors, rather than merely passive subjects, long before the emergence of contemporary historiographical and ethnological trends.

Ibiapaba: A Diplomatic Mission

Ibiapaba was one of the first missions planned by Vieira after returning from Lisbon in 1654. His aim with this mission was more political than religious. He wanted to win the trust of the Indigenous people there, who were trapped between the Portuguese territories of Pernambuco and Maranhão. Many Indigenous groups were living in this area when the mission was founded. Amid the mountain ranges of the Serra de Ibiapaba were Tobajara people (three large settlements), Tapuian nations, and Indigenous groups from Pernambuco.[4]

After 1607, when the priest Francisco Pinto was killed, the Indigenous people in this mountain range stayed independent. This remained the case until 1630, when the Dutch captured the fort of Ceará. According to Vieira, they not only made friends with some of the local Indigenous groups but also "reduced the Indians there" (Vieira 1951, 77). Until 1642, these Indigenous groups were Dutch allies against the Portuguese and sided with them during the war in Maranhão. The Tobajara were later joined by nations that had fled Pernambuco in 1654 and were fearful of possible revenge from the Portuguese after the conquest of Recife. According to Vieira, these groups from Pernambuco had previously been Christians and Portuguese subjects, but they had become "domestic enemies" of the Portuguese (Vieira 1951, 80). They taught the Indigenous people in the Serra de Ibiapaba what they had learned in Pernambuco and were "received and venerated by the Tobajara as literate and wise men" (Vieira 1951, 82).

Vieira called Serra de Ibiapaba the "Geneva of all the Brazilian *sertões*" because it was full of Protestants (i.e., Indigenous people converted by the Dutch) (Vieira 1951, 81). As a Jesuit missionary, he did not know whether the Indigenous groups there were gentiles or heretics. For him, while the Maranhão mission had three main objectives, which included attending to the spiritual lives of both the Portuguese and Christian Indigenous people, the most important was the conversion and reduction of these "gentile" Indigenous people.[5] In this sense, Serra de Ibiapaba was Vieira's greatest challenge in his efforts at missionization.

Before starting his career as a missionary among the Indigenous people of Maranhão, Vieira had significant diplomatic experience in European courts. As a diplomat, he had tried to find a solution to the Portuguese-Dutch war. The Dutch had remained in Pernambuco for twenty-four years. During this time, they had expanded not only sugar production but also commercial contacts with the Indigenous people of the interior region, to whom they supplied various small goods and desiderata. Vieira's challenge was to regain their "will" (*vontades*). Since the disputed territory with the Dutch was the Pernambuco hinterlands, which was the passage to Maranhão, Vieira's goal hinged on the alliance, friendship, trade, and particularly the loyalty of its Indigenous inhabitants. Through political agreements, Vieira managed to persuade the Indigenous people to accept Portuguese authority in advance of converting them to Christianity. As such, the Ibiapaba mission can be best understood as the second stage in António Vieira's diplomatic career, rather than as merely an ordinary "mission" stage of his life.[6]

The Embassy

Before starting the first diplomatic mission to Ibiapaba, Vieira sent a letter to the *principais*, that is, regional leaders, through an Indigenous man named Francisco.[7] After nine months without response, he decided in 1656 to send the priests Manuel Nunes and Tomé Ribeiro on a sea route there. They were unable to reach the area of Ibiapaba, however, because of headwinds, which hindered sea travel from Maranhão to northeastern Brazil. After trying for fifty days to reach Ibiapaba, they gave up and returned. On the way back, by coincidence, they met Francisco carrying the leaders' response, which was written, according to Vieira, on Venetian paper in India ink. This is evidence of existing and well-established relationships with foreigners at the time. The answer to the Jesuit's entreaties was positive, so Vieira sent another two priests. This time he sent Antonio Ribeiro, who was an expert in languages, and Pedro Pedrosa, who had just arrived from Portugal. In light of the prior difficulties with sea travel, they went overland and managed to reach Ibiapaba. With this description, Vieira begins the second part of the text, which narrates the diplomatic mission that these two men initiated.

The priests arrived at Serra de Ibiapaba on July 4, 1656, although on arrival they were reportedly "without breath, color or any resemblance to the living" because of the arduous nature of the travel (see Vieira 1951, 95). They were received by the local Tobajara with "great demonstrations of pleasure and humanity" (Vieira 1951, 98; see also Van Valen 2013; and Van Valen's and Whitaker's chapters in this volume). After building churches, the priests began to teach religious doctrine, especially to the children. The baptism of many adults and children followed. It seemed easy, but soon the Indigenous people began to distrust the priests.

Vieira attributed the mistrust of the Tobajara to the work of the devil. He believed that on certain occasions, the devil would put into the minds of the local Indigenous people the idea that the priests wanted only to deceive them and to make them slaves of the Portuguese. The first occasion was when the Tobajara heard that the governor of Maranhão, André Vidal, was coming by land with a group of soldiers. They suspected the intention was to conquer them, so they called their Tapuia neighbors and made a trap for the Portuguese.

When this fear had passed, the devil allegedly acted again, according to Vieira. In this case, two Tapuia nations (i.e., the Ganacé and the Juguaruana) lived near the Ceará fort and were allies of the Portuguese but enemies of each other. When the Juguaruana were collecting wood for the fortress, the Ganacé attacked them, kidnapping the women and children. In response, twenty-four Portuguese soldiers were sent to assist the Juguaruana, who finally killed all their attackers without Portuguese assistance. But the episode caused a stir among the Indigenous communities in the Ibiapaba region, especially among those who were already allies and vassals of the Portuguese.

According to Vieira, this was a case in which the "reason of greed" prevailed over "that of the state" (Vieira 1951, 102). The first centered on desires. The second focused on diplomacy, stipulating that neutrality be kept toward both nations, since both were Portuguese allies. Notably, according to Vieira, the Portuguese assistance to the Juguaruana against the Ganacé, who were also allies, caused just wrath among the various Indigenous communities involved, since it meant selecting one allied Indigenous group over another. The priests were called to mediate. And finally, Father Antonio Ribeiro was able to make peace.

Around this time, another episode caused distrust of the Portuguese among the Indigenous groups in the region. The Tobajara received a letter from Vieira in which he sent them news that the mission Visitor, Francisco Gonçalves (1656–58), wanted to end the mission and had ordered the priests return to Maranhão.[8] He proposed that those communities willing to accompany the priests to São Luís should do so. When Pedro Pedrosa read this proposal to the leaders, they were seemingly convinced that they were being deceived by the Portuguese, which could be seen "in the countenances of the Indians" (Vieira 1951, 110).

On all three occasions, Vieira imagined the devil allegedly manifesting through the interference of local authorities, settlers, and the hierarchy of the order itself to instill in local Indigenous people a distrust of priests, which was always expressed in terms of a breach of contract. Vieira positioned himself as a privileged intermediary in relations with local Indigenous people, despite everything and everyone. At this point in his text, Vieira ascribes to them a voice. He writes that the "Indians" told him that "what we all worried about until now had become true, the priests never had any other intention, other than to uproot us from our lands to make us slaves to their white relatives" (Vieira 1951, 110). Once again, the Tobajara asked the Tapuias for help in covertly killing the priests. Warned about this possibility, the priests waited for "the day of [their] death." When it did not arrive, they went to talk to a *principal*, who was disconcerted to discover that they knew the secret. Nonetheless, although the "Indians" remained suspicious, the priests decided to remain against the orders of their supervisors.[9]

In addition to these difficulties, the missionaries' greatest challenge was achieving their goal of converting the Indigenous people to Christianity and changing their customs to suit Portuguese rule, as well as colonial and church interests. Although all three Tobajara leaders were already Christians, none was married in the church. They did not want to be married in that way, despite the insistence of the priests that they should be. All three of them had concubines. Evoking Protestantism, they questioned and mocked Catholic doctrines. They said that when they died, they would go underground to live in peace. According to Vieira, "in the veneration of the temples, the images, the crosses, the priests and the sacraments, many of them are as Calvinist and Lutheran as if they were born in England or Germany" (Vieira 1951, 114). In this way, his previous contentions with the Dutch were reflected in his missionary activities with the Indigenous people of Brazil.

Best known for his metaphor of marble and myrtle, which posited an "inconstancy" of the "savage" soul, Vieira used a similar metaphor to describe the difficulties faced in the Ibiapaba.[10] He compared the mountain range to its inhabitants, describing the range as formed of "a single very hard rock and in parts that are bare and hideous, in others covered with greenery and plowed earth, as if nature portrays in these black cliffs the condition of their inhabitants, who, always being hard and like stones, sometimes give hope and let themselves be cultivated" (Vieira 1951, 96).

The allusion resonates with "desert of stones," evoked by Manuel da Nóbrega, who was an earlier Jesuit priest in Brazil, in his "Dialogue on the Conversion of the Gentile" (1557).[11] Although the metaphor provides an apology for Vieira's mission work (Pécora 2009), the hopes he had for the Serra's inhabitants differed from Nóbrega's view in relation to "reducing" the local Indigenous people. For Nóbrega, the "savagery" and hardness of the Indigenous people justified Portuguese political power over them, whose consent could be obtained by fear (Eisenberg 2000). For Vieira, on the contrary, the Indigenous groups' fear made his work more difficult and was something he sought to obviate and neutralize through a different approach.

The Agreement

In the third part of Vieira's text, the results of the mission emerge. Many of the adults among the missionized Indigenous groups in Ibiapaba still apparently continued to resist the missionaries, but more than five hundred infants were baptized, and three churches had been formed in the villages. These three later merged as one church.

The Tobajara were "reduced" without violence and with little expense to the missionaries. According to Vieira, they were almost "civilized" and would soon become Christians. He also reports that the overland road from Maranhão to Pernambuco was now open and safe, as well as that the amber and timber trade had become possible again. This drew a line connecting the missions with broader economic interests in the region.

Vieira wrote to the Indigenous *principais*, and all three subsequently sent ambassadors to visit him and the governor of the Captaincy of Maranhão in São Luís. The ambassadors were very satisfied with the reception they received. Vieira vowed to visit them for St. John's Day. The Indigenous people were employed in building a church, and it seemed that their fears had been assuaged. Yet, further problems soon emerged. When Jorge da Silva (the son of the oldest leader) went to visit the Portuguese king, he inadvertently left letters of recommendation from Vieira behind in Maranhão. Nevertheless, the Count of Odemira received him, presented him to the king in Portugal, "and sent him back again to Maranhão full of titles from his Majesty" (Vieira 1951, 129). Meanwhile, a few months before St. John's Day, the Portuguese leaders in Ibiapaba sent several "Indians" to fetch Vieira, but he was ill and remained in the Captaincy of Pará until the beginning of the following year. At this point, distrust of the priests once more emerged among the local Indigenous groups. As Silva was taking too long to return, some of them said that he had not been sent to Portugal but that he had drowned. Others said he had been enslaved. They decided that if this was true, they would kill the priests.

Arriving from Pará, Vieira set out for the Serra de Ibiapaba with Silva, who had arrived two months prior with Father Gonçalo Veras and an Indigenous group from the Serra de Ibiapaba, which included both Tobajara and Pernambucos. Vieira and the Indigenous principals agreed that all the Pernambuco Indians should go to Maranhão. According to Vieira, once the people of Pernambuco made a commitment to becoming subjects, they could be compelled to fulfill their assumed obligations by force if they did not do so willingly. Moreover, it would be easier to convert the Indians in the Serra de Ibiapaba, without the influence of the Pernambucos.

Vieira also agreed with the Tobajara principals that the three large villages would be merged, all the people would be baptized, local children would receive religious education, polygamy would be prohibited, and confession would be required at least annually during Lent. Finally, the people there pledged to keep "the law of God and obedience to the Church entirely" and put the greatest principal's brother in charge of mandatory church attendance, discipline, and other matters. As reported by Vieira, "All of this was put on paper, and a copy was given to each of the principals, . . . so that they could take care of it, and see who best fulfilled it" (Vieira 1951, 134).

How to "Reduce" the Indigenous People

The term "reduce" refers to the process of bringing Indigenous people under the control and influence of the Catholic Church and the Portuguese Crown. It often involved conversion to Christianity and acceptance of colonial rule. In this sense, Vieira's strategy to reduce the Indigenous people cannot be discerned in his account of the Ibiapaba mission, but it can be found in at least two texts written in the context of his expulsion shortly after his mission, as well as (some years later) in a document that he wrote by order of the Overseas Council.[12]

According to Vieira, the Indigenous people were not enemies of the faith and did not even know what it was. For this reason, the missionaries' strategy to reduce them was not faith based but centered on "reasons," "promises," and "human convenience" (Vieira 1951, 333). This assessment, written in 1678, summarizes the almost ten years of his missionary experience (1652–61) among the Indigenous people from Maranhão and takes up the arguments he had addressed to the settlers when he was expelled from there and had to defend himself against their accusations.

In 1661, while trying to persuade the colonists to end their revolt against the Jesuits, he writes that the missionaries preached with the gospel in one hand and the law in the other. It was necessary to convince the Indigenous people that colonial laws would be respected in relation to their rights and protections. This required good treatment of Indigenous people by European settlers and respect for the contracts established with Indigenous authorities regarding Indigenous labor for the Portuguese. Vieira notes the importance of the Ibiapaba Indians' friendship for trade with and passage to Maranhão and argues that all would be lost if the Portuguese did not respect their contracts with the Indigenous people (Vieira 1951, 145).

He develops these arguments later in response to the accusations against him:

> The conversion and reduction of the Indians of Maranhão not only consist of the missionaries preaching to them the mysteries of the faith and giving them knowledge of the true God, but it depends mainly on holding them back and persuading them that the Portuguese will not capture or mistreat them, and neither will they take their wives and their children, nor will they use them, but voluntarily, for their stipend, and finally that they will live together in their villages as free, without any force or violence. In addition, when this is fulfilled and kept as fully as it is promised, it is still a great efficacy of the divine grace that Gentile and barbaric men, raised without any law, nor even that of nature, want to be uprooted from their homelands and come to strange lands to receive the faith of God and the subjection of a King they do not know and are obliged in everything to such different styles and precepts of life. However, when this is not observed, but quite the contrary, and instead of the promised freedom and good treatment, the Indians find captivity, violence, robbery, impiety, would a Gentile, no matter how barbaric, believe in such a law, or receive the God of such ministers or submit to the prince of such vassals? (Vieira 1951, 288)

In the same response to the accusations, Vieira lists three conditions without which the conversion of Indigenous groups from Maranhão would not have been possible. These included, first, the Portuguese not waging war against them without the king's authorization, as well as not using gratuitous violence against them. Second, those who were converted could not be forced to work more than what had been agreed on and should be governed by their traditional authorities and leaders in conjunction with the missionaries. Finally, placing missionaries as privileged mediators of Indigenous-Portuguese relations, Vieira argued that the missionaries should be independent in their missions and receive all necessary help from the Portuguese colonial authorities and colonists.

In addition to respecting contracts and nonviolence agreements, more was needed, according to Vieira, to convince the Indigenous people to accept Portuguese rule. It was also necessary to supply them with "human conveniences," which meant (similar to the situation with the Dutch) gifts that included "axes, sickles, knives, mirrors, combs, glass beads, cotton shirts, and . . . hats and brightly colored garments" (Vieira 1951, 310; see also Whitaker 2016).

Vieira viewed the absence of these conditions as precisely the cause of the difficulties that he narrated in his Ibiapaba mission report. We do not know exactly what Vieira and his fellow missionaries promised the Tobajara to convince them to submit to Portuguese rule. But once expelled by the settlers, they probably could not keep their promises, so the Indigenous people were likely right in their suspicions against them.

Consequently, for Vieira, the Portuguese (through the religious mission) should employ, in their colonization efforts, peaceful means that respected the sovereignty of the Indigenous communities, not only because these communities had these rights, which were highlighted by theologians and recognized by the legislation of the Iberian empires, but especially because this was the only way to have them as friends, allies, and finally vassals. As such, Vieira saw the "Indian" as a political human being with natural freedom and therefore sovereignty. For him, it was necessary to make agreements with the Indigenous groups in a symmetric way, no matter how "barbaric" they were perceived to be by European colonists or colonial governments.

These ideas reappear in another context many years later, in Vieira's (1694) "Voto sobre as dúvidas dos moradores de S. Paulo acerca da administração dos índios," which he wrote when he was eighty-six years old. Ricardo Ventura (2016) describes this text as a "conclusive testimony of his position," while João Viegas calls it "the final text of his life where he seeks conceptual elevation" (see Vieira 1998). More simply, André de Barros refers to it as a "doctrinal voice" (see Vieira 1736). In any case, with almost seventy years of diplomatic experience involving European courts and Indigenous leaders, Vieira states again that the Indigenous people had lived "in their political way" and that they should have sovereignty over their lives. As free people, they had no obligations to the Portuguese. Referring to the free Indigenous groups who were subjugated and forced to work by the settlers from São Paulo Captaincy, Vieira states that:

> The so-called Indians are those who, living free and natural masters of
> their lands . . . are not slaves, nor subjects. They are not slaves, because
> they are not captured in a just war; and nor are they subjects, because like
> the Spanish or Genoese captive in Algiers, he is also a vassal of the king
> and his republic, so the Indian is not, since he is forced and captive, as a
> member of the body and political head of their nation, equally mattering
> for the sovereignty of freedom, both the crown of feathers and the crown
> of gold, and both the bow and the scepter . . . although brought to the lands
> subject to the domination of Portugal, they are in no way subject to the
> same domain. (Vieira 1951, 341–42)

His definition of freedom as the "the right and the faculty of each one to
do what he wants with his goods and people" (Vieira 1951, 342) refers to
those Indigenous people who had not yet been brought under colonial
subjugation by the Portuguese (i.e., "reduced"). For Vieira, it was fundamental that Portuguese political dominion over Indigenous communities
should—except in cases of "just war"—be based on the consent of those
communities. Consent is understood by him in line with the Dominican
reading of Thomism rather than with the Jesuit one.[13] Indigenous people
were free by nature, with sovereignty over their territories, and had life
that was "somehow human and political," which meant that neither force
nor fear should intervene in the establishment of contracts or pacts of
vassalage with them (Vieira 1951, 351).

To summarize, Vieira left his career as a diplomat in Europe to take
over governance of the missions in Maranhão. The Serra de Ibiapaba
had special geopolitical importance, as it was the land connection between Brazil and Maranhão. But the region was under the influence of
the Dutch, so Vieira understood that he needed to regain the trust of its
inhabitants to make pacts of alliance and eventually vassalage. According
to him, for these pacts to be realized, it was necessary to respect the sovereignty of the Indigenous peoples, which they possessed not only in law
but in fact, and to respect the agreements that had been established with
them by consent. Effectively, within a context of imperial dispute, Vieira
recognized that Indigenous groups established strategic alliances to defend their interests and to limit threats from outsiders (see Roller 2021;
and Whitaker 2025). The Jesuit acted as a diplomat and sought to respond to the expectations of Indigenous groups regarding conveniences

(e.g., trade goods) and security guarantees. With this goal in mind, he wanted to converge his aims with Portuguese interests.

Revisiting António Vieira's texts about the Indigenous people in Brazil can elucidate that, even in a colonial context, political subordination was not always assumed a priori. To understand the importance of this assertion, it is necessary to free ourselves of our contemporary lenses and to read propositions from writers such as Vieira within the intellectual framework of their day. In doing so, we find that, despite notions of arrogated superiority, characteristic of the time, there was also the idea that the relationships should be symmetric. Although it is difficult to distinguish the Indigenous peoples' perspectives in the *Report*, which could simply be projections of Vieira's rhetoric, it is clear in his writings that Indigenous people were historical actors, who chose to engage with outsiders based on their interests in a symmetric relationship. Although part of the colonial project, Vieira's strategy emphasized persuasion through promises and provisions for human needs and desires rather than force, arguing that successful "reduction" required respecting Indigenous people's autonomy and treaties. Vieira believed in achieving political submission through diplomacy and mutual agreements, contrasting with the more coercive colonial practices sometimes pursued by others.

Once the Indigenous people accepted Portuguese dominion, according to Vieira, they transitioned from sovereignty to vassalage. Acknowledging this vassalage, the relationship turned asymmetric; the Indigenous groups became subjects with well-defined obligations, who could receive titles and privileges but also punishments, in line with their loyalty to the king. Vieira indicates this when commenting on the obligations of the already-reduced Pernambuco Indians and on the title received by Jorge da Silva. Therefore, for Vieira, there was a line that separated sovereignty from vassalage, autonomy from subordination; he made the Ibiapaba people sign on paper that they had crossed this line.

Notes

1.   The full title in Portuguese is the *"Relação da Missão da Serra de Ibiapaba escrita pelo P. António Vieira, e tirada do seu mesmo original"* (Vieira 1736, 3–89). For this chapter, I have used the edition in Vieira's collected works edited by Hernâni Cidade (Vieira 1951, 72–134), *"Relação da Missão da Serra de Ibiapaba."*

2. The term New Christians refers to Jewish people in Portugal and Spain who converted to Christianity because of religious persecution. Vieira acted in favor of their interests, since he believed they played an important role in the economy of the Portuguese empire.

3. João Lúcio de Azevedo ([1918] 1992) believes that Vieira's move to Maranhão allowed him to stay away from the court. Ricardo Ventura (2016, 20–21), however, recently pointed out that Maranhão had already been cited several times by Vieira in his political plans for the Portuguese empire after the 1640 Restoration.

4. In the seventeenth century, the Serra de Ibiapaba harbored a diversity of Indigenous groups that had migrated and settled in the area as a result of a series of factors, including colonial pressures and internal dynamics. Ethnographic information from sixteenth- and seventeenth-century sources is sparse and residual. Europeans established a broad division between Tupi-speaking groups and other groups, often resistant to contact, designated as Tapuias. It is worth noting that the terms and designations used by Europeans may have influenced how different Indigenous groups identified socially and how they were perceived by others. Among the most prominent ethnic groups settled in Ibiapaba were the Tupinambá, Caetés, and Potiguara. Part of them appropriated, according to Jesuit reports, the designation Tbajara (Tobajara) as a social distinction. Additionally, Tapuian groups like the Reriíu, Anacé, Carariju, Acongruaçu, Caratiú, Tremembé, and Quixariú also inhabited the region; see Maia (2010).

5. This quotation refers to the letter by Vieira (1951, 174–315), "Resposta aos capítulos que deu contra os religiosos da Companhia de Jesus, em 1662, o procurador do Maranhão Jorge de Sampaio."

6. João Lúcio de Azevedo ([1918] 1992), in his biography, first suggested these different stages in Vieira's life. His idea has been taken up by other authors.

7. According to Rafael Bluteau's (1789) eighteenth-century dictionary of the Portuguese language, *principal* "is the title given in Brazil to the most esteemed gentile of the village, who governs as its captain."

8. The Visitor was a member of the order tasked with supervising Jesuits in a given region to ensure they were following the principles of the order. He visited different communities, overseeing the activities of the missionaries in their various works and providing particular instructions.

9. All these elements make this text curious. As a missionary, Vieira's description of challenges in converting the people would presumably serve to justify his work, but he positioned himself to gain enemies by attributing these challenges to the behavior of his colleagues. In the letters he wrote while he was in Maranhão, Vieira refers to his project of writing a *Relação*. In letters from 1656 to 1661, and in the *Ibiapaba Report*, however, Vieira describes several conflicts with his colleagues. In 1658, he complained that missionaries were not being sent to Maranhão, despite the insistent requests made to the provincial of Brazil. In 1660, he justified to the Provincial Simão de Vasconcelos his noncompliance with the order of Francisco Gonçalves, the Visitador do Maranhão, to

leave Ibiapaba. He also complained about the attitudes of the Visitador, according to Vieira, contrary to Portuguese laws. In 1661, he responded to the general's numerous accusations against him in Lisbon. At this point, he was in conflict with foreign colleagues who were opposed to his intervention in the temporal governance of the Indians of Maranhão; see the two volumes of letters edited by Franco and Calafate: Vieira (2014) vol. 1, *Epistolografia*, and vol. 2, *Cartas da missão: Cartas da prisão*.

10.   This is a reference to António Vieira's "Sermão da Epifania," given in Lisbon in 1662, shortly after he was expelled from Maranhão; for a discussion of some of its themes, see Viveiros de Castro (1992, in Portuguese; and in English, 2011).

11.   Manuel da Nóbrega (1517–70) was a Portuguese Jesuit who came to Brazil in 1549, along with the first general-governor of the colony. He was responsible for founding several religious missions in different regions of the country. He also had a relevant political role, being adviser to the general-governor. Nóbrega participated in the elaboration of guidelines for the administration of the colony, particularly concerning the relationship with Indigenous communities. He was responsible for formulating the project for the conversion of Brazilian Indigenous people based on bringing together different ethnic groups in a single location. In "Diálogo sobre a Conversão do Gentio" (1577) as well as in *Plano Civilizador* (1558), Nóbrega (1955) systematized the theological and political justification for using fear in conversion.

12.   The three texts are "Representação ao Senado do Pará" (1661), in Vieira (1951, 140–50); the "Resposta aos capítulos que deu contra os religiosos da Companhia o Procurador do Maranhão Jorge de Sampaio" (1662), in Vieira (1951, 174–315); and "Informação que por ordem do Conselho Ultramarino deu sobre as cousas do Maranhão ao mesmo Conselho," in Vieira (1951, 324–39).

13.   José Eisenberg (2000, 92, 116–17) identifies conceptual changes in the plan formulated by Manuel da Nóbrega in the 1550s. While for the Dominicans, the legitimacy of political power should be based on the voluntary consent of subjects, Nóbrega, and afterward Juan de Mariana, argued that fear was the cause of consent. Fear, and not coercion, was not only an efficient cause of political power but also a source of legitimacy. It seems that for Vieira, however, fear should not intervene in the persuasion of the Indigenous folk, thus bringing him closer to the Dominican reading of the Thomist theory, according to which consent was the material and efficient cause of political authority.

References

Azevedo, João Lúcio de. (1918) 1992. *História de António Vieira*. Lisbon: Clássica Editora.

Bluteau, Rafael, ed. 1789. *Diccionário da lingua portugueza: Reformado e acrescentado por António de Moraes Silva*. Vol. 1. Lisbon: Officina de Simão Thaddeo Ferreira.

Boxer, Charles R. 1969. *The Portuguese Seaborne Empire, 1414–1825*. London: Hutchinson.

Cardoso, Alírio. 2019. "The Dutch in Portuguese Amazonia: War, Trade and Navigation (1620–1641)." In *Rivers and Shores: "Fluviality" and the Occupation of Colonial Amazonia*, edited by Rafael Chambouleyron and Luís Costa e Sousa, 62–82. Peterborough, ON: Baywolf.

Eisenberg, José. 2000. *As missões jesuíticas e o pensamento político moderno: Encontros culturais, aventuras teóricas*. Belo Horizonte, Brazil: Editora UFMG.

Maia, Lígio José de Oliveira. 2010. "Serras de Ibiapaba: De aldeia à vila de Índios: Vassalagem e Identidade no Ceará colonial—século XVIII." PhD diss., Universidade Federal Fluminense, Niterói.

Nóbrega, Manuel da. 1955. *Cartas do Brasil e mais escritos do Pe. Manuel da Nóbrega*. With introduction and annotations by Serafim Leite. Coimbra: Universidade de Coimbra.

Pécora, Alcir. 2009. *O bom selvagem e o boçal: argumentos de Vieira em torno à imagem do "índio boçal"*. In *Entre a selva e a corte: Novos olhares sobre Vieira*, edited by José Eduardo Franco, 65–76. Lisbon: Esfera do Caos.

Roller, Heather F. 2021. *Contact Strategies: Histories of Native Autonomy in Brazil*. Stanford, Calif.: Stanford University Press.

Van Valen, Gary. 2013. *Indigenous Agency in the Amazon: The Mojos in Liberal and Rubber-Boom Bolivia, 1842–1932*. Tucson: University of Arizona Press.

Ventura, Ricardo, ed. 2016. *Padre António Vieira, Escritos sobre os Índios*. Lisbon: Temas e Debates.

Vieira, António. 1736. "*Relação da Missão da Serra de Ibiapaba* escrita pelo P. António Vieira, e tirada do seu mesmo original." In *Vozes Saudosas*, edited by André de Barros, 3–89. Lisbon: Officina de Miguel Rodrigues.

Vieira, António. 1951. *Obras escolhidas*, vol. 5, *Obras várias: Em defesa dos índios*. Preface and notes by Hernâni Cidade. Lisbon: Sá da Costa.

Vieira, António. 1998. *La mission d'Ibiapaba: Le père António Vieira et le droit des Indiens*. Edited and translated by João Viegas. Paris: Chandeigne.

Vieira, António. 2014. *Obra Completa Padre António Vieira*. Vols. 1 and 2, edited by José Eduardo Franco and Pedro Calafate. São Paulo: Loyola.

Viveiros de Castro, Eduardo. 1992. "O mármore e a murta: Sobre a inconstância da alma selvagem." *Revista de Antropologia* 35:21–74.

Viveiros de Castro, Eduardo. 2011. *The Inconstancy of the Indian Soul: The Encounter of Catholics and Cannibals in 16th-Century Brazil*. Chicago: Prickly Paradigm.

Whitaker, James Andrew. 2016. "Amerindians in the Eighteenth Century Plantation System of the Guianas." *Tipití* 14 (3): 30–43.

Whitaker, James Andrew. 2025. *The Shamanism of Eco-Tourism: History and Ontology among the Makushi in Guyana*. Cambridge: Cambridge University Press.

CHAPTER 2

"These Fathers Make Us People"

Mojo Ideas of Humanity and the Encounter with the Jesuits

GARY VAN VALEN

In the late seventeenth century in the Llanos de Mojos, an ex-shaman who became a Christian and a cacique (local leader) explained the impact of Spanish Jesuit missionary work as follows: "Since we became acquainted with God, we do not live like brutes; we [now] see cows, horses, machetes, knives, needles, beads, fish hooks, bells, clothes, hats; these Fathers make us people" (Eguiluz 1884, 54). Although ethnohistorians sometimes view such trade goods merely as the material incentive for Indigenous people to accept missions, the cacique's words indicate that his people desired European manufactured goods and livestock for more than the material benefits they provided (Block 1994, 65–66, 102; Sarreal 2014, 74–77; Van Valen 2013, 13–14). As other scholars have pointed out, trade goods can have a cultural and social dimension for Indigenous people, which often outweighs their utility in material life (Gow 1991, 35, 62–65, 265–66; Walker 2012, 146; Walker 2013; Whitaker 2025).

The concept of being made people, as well as the possibility of transformation from "brutes" to people, refers to important understandings among the Mojo that humanity (1) is constructed rather than a given, (2) emerges from a general condition of nonhumanity, and (3) is an unstable bodily status that can be lost or surpassed through transformation (see Fausto 2007; McCallum 2001; Micarelli 2015; Opas 2005; Rival 2005; Santos-Granero 2012; Seeger, Da Matta, and Viveiros de Castro 2019;

Vilaça 2005; Vilaça 2010; Viveiros de Castro 1998; Whitaker 2021; and
Yvinec 2014). This chapter suggests that conversion to Christianity became one way among the Mojo through which humanity could emerge
from nonhumanity. As the Mojo accepted Christianity, they defined it
as a new way of being human. For the Jesuits, success in the missionary
enterprise depended on phrasing Christian concepts in ways that res-
onated with Mojo notions of humanity and nonhumanity, addressing
existing notions of alterity in order to be accepted among the Mojo, and
creating new notions to differentiate Christians from non-Christians. For
the Mojo, a mission presence brought the material benefits listed by the
cacique, but they interpreted these through their own cosmology. The
cacique's statement implies that alliance and partnership with the Jesuits allowed them to achieve or maintain their humanity. As the ultimate
source of these material benefits, the Christian God also became a kind
of ally or partner to the Mojo through Jesuit mediation.

Jesuit primary sources, including the grammar, dictionary, and catechism of Father Pedro Marbán, as well as accounts by lay brother José
del Castillo and provincial of Peru Diego de Eguiluz, provide a wealth of
information on Mojo ideas of humanity, which can best be understood
through definitions of the attributes that would make one *not* human.
The Mojo, like many other Amazonian peoples, defined humanity as an
absence of those qualities that would make one not human (cf. Opas
2005, 112–13, 122–23; Rival 2005, 106; Rosengren 2006, 96; Schindler
1977, 71).[1] In a situation in which humanity is understood as constructed
and always in danger of being lost, it is comprehensible that people would
focus on the ways in which the latter could happen.

The most common Mojo term that Marbán provides for nonhuman is
voi achaneiná, meaning "not human," which is composed of the negation
marker *voi* plus *achane* (human) plus the irrealis marking *-ina*. A variant
is *voi achanenuiná*, "I am not human" (Marbán 1702a, 14–15, 305, 336;
Rose 2014). Marbán translated *voi achaneiná* variously as *no es cosa viva*
(is not a living thing); *bruto, es un bruto* (brute, is a brute); *no es una
persona* (is not a person); *no es gente* (is not people); *hombre perdido*
(lost man); *indigna persona* (unworthy person); and *salvaje* (savage), and
voi achanenuiná as *bárbara persona* (barbarous person) (Marbán 1702a,
155, 163, 258–59, 290, 305, 333, 368; Marbán 1702b, 40–41). Another
Spanish term, *inhumano* (inhuman, inhumane), can be linked indirectly

to *voi achaneiná*. Several of these Spanish terms also translate into other Mojo terms, which subsequently translate into other Spanish terms, and so on.

Using a concept map in the form of an extended Venn diagram, the relationship of all these terms to one another can be visualized (figure 2.1). The result of this mapping is a series of branching chains of circles leading from the central concept of *voi achaneiná* to several vectors of nonhumanity: (1) not compassionate, (2) several qualities regarded as "unworthy," (3) a lack of knowing or understanding to a lesser extent, (4) a lack of knowing or understanding to an extreme extent, (5) animals, and (6) not baptized. Spanish contact led to new interpretations of several Mojo notions of nonhumanity, most notably adding "not baptized" to their list.

These notions of nonhumanity form a starting point for further analysis of Mojo society at the time of their encounter with the Jesuits. Each one also suggests how the Mojo understood humanity, and hence how they classified living beings as either "same" or "other." Jesuit sources provide evidence that conversion involved a conversation between missionaries and Mojo people, during which individuals from both sides actively tried to frame each other's humanity in concepts familiar to them. Further analysis is organized below according to each notion of nonhumanity. Along with material from Jesuit sources, I also use comparison with more recent ethnographies of lowland South American Indigenous groups in this analysis. Although there is no direct connection between most of these recent studies and the seventeenth-century Mojo, scholars recognize cultural similarities among many Indigenous peoples across the region, and historical processes allow for continuity as well as change over time. Thus, these ethnographies can provide important clues for how to interpret information in Jesuit sources from an Indigenous Amazonian, rather than a European, perspective. Much of this ethnographic writing falls into broad and distinct trends: one focuses on Indigenous ideals of humanity as living together in "harmonious conviviality," while the other concentrates on the differentiation of humans from dangerous, predatory, nonhuman others (Overing and Passes 2000; Viveiros de Castro 1996). As the two styles respectively emphasize social relations internal and external to Indigenous groups, I consider them to be complementary and find inspiration in both.

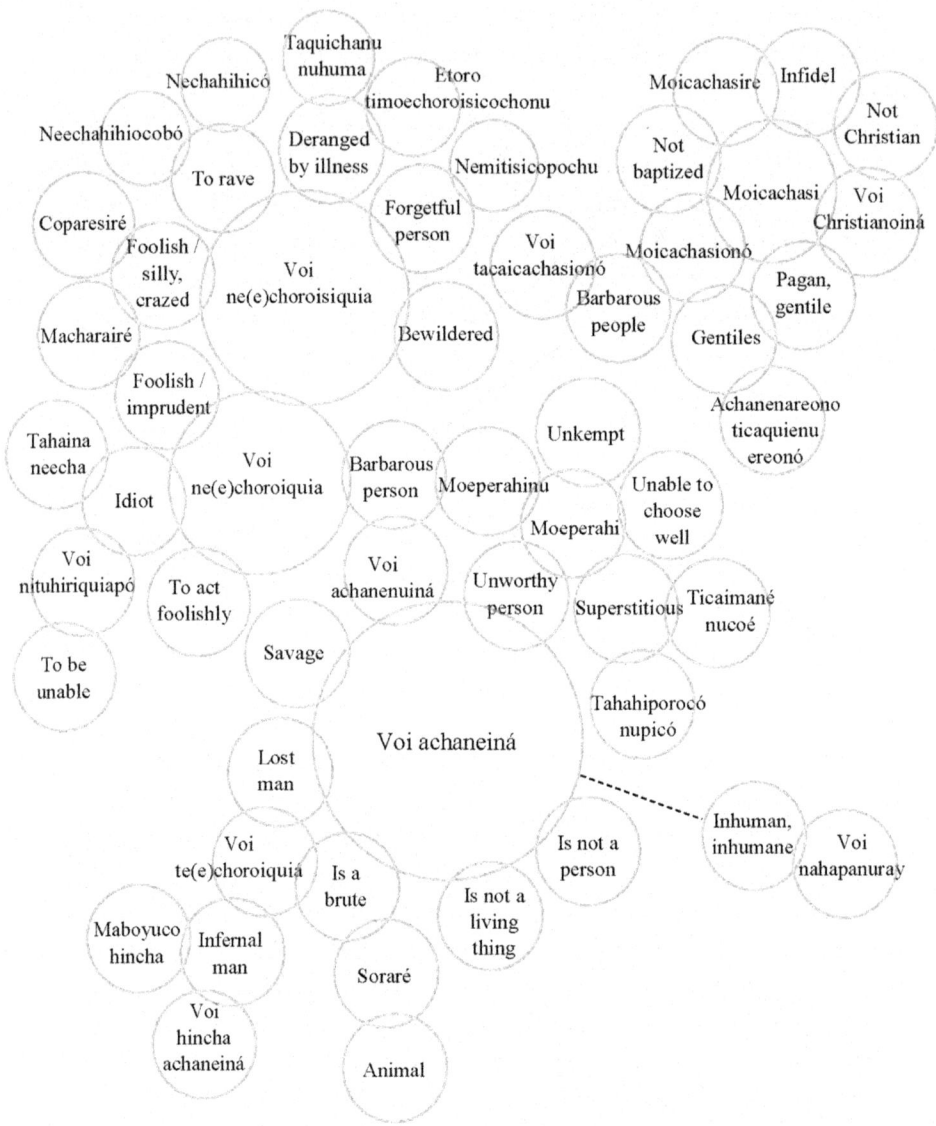

FIGURE 2.1 Mojo terms for nonhuman qualities centered on *voi achaneiná*.
Spanish terms are translated into English, and some terms connected to *voi ne(e)
choroiquia* are omitted for lack of space. Figure made by Gary Van Valen based
on data from Marbán (1702a, 1702b).

Since scholars often depict the concepts of structure and agency as existing in tension or in conflict with each other, a word is necessary about how a focus on what are essentially structures of thought about humanity and nonhumanity can contribute to this volume's theme of Indigenous agency (Rapport and Overing 2000, 1–3). Scholars clearly distinguish "agency" from mere "resistance" to domination but often use the concept of agency to describe creative responses to situations of domination. For example, in the case of the Peruvian Urarina, Harry Walker (2012, 156) has demonstrated how agency can emerge from structures of subordination and even owe its existence to those structures. Yet when the Mojo and the Jesuits formed their alliance, neither was subordinate to the other. The context of that historical moment was one of change rather than conquest and domination, and the Mojo exercised agency in negotiating the course that change would take. They taught Marbán their language, and he relied on their interpretations of meaning. As the Jesuit missionary attempted to translate Christian concepts into Mojo, he did so in partnership with, and guided by, the Mojo. In the following sections, I examine the evidence for different aspects of Mojo definitions of humanity and nonhumanity, noting where new, Christian interpretations were being negotiated. I end by describing the fuller, interconnected sense of Mojo humanity that we can assemble from this evidence, and how its evolution reflects the Mojo people's formation of alliance with the Jesuits.

Not Compassionate

The Spanish word *inhumano* can mean both "inhuman" and "inhumane," just as *humano* can mean both "human" and "humane." We can link *inhumano* to *voi achaneiná* because of the first meaning. Marbán recorded a translation of *inhumano* as *voi nahapanuray*, "I am not compassionate," which may imply a lack of humaneness, or faulty humanity, more than a literal condition of nonhumanity (Marbán 1702a, 259). Similarly, *voi nahapanu* can mean "I do not have *lástima*," a Spanish concept signifying pity, compassion, grief, or empathy from having witnessed someone's suffering or grief (Marbán 1702a, 60).

The opposite term, *nuhapanuray*, which means "I am compassionate" or "I am charitable," is based on a root, *-hapanu*. The latter refers to having compassion or charity and is the basis for several related words listed by Marbán (1702a, 93, 172, 210, 305, 413; Marbán 1702b, 70). Compassion, or nonreciprocal love and generosity, is a value of humanity held by many other Indigenous Amazonians (Killick 2009, 704–10; Santos-Granero 1991, 201–3; Walker 2020, 155–56). *Nuhapanuray* forms part of a second constellation of terms centered on the term *nuuremo*, which Marbán translated as "human/humane," "merciful," "soft of heart," "well-disposed," "affable," and "to be gentle, mild, calm, pleasant or quiet" (Marbán 1702a, 125, 139, 159, 160, 282, 659; see figure 2.2). All of these definitions reflect positive attributes of humanity for the Mojo.

Although Marbán (1702a, 30–31, 52–53; Marbán 1702b, 97–98, 170) used terms based on another root (*-emuna*) for the reciprocal love between God and humans, he found Mojo ideas of compassion useful in teaching Christianity. He employed words based on *-hapanu*. Compassion, he taught, is foremost a quality of God (Marbán 1702b, 163). Those who say that God is not merciful break the second commandment, "because God is extremely good, and without equal, and extremely compassionate" (Marbán 1702b, 42–44). He claims that people should thank God and recognize his compassion after receiving communion. When praying, people should ask God to show compassion for gentiles by sending a missionary to convert them. Compassion also characterized relations between parents and children, as Marbán explained when describing the fourth commandment. Parents should show compassion for their children, as young children relied on their parents' protection. Grown children should aid their aged parents in their need and with piety. "Do you not have compassion for them when they are sick?" he asked children of their parents (Marbán 1702b, 117). He used words based on *-hapanu* for works of charity and almsgiving (Marbán 1702a, 266; Marbán 1702b, 70–78, 97–98). Finally, he employed Mojo concepts of compassion to justify the new mission government. The Mojo must have questioned the humanity of newly installed leaders who exercised powers of command and punishment unprecedented in Mojo society. Marbán (1702b, 51–52) had to explain that caciques and alcaldes (local magistrates) who jail and whip evildoers, thieves, and adulterers do not offend God, because they punish those lawbreakers out of compassion for the victims rather than

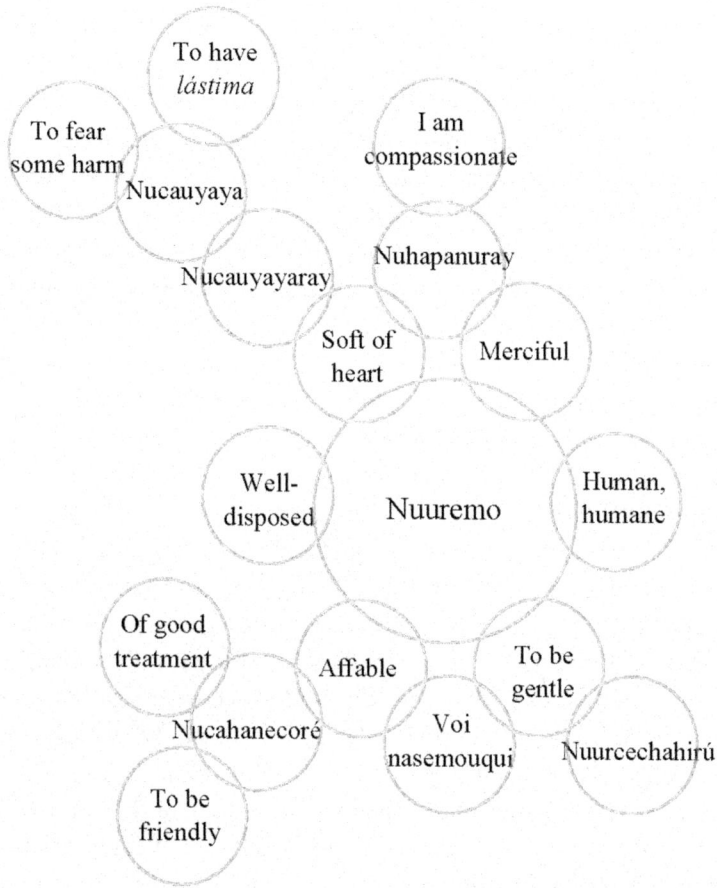

FIGURE 2.2 Mojo terms for human qualities centered on *nuuremo*. Spanish terms, except *lástima*, are translated into English. Figure made by Gary Van Valen based on data from Marbán (1702a, 1702b).

hatred. In all cases, compassion was a love that the strong demonstrated for the weak.

Several Qualities Regarded as "Unworthy"

In the Mojo language, an "unworthy person" is both *voi achaneiná* and *moeperahi* (Marbán 1702a, 258). The term *moeperahi* is also translated as *ser desaliñado* (meaning "to be unkempt, scruffy, disheveled, untidy"), "to be unable to choose well," and "superstitious" (Marbán 1702a, 198, 342, 417, 518). Other, related terms indicate that the Mojo regarded courtesy and conscientious work as worthy qualities, and their lack as unworthy ones. *Moeperahinu* (I am unworthy) is translated as "barbarous person" and thence is connected to *voi achanenuiná* and *voi nechoroiquia* (see below) (Marbán 1702a, 155, 183, 200, 228–29, 519). Marbán (1702a, 172) adapted the "unclean" aspect of *moeperahi* to describe nonfasting days, when Catholics are allowed to eat meat, as *moeperahibi tahahiporocó binicó*, meaning "when we eat any unclean thing."

Some other Amazonian peoples hold similar concepts of worthiness and unworthiness based on social behavior and bodily adornment; a lack of cleanliness and adornment is related to asocial behavior, which is interpreted as a lack of humanity (Fausto, Franchetto, and Heckenberger 2008, 149n21; Gregor 1977, 153–76; Lagrou 1998, 15, 45; Muratorio 1991, 210; Opas 2005, 112; Robbins, Schieffelin, and Vilaça 2014, 575–76; Vilaça 2002, 354, 357–58; Vilaça 2005, 453). Jesuit accounts indicate that the Mojo had high standards of dress, adornment, and cleanliness. They used cotton tunics and adorned themselves with silver and tin ornaments, feathers, and paint. They also took great care to wash and dress their hair (Barnadas and Plaza 2005, 36, 56, 70, 97–98; Castillo 1906, 303, 319, 324–25, 330, 347; Marbán 1702a, 399, 457).

Adornments were so much a part of being human that they had to be removed when a person entered the liminal state of contact with the spirit world during initiation as a shaman. Castillo wrote about a Mojo girl who went through what he interpreted as an emotional crisis. Her father decided that this was evidence that she was to become a *tiarauqui* (shaman). The Jesuit brother noted that she began abstaining from eating fish and that "she had taken off her *yupesires* [tin nose studs] as if protesting that she was not now of the world; the father, when we left, finished stripping her of beads and of all adornment." The girl only put on adornments again, and ended her abstention from fish, for the next chicha drinking ceremony, indicating that her initiation as a shaman was complete (Castillo 1906, 357; see also Cortés Rodríguez 2005, 52–53).

Access to Spanish goods caused the Mojo to reassess the role of bodily accessories in constructing humanity. By Castillo's (1906, 348) time, they considered a person with a complete set of beads and other adornments to be "blessed and rich," and one with a knife, axe, and machete to be "very powerful." Thus, the body, strengthened and stabilized as human by adornment, could be made even stronger by wielding Spanish metal tools, which the Jesuits brought as gifts to facilitate conversion. The Mojo believed that their own gods had provided the silver and tin that they used for adornments, and so the Jesuits encouraged the Mojo to believe that the Spanish acquired their abundance of iron implements from the Christian God, and that conversion would ensure a steady supply of these items. As Castillo (1906, 348) explained, God gave his children, among other things, "the iron for tools and other necessary things, so that we don't lack them."

A Lack of Knowing or Understanding to a Lesser Extent

The Mojo expression *voi achanenuiná* (I am not human) leads to "barbarous person" and thence to *voi nechoroiquia*, the key to another vector of nonhumanity (Marbán 1702a, 288). This and other negative terms based on the root for "to know," *-echo*, form the core of this vector, (Marbán 1702a, 132, 267, 288, 348). The Mojo terms clustered around *voi nechoroiquia* refer to perceived intellectual disability (Marbán 1702a, 162, 257, 288, 198, 359). Some meanings clustering around the related term *voi ne(e)chorosiquiá* suggest more serious states of mental impairment, some temporary (Marbán 1702a, 132, 150, 198, 209, 267, 294, 348).[2] In these understandings, the Mojo are comparable to some other lowland South Americans, who relate intellectual disability, mental illness, and physical illness to a loss of humanity (McCallum 1996, 347, 357; Severi 1996, 63–73, 106). Nevertheless, the Mojo's compassionate ethos apparently allowed them to care for these people and hope for their recovery, which they interpreted as a return to humanity. One Mojo term for "to convalesce" or "to have health" was *achanenú* (I am human) (Marbán 1702a, 181, 333).

One translation of *achane* (human) was "understood," and humanity is expressed by terms based on *-echo*, including *neechó* ("I know, I understand," or "to conjecture"). The words *neechoroicó* (unelided) and *nechoroicó* (elided) have meanings including "I am understood," "sagacious," "wise person," "courteous," *cuerdo* (meaning "prudent, discreet, sensible, wise, judicious, in one's senses, not mad"), "to be *cuerdo*, understood, obedient," "respectable man," and "industrious," all positive attributions of humanity for the Mojo (Marbán 1702a, 179, 183, 186, 222, 253, 258, 322, 332, 368, 463). Adapting these positive *-echo* terms to Christianity, Marbán (1702a, 259, 470; Marbán 1702b, 14) chose *echoroicache* to describe God as "exceedingly wise."

Indigenous theories of knowledge and being have commanded much attention recently in Amazonian anthropology. A prominent theme is that humanity is often produced through the embodiment of knowledge, with "mind" or "soul" not necessarily separate from "body" (see Whitaker 2016). Embodied knowledge is an essential part of the definition of humanity to many peoples in the region (Ellis 1997, 23; Kensinger 1995; Lagrou 1998; McCallum 1996; Micarelli 2015, 75, 79; Muratorio 1991, 204–5, 211, 214; Robbins, Schieffelin, and Vilaça 2014, 573–74; Severi 1996, 87–91; Werlang 2006, 104, 107). The idea that the accumulation of knowledge was necessary to achieve human status may explain one custom that the Jesuits found repugnant: when a Mojo mother died from complications with childbirth, the Mojo would bury her baby alive with her (Barnadas and Plaza 2005, 56, 69–70; Castillo 1906, 335, 361, 366, 375; Eguiluz 1884, 9). The baby was probably considered still not a separate being from the mother and incapable of surviving independently.

The Mojo language provides evidence for comparison with other ethnographic cases that emphasize the role of the senses in acquiring embodied knowledge. The positive "I know, I understand" is both *neechó* and *nusamo*, and words based on the root *-samo* indicate that the Mojo thought of knowing as something bodily and related to the senses. These *-samo* words signify hearing (with negative forms referring to the inability to hear), informing oneself (through hearing), understanding (what is heard), thinking what is best (by hearing yourself), perceiving, tasting something, trying something, smelling, feeling physically bad (through illness and pain, including birth pains), and having a sense of touch (or feeling through the skin) (Marbán 1702a, 164, 222, 246, 259, 293–94, 388, 596–98; Marbán 1702b, 178–79). Out of all the senses, hearing was very important for the Mojo, as for many other Amazonians. The Kayapo and Cashinahua, for example, associate hearing with understanding, and recent studies also point out that the privileging of sight is a Western conceit (McCallum 1996, 347, 357; Micarelli 2015, 81; Santos-Granero 2006, 62, 69, 71–72; Turner 1995, 153).

The Jesuits took hearing as the principal meaning of -*samo* and probably arrived in South America predisposed to emphasize hearing in the reception of the Christian message. In other mission fields, they stressed the precept *fides ex auditu* from Romans 10:17, meaning "faith comes from hearing" (Agnolin 2018, 74; Dorsey 1998, 410). Consequently, they used -*samo* words for hearing a Mass (or a sermon), missing Mass, and not coming to Mass. They extended these meanings (1) to the church (as the place to hear Mass); (2) to the verbs for "to preach," "to say Mass," and "to be in prayer"; (3) to articles pertaining to the church; and (4) to frequently attending church (Marbán 1702a, 238, 313, 336, 428, 597; Marbán 1702b, 178–79). By this interpretation, the church became the place where one could "know" through hearing (-*samo*). Such knowledge could accumulate, and one could "know" (-*echo*) enough to be a mature and complete human being.

A Lack of Knowing or Understanding to an Extreme Extent

In Mojo, *voi achaneiná* shares a meaning with "lost man," which in turn leads to *voi techoroiquiá*, the nonspecific third-person meaning "he/she/it does not know; they do not know" (Marbán 1702a, 305). Marbán's catechism used the unelided form *voi teechoroiquiá* to refer specifically to animals' lack of understanding. *Voi techoroiquiá* is linked to "infernal man," a term that overlaps with *voi hincha achaneiná* (very not human, truly not human), as well as *maboyuco hincha* (very excessively [bad]) (Marbán 1702a, 258–59; Marbán 1702b, 164–65).

The "infernal man" refers to a well-known concept from lowland South America, the human being who leaves human society to be converted into a forest monster (Jackson 1983, 108–12, 196–97; Kensinger 1995, 234; Lagrou 1998, 102–4; McCallum 1996, 359; Smith 1996, 53–55). Disease and irrational behavior are sometimes seen as a transformation into an animal. At times, the afflicted person never returns to humanity. What humans see as disease, animals see as warfare, and disease is a process of being captured or eaten by animals, who increase their numbers by incorporating humans as kin (Fausto 2007, 501–2; Lagrou 1998, 45–54; McCallum 1996, 363; Severi 1996, 66; Vilaça 2002, 354, 357–58; Vilaça 2005, 453). Unethical behavior, including sexual immorality, thievery, and murder, can transform a human person into this type of otherly being (Jackson 1983, 200–220; Opas 2005, 118; Severi 1996, 68, 71). Similarly, an anonymous Jesuit text, the "Descripción de los Mojo," noted that "the souls of homicides convert or pass to animate the bodies of [maned] wolves, jaguars, etc." (Barnadas and Plaza 2005, 113).

Among some Amazonian Indigenous peoples, the forest monster is identified with the soul (or one of the souls) of a deceased person (Holmberg 1969, 160, 235–36, 239–40, 243; Opas 2005, 117; Werlang 2006, 107–8, 113). The fact that *voi techoroiquiá* is "not knowing" in the nonspecific third person suggests that the Mojo conceived of this type of person as irredeemably lost to humanity, as well as further removed than the first-person singular *voi nechoroiquiá*. Unlike the latter term, which has an opposite (*nechoroicó*) indicating humanity, Marbán recorded no opposite for *voi techoroiquiá*. Instead, his usage of the concept "infernal man" translated the forest monster into the "damned soul" in Christianity, which is also irredeemably lost to humanity.

Animals

Marbán's (1702a, 163) dictionary of Mojo translates "brute, it is a brute" as *voi achaneiná* and *voi techoroiquiá*. In turn, "brute, animal" is *soraré*. This is the only category that modern Western science would regard as nonhuman. To the Mojo, however, it was both a way to be nonhuman and a possible result of transformation from humanity. According to the "Descripción de los Mojo," they "almost do not distinguish brutes from men and in consequence of their reasons, they see brutes as rational, believing that the bellows of animals and the songs of birds were conversations and speeches in a foreign language" (Barnadas and Plaza 2005, 114). Not only did homicides transform into beasts of prey, but ordinary Mojo could become deer, birds, or other animals after death (Barnadas and Plaza 2005, 113–14). In the catechism's Statement of the Lord's Prayer, Marbán found it necessary to directly address Mojo ideas about the interchangeability of human and animal souls. He uses each phrase of the Lord's Prayer to elaborate on Catholic belief through a series of questions and answers. The first words, "Our Father," inspire the question, "God, perchance, is Our Father?" to which Marbán (1702b, 165–67) replies:

Yes, because he created us, and we are similar to him, since we have understanding, and speak with judgment, because we have a soul, also of his
creation, immortal, which works those effects in us, in which we resemble
God. And God has us as children. And we are not like the animals, which,
although they are God's creatures, are not his children. They are another
type of creatures, that neither speak, nor have judgment, nor know about
God. It is true, that they have a soul, that makes them living beings, but it
is not like ours. It is mortal, and for that reason they are neither similar to
God, nor does God have them as children, being thus that he has us as his
children, because we are similar to him.

Marbán drew on his university education in theology and philosophy for
this discourse on human and animal souls, which reflects a late-medieval
Catholic interpretation of the basic ideas in Aristotle's *De Anima*. According to this interpretation, the animal soul was mortal because animals
possess only the material qualities of nutrition, growth, and reproduction
(shared with plants), as well as an equally material perception based on
sensory organs. The human soul was immortal because, in addition to
these powers, humans also possess reason, intellect, or judgment, which
can survive death because it is immaterial (Oelze 2018, 28–42). Despite
the Western philosophy behind Marbán's discourse, it is striking that he
felt the need to explain how human and animal souls differed in response
to a simple question about why God is our father. Marbán likely found
this elaboration necessary after discussing humans and animals with the
Mojo themselves. The Mojo text of this section is notable for several us-
ages. "We have understanding, and speak with judgment" is *bechoroicó*,
the first-person plural of -*echo* (to know), while for animals, "nor have
judgment, nor know" is *voi teechoroiquia voi teecha*, which are negative
and nonspecific third-person forms of -*echo* (Marbán 1702b, 164).

The Statement of the Lord's Prayer returns to animal imagery in Marbán's discussion of the final phrases of the prayer. When explaining "And
lead us not into temptation," Marbán compares the devil to the jaguar, as
a predator that attacks people when they are alone:

As happens with you all when, accompanied by others, you meet a jaguar
in the middle of the pampa, you do not fear it; rather, it fears you, and
flees from you. But not so, if it catches you alone, and without arrows with

which to defend yourselves; then you are afraid, and shake in fear of death, and say "Poor me, this time it will kill me." You do not have spirit, nor are you able to do anything out of fear, and the jaguar attacks you, bites you, and kills you. (Marbán 1702b, 191)

To many Indigenous Amazonians, according to the theory of perspectivism, becoming prey would mean a loss of humanity. In the Mojo case, resisting the devil-as-predator would conserve one's humanity, so that the category of Christians could become conflated with the category of human beings. The jaguar was the nonhuman enemy par excellence, and its predation was equated with warfare, so the Mojo kept trophy skulls of both jaguars and non-Mojo human enemies in their communal drinking houses (*bebederos*). To explain "But deliver us from evil," Marbán (1702b, 201) lists familiar dangers as evils: "And so we ask God that he deliver us from a tree falling on us, and that he deliver us from the lightning bolt, the snake, and the jaguar, and all of the other bad things." Here, the Mojo may have understood that the Christian God would protect them from capture and incorporation as kin by such powerful predators as the anaconda, the supernatural *Oé* serpent, and the jaguar. Thus, God could be conceived of as a kind of powerful ally or partner, while the devil, identified with predators in Jesuit teachings, perhaps was understood as an enemy.

The Mojo fear of predation might have made it more difficult for the Jesuits to convince several dispersed kin groups (*parcialidades*) to settle in one town. The first attempt at such settlement, which was made in 1669, failed as a result of Mojo suspicions regarding Spanish intentions (see also Loureiro Dias's chapter in this volume): "They thought that the gathering of them together for the Christian doctrine, was to prepare them to turn them over, in opportune time, to the Spaniard; that the attempt to reduce them to larger towns was to secure the prey in order that they not be lost by being dispersed" (Eguiluz 1884, 3; see also Renard-Casevitz 2002, 129). In accordance with ontological frameworks common among many Indigenous Amazonians, becoming "prey" would be more serious than merely losing their liberty; it would mean losing their humanity.

When trying to understand Mojo ideas of warfare, Castillo asked Mojo people questions that help elucidate their ideas about humanity and alterity:

They say that they who fight naked are brave; the Spanish are not, who fight so well-armed that they do not do much in being brave. Asking them, why they do not fight the jaguar alone and without weapons, tooth and nail, as he does, but rather they go in the company of others, all with dogs, bows, and arrows, [they responded] that they do this because they have understanding and reason, and that because of that, they are braver than the jaguar and kill very many. Thus, the Spanish look upon them [the Mojo] as animals, and because of that, they arm themselves with better weapons and triumph with more understanding, and thus they are braver, a few being enough for thousands of them. (Castillo 1906, 342–43)

After initially claiming that fighting with inferior arms proved their greater bravery, the Mojo quickly changed their argument when Castillo asked them to consider the jaguar. Those with better arms had more understanding (and thus more humanity) and could view their opponents, in comparison, as animals. The Mojo seemed to think that it was only natural for the better-armed Spanish to view them as animals. What modern scholars would consider as merely historically conditioned differences in military technology, the Mojo saw as differences in understanding and humanity.

The Mojo acceptance of missionaries brought Spanish goods and an increased knowledge of Spanish technologies, for example, in ironworking (see Whitaker's chapter in this volume) and was desirable as a way to maintain their humanity. Adapting their ideas of humanity and nonhumanity to changing conditions is an example of Mojo agency (see Van Valen 2013). Conversion was attractive because it offered the Mojo an opportunity to maintain a position of humanity in these new circumstances. As with some other Indigenous groups in Amazonia, such as the Wari', Christianity gave the seventeenth-century Mojo "an additional tool for the continual work of differentiating themselves from animals" (Robbins, Schieffelin, and Vilaça 2014, 576).

Not Baptized

The previous qualities of nonhumanity likely predated the arrival of Jesuit missionaries among the Mojo. Being fully human probably already required one to have the physical form of a human being (as opposed to an animal), as well as "knowing" or understanding, compassion, and "worthy" qualities of character. With the Mojo decision to accept Christianity, not being baptized became a new way to be nonhuman, and baptism as a Christian became a new way to be human. From *voi achaneiná*, "barbarous people" overlaps with plural terms for the unbaptized: *moicachasionó* and *voi tacaicachasionó*, which lead to further terms for non-Christians (infidels, pagans, gentiles) (Marbán 1702a, 155, 241–42, 259, 520, 297; Marbán 1702b, 8). The most common terms for baptism (or lack of baptism) are based on the root *-cachasi*, meaning "to wash the head." The basic form *moicachasi* means "not baptized/head washed," or "without baptism/head washing" (Marbán 1702a, 72–73).

Why did the Mojo consider the "head washing" of baptism to be the most important element of Christianity? The Jesuits probably contributed to this idea, since baptism was the first of the sacraments to be administered. Baptism made one a Christian, and baptisms allowed the Jesuits to report on the success of their mission and to retain the support of the ecclesiastical and civil authorities who financed and supported their efforts. Additionally, the Jesuits' success depended on their willingness to accept many of the practices and beliefs of the Indigenous people, so they did not initially demand much more than baptism. Nevertheless, a ritual pouring of water on the head, often performed on the gravely ill, resonates with other Indigenous Amazonian ideas of health and curing. Several Indigenous groups in Amazonia (including the modern Trinitario Mojo) regard the application of paint or medicines to the skin as important to health, and medicinal baths serve a similar function (Thomas et al. 2009, 305–310).

The seventeenth-century Mojo had a curing ritual that involved bathing the body to remove illness in the form of an invisible snake. Castillo described it thus:

> These [curers] take it [the snake] out, making from the root of a certain plant a foam which is not different from that of soap, in great quantity. They make the sick person lay stretched out and they put a lot of this foam on him, on the whole back, from the waist to the shoulders. They make him turn over and they also put it on the belly and the chest. With this, and

with telling them that the snake came out, they [the patients] go, grateful and content. (Castillo 1906, 353; cf. Kensinger 1995, 227)

Two terms for the Mojo ritual, *nusipoocó* and *nucasipoó*, meant both to wash or bathe the body and to cure with foam. The related term *nusipocuó* meant to wash. These and many other washing terms were based on the root *-sipo*. Marbán (1702a, 157, 428, 606) recorded other expressions for "to baptize" (*nusiposicó*) and "to be baptized" or "to wash the head" (*nucasiposi*) based on this same root. Since the Mojo built terminology for "to cure with foam" and "to baptize" around the same root, they may have categorized these procedures together.

Castillo (1906, 389) recorded a case that confirms this conflation of baptism with a medicinal bath applied to the whole body. One gravely ill cacique wanted to become a Christian: "He disposed himself to receive the sacred baptism, and pouring the water on his head, he said, 'And why do you not wash the rest of me?' The fathers responded that it was enough."

The Mojo initially referred to the Jesuits as shamans (*tiarauqui*); despite being told many times not to call the Jesuits this, the Mojo would not desist (Castillo 1906, 357; see also Castelnau-L'Estoile 2006, 2019; Van Valen 2013; and Whitaker 2025). This identification with Indigenous curers is not surprising, since Marbán defined the sacraments as "some spiritual remedies which Christians use to cure their souls of the pains of their sins" (Marbán 1702b, 79).

Marbán (1702b, 71) explained how gentiles (*moicachasireono*) differed from Christians (*Christianono*) in their relationship to God when answering the catechism's question, "How are we to pray to God for the living?"

I will tell you all, you all have to know, that there are two sorts of living men, some are Christians, and they are our brothers, because we all know God as Father, who deigns to have us as his children. For these we must ask God to give them health, to free them from the devil's deceits, and to give them his grace, in order to keep his Holy Commandments. The others are the Gentiles; it is true these are of our same nature, but they are not our brothers, because they do not know God as their Father, nor do they have him as such. For these we must ask God, that he have compassion for them, and send to them someone who will teach his Holy Law to them, in order that they know God as their Father, and thus be baptized, and come to be our brothers.

Although Marbán regarded both Christians and gentiles as human, his teaching could easily have been interpreted differently by the Mojo, especially considering what the Jesuit missionary had taught them about humans and animals. Like the animals, the gentiles do not "know" God as their father, nor do they seem to "have" God as their father, since they are not brothers to the Christians. Being thus like the animals, the gentiles could (according to this logic and from a Mojo perspective) be classified conceptually as nonhuman until baptism made them human. By becoming brothers and recognizing the same father, they would become kin. Until then, they would remain non-kin enemies (or perhaps affinal enemies).

Mojo Notions of Humanity in a Time of Change

Evidence from Marbán and other Jesuit sources shows that the Mojo held clear and multifaceted notions of humanity during the seventeenth century. Some of these notions involved ideals concerning how humans should treat each other convivially, including compassion, courtesy, and conscientious work or industriousness. Other notions described a condition of mental and physical soundness that promoted this human sociability. This state of sound humanity was expressed partly through cleanliness and adornment. It was exemplified by a "knowing" state of clear-mindedness, judgment, understanding, and reason. And it was made possible through the ability to perceive knowledge through hearing and other senses.

The Mojo also conceptualized their humanity as a form of differentiation that contrasted them with other beings who did not share these human qualities. Based on their perspectivist understanding of the world, they knew that the possibility of transformation into nonhuman beings existed. The Jesuit sources give indications that the Mojo believed humanity could be lost by falling prey to such otherly beings (e.g., jaguars and other animal predators). Such a loss of humanity could be temporary, for example, through mental or physical illness, intoxication, or removal of adornments, or it might be permanent, such as through the loss of reason and conversion into a murderer, a monster, or some kind of animal.

The Jesuits appealed to Mojo conceptualizations of humanity when they taught them that compassion was a Christian value. Unlike some of the secular Spanish who had entered the Llanos de Mojos, the Jesuits demonstrated this value, as well as perhaps courtesy and conscientious work. They exhibited a state of sound humanity through their knowledge, which became clear once they had learned the Mojo language and begun to translate Christian concepts with the guidance of their Mojo teachers. The Mojo and Jesuits found common ground in their agreement that knowledge came from hearing and that animals lacked human reason or understanding. The Jesuits also offered new material goods, which the Mojo found desirable. This desirability may have been, in part, because these goods helped facilitate Mojo goals of human sociability and differentiation from animals. The Mojo accepted Christian baptism, which resembled Mojo curing rituals that restored endangered humanity, because this baptism sealed an alliance and partnership with the Jesuits and the Christian God. It ensured access to the Jesuit goods and knowledge that helped maintain their humanity in a time of change and became a new way in which the Mojo could differentiate themselves from both animals and non-Christians.

Throughout this chapter, the analysis of Jesuit primary sources has shown that Mojo conceptualizations of humanity and nonhumanity are significant for understanding the alliance and partnership between Mojo and Jesuits. Initially defined by the Mojo as shamans, the Jesuits would have appeared as liminal figures with the power to transform, as well as to translate or mediate between worlds (Vilaça 2010, 315; Whitaker 2025). They brought gifts of metal, other manufactured goods, and livestock to gain Mojo goodwill. To successfully establish a mission presence in the Llanos de Mojos, the Jesuits needed to engage with Mojo concepts of alterity and humanity by demonstrating compassion; "knowing," or understanding; and worthy qualities of character, as locally defined by the

Mojo. In several cases, a dialogue between the Jesuits and Mojo people resulted in conflations of the categories of Christian and human.

The Mojo adapted their conceptualizations of humanity and nonhumanity in the new situation created by the arrival of the Spanish. At least some of the Mojo judged the Spanish to have more understanding, as well as the ability to defeat and capture them, both of which threatened to conceptually reclassify the Mojo as animals. At the same time, the Jesuits demonstrated that, as well as "knowing," some of the Spanish were perhaps compassionate and worthy through their kindness, peacefulness, and learning, although the behavior of many of the Spanish undoubtedly did not meet the standards and expectations of the Mojo concerning how real people ought to behave. In this new situation, the Mojo sometimes adjusted their criteria for humanity. For example, such criteria were altered to include Christianity as a humanizing predication. They converted to Christianity and allied with the Spanish in accordance.

The Mojo and Jesuits eventually came to see one another as human, as shown by their use of a lack of baptism to jointly redefine the other. This mutual recognition was necessary before relations of alliance and partnership (between both the Mojo and the Jesuits and the Mojo and the Christian God) could be made permanent. This new way of being human resulted in defining the unbaptized as nonhuman, but it also allowed other baptized peoples to enter the category of human. As the classification of others as non-kin enemies shifted to allow other baptized peoples to be treated as allies, partners, and kin, the Jesuits went on to introduce Christianity to the Canichana, Movima, Cayubaba, Baure, Itonama, and other groups of the Llanos de Mojos. What the Jesuits saw as an expanded mission field was likely interpreted by local people as a new system of alliance, mediated by the Christian God, and made possible by shared humanity.

Notes

1.   A modern comprehensive study of the Ignaciano Mojo language indicates that
      most terms associated with human and nonhuman qualities in the seventeenth
      century have comparable meanings in modern times. See the following examples in Olza Zubiri, Nuna de Chapi, and Tube (2004), with page references:
      nujápanurahi ("I am compassionate," 411); the root *-uri* ("good, to be good,"
      75–77); *máeperaji* ("dirty," 685, 802) and *-máeperajica* ("to make dirty," 802);

-*echareca* ("to be understood, to be intelligent," 934) and *néchareca* ("I am intelligent," 934); *máecharaire* ("foolish and silly, without intelligence," 792); and *máicachasiana* ("the barbarians," 487, 521).

2. Mojo terms clustering around *voi ne(e)choroiquiá* are translated as "imprudent," "foolish," "stupid person," "idiot," "to act foolishly," "to talk nonsense," "to be unable," and "to speak in a language that is not understood" (Marbán 1702a, 162, 257, 288, 198, 359). Meanings clustering around *voi ne(e)chorosiquiá* include "to be lacking in judgment," "to be crazy," "bewildered, dazed, perplexed," "to rave or rant," "forgetful person," and "deranged by illness" (Marbán 1702a, 132, 150, 198, 209, 267, 294, 348). *Voi ne(e)chorosiquiá* incorporates the quantitative infix *-sí-* (meaning "many," "very," etc.) and is an intensified version of *voi ne(e) choroiquiá* (Olza Zubiri, Nuna de Chapi, and Tube 2004, 828–31). Other negative terms include *macharairé* (a privative form based on the regional variant *-echa*) and *coparesiré* (probably referring to intoxication caused by chewing the beans of *Anadenanthera colubrina* var. *cebil*), both translated as "crazed" (Marbán 1702a, 132, 267, 288, 348).

References

Agnolin, Adone. 2018. "Violence and Adaptability of the Word: Jesuits and Natives in Portuguese America (16th-17th Centuries)." In *Compel People to Come In: Violence and Catholic Conversions in the Non-European World*, edited by Vincenzo Lavenia, Stefania Pastore, Sabina Pavone, and Chiara Petrolini, 69–88. Rome: Viella.

Barnadas, Josep M., and Manuel Plaza. 2005. *Mojos: Seis Relaciones Jesuíticas, Geografía—Etnografía—Evangelización*. Cochabamba, Bolivia: Historia Boliviana.

Block, David. 1994. *Mission Culture on the Upper Amazon: Native Tradition, Jesuit Enterprise, and Secular Policy in Moxos, 1660–1880*. Lincoln: University of Nebraska Press.

Castelnau-L'Estoile, Charlotte de. 2006. "The Uses of Shamanism: Evangelizing Strategies and Missionary Models in Seventeenth-Century Brazil." In *The Jesuits II: Cultures, Sciences, and the Arts, 1540–1773*, edited by John W. O'Malley, Gauvin Alexander Bailey, Steven Harris, and Frank Kennedy, 616–37. Toronto: University of Toronto Press.

Castelnau-L'Estoile, Charlotte de. 2019. "Jesuit Anthropology: Studying 'Living Books.'" In *The Oxford Handbook of the Jesuits*, edited by Ines G. Županov, 811–30. Oxford: Oxford University Press.

Castillo, Joseph [José del]. 1906. "Relación de la provincia de Mojos." In *Documentos para la historia geográfica de la República de Bolivia, serie primera: Época colonial*, vol. 1, *Las Provincias de Mojos y Chiquitos*, edited by Manuel V. Ballivián, 294–395. La Paz: J. M. Gamarra.

Cortés Rodríguez, Jorge. 2005. *Caciques y hechiceros: Huellas en la historia de Mojos*. La Paz: Plural Editores.

Dorsey, Peter A. 1998. "Going to School with Savages: Authorship and Authority among the Jesuits of New France." *William and Mary Quarterly* 55 (3): 399–420.

Eguiluz, P. Diego de. 1884. *Historia de la misión de Mojos en la república de Bolivia escrita en 1696 por el P. Diego de Eguiluz.* Lima: Imprenta del Universo.

Ellis, Rebecca. 1997. "A Taste for Movement: An Exploration of the Social Ethics of the Tsimanes of Lowland Bolivia." PhD diss., University of St. Andrews.

Fausto, Carlos. 2007. "Feasting on People: Eating Animals and Humans in Amazonia." *Current Anthropology* 48 (4): 497–530.

Fausto, Carlos, Bruna Franchetto, and Michael Heckenberger. 2008. "Language, Ritual, and Historical Reconstruction: Towards a Linguistic, Ethnographic and Archaeological Account of Upper Xingu Society." In *Lessons from Documented Endangered Languages,* edited by K. David Harrison, David S. Rood, and Arienne Dwyer, 129–58. Amsterdam: John Benjamins.

Gow, Peter. 1991. *Of Mixed Blood: Kinship and History in Peruvian Amazonia.* Oxford: Clarendon.

Gregor, Thomas. 1977. *Mehinaku: The Drama of Daily Life in a Brazilian Indian Village.* Chicago: University of Chicago Press.

Holmberg, Allan R. 1969. *Nomads of the Long Bow: The Siriono of Eastern Bolivia.* Garden City, N.Y.: Natural History Press.

Jackson, Jean E. 1983. *The Fish People: Linguistic Exogamy and Tukanoan Identity in Northwest Amazonia.* Cambridge: Cambridge University Press.

Kensinger, Kenneth M. 1995. *How Real People Ought to Live: The Cashinahua of Eastern Peru.* Prospect Heights, Ill.: Waveland.

Killick, Evan. 2009. "Ashéninka Amity: A Study of Social Relations in an Amazonian Society." *Journal of the Royal Anthropological Institute* 15 (4): 701–18.

Lagrou, Elsje Maria. 1998. "Cashinahua Cosmovision: A Perspectival Approach to Identity and Alterity." PhD diss., University of St. Andrews.

Marbán, Pedro. 1702a. Arte, Vocabulario. In *Arte de la lengua moxa con su vocabulario y cathecismo.* Lima: Imprenta Real de Jospeh de Contreras.

Marbán, Pedro. 1702b. Cathecismo. In *Arte de la lengua moxa con su vocabulario y cathecismo.* Lima: Imprenta Real de Joseph de Contreras.

McCallum, Cecilia. 1996. "The Body That Knows: From Cashinahua Epistemology to a Medical Anthropology of Lowland South America." *Medical Anthropology Quarterly* 10 (3): 347–72.

McCallum, Cecilia. 2001. *Gender and Sociality in Amazonia: How Real People Are Made.* Oxford: Berg.

Micarelli, Giovanna. 2015. "Finding the Taste of Knowledge: The Orphan in Indigenous Epistemologies." *Tipití* 13 (2): 74–90.

Muratorio, Blanca. 1991. *The Life and Times of Grandfather Alonso: Culture and History in the Upper Amazon.* New Brunswick, N.J.: Rutgers University Press.

Oelze, Anselm. 2018. *Animal Rationality: Later Medieval Theories, 1250–1350.* Leiden: Brill.

Olza Zubiri, Jesús, Conchita Nuna de Chapi, and Juan Tube. 2004. *Gramática moja-ignaciana (morfosintaxis)*. Cochabamba, Bolivia: Editorial Verbo Divino.

Opas, Minna. 2005. "Mutually Exclusive Relationships: Corporeality and Differentiation of Persons in Yine (Piro) Social Cosmos." *Tipití* 3 (2): 111–30.

Overing, Joanna, and Alan Passes. 2000. *The Anthropology of Love and Anger: The Aesthetics of Conviviality in Native Amazonia*. London: Routledge.

Rapport, Nigel, and Joanna Overing. 2000. *Social and Cultural Anthropology: The Key Concepts*. London: Routledge.

Renard-Casevitz, France-Marie. 2002. "Social Forms and Regressive History: From the Campa Cluster to the Mojos and from the Mojos to the Landscaping Terrace-Builders of the Bolivian Savanna." In *Comparative Arawakan Histories: Rethinking Language Family and Culture Area in Amazonia*, edited by Jonathan D. Hill and Fernando Santos-Granero, 123–46. Urbana: University of Illinois Press.

Rival, Laura. 2005. "Introduction: What Constitutes a Human Body in Native Amazonia?" *Tipití* 3 (2): 105–10.

Robbins, Joel, Bambi B. Schieffelin, and Aparecida Vilaça. 2014. "Evangelical Conversion and the Transformation of the Self in Amazonia and Melanesia: Christianity and the Revival of Anthropological Comparison." *Comparative Studies in Society and History* 56 (3): 559–90.

Rose, Françoise. 2014. "Negation and Irrealis in Mojeño Trinitario." In *Negation in Arawak Languages*, edited by Lev Michael and Tania Granadillo, 216–40. Leiden: Brill.

Rosengren, Dan. 2006. "Matsigenka Corporality, a Nonbiological Reality: On Notions of Consciousness and the Constitution of Identity." *Tipití* 4 (1): 81–102.

Santos-Granero, Fernando. 1991. *The Power of Love: The Moral Use of Knowledge amongst the Amuesha of Central Peru*. London: Athlone Press.

Santos-Granero, Fernando. 2006. "Sensual Vitalities: Noncorporeal Modes of Sensing and Knowing in Native Amazonia." *Tipití* 4 (1–2): 57–80.

Santos-Granero, Fernando. 2012. "Beinghood and People-Making in Native Amazonia: A Constructional Approach with a Perspectival Coda." *HAU: Journal of Ethnographic Theory* 2 (1): 181–211.

Sarreal, Julia J. S. 2014. *The Guaraní and Their Missions: A Socioeconomic History*. Stanford, Calif.: Stanford University Press.

Schindler, Helmut. 1977. "Carijona and Manakïnï: An Opposition in the Mythology of a Carib Tribe." In *Carib-Speaking Indians: Culture, Society, and Language*, edited by Ellen B. Basso, 66–75. Tucson: University of Arizona Press.

Seeger, Anthony, Roberto Da Matta, and Eduardo B. Viveiros de Castro. 2019. "The Construction of the Person in Indigenous Brazilian Societies." *HAU: Journal of Ethnographic Theory* 9 (3): 694–702.

Severi, Carlo. 1996. *La memoria ritual: Locura e imagen del blanco en una tradición chamánica amerindia*. Quito, Ecuador: Ediciones Abya-Yala.

Smith, Nigel J. H. 1996. *The Enchanted Amazon Rain Forest: Stories from a Vanishing World*. Gainesville: University Press of Florida.

Thomas, Evert, Ina Vandebroek, Patrick Van Damme, Lucio Semo, and Zacaria Noza. 2009 "*Susto* Etiology and Treatment according to Bolivian Trinitario People: A 'Masters of the Animal Species' Phenomenon." *Medical Anthropology Quarterly* 23 (3): 298–319.

Turner, Terence. 1995. "Social Body and Embodied Subject: Bodiliness, Subjectivity, and Sociality among the Kayapo." *Cultural Anthropology* 10 (2): 143–70.

Van Valen, Gary. 2013. *Indigenous Agency in the Amazon: The Mojos in Liberal and Rubber-Boom Bolivia, 1842–1932*. Tucson: University of Arizona Press.

Vilaça, Aparecida. 2002. "Making Kin out of Others in Amazonia." *Journal of the Royal Anthropological Institute* 8 (2): 347–65.

Vilaça, Aparecida. 2005. "Chronically Unstable Bodies: Reflections on Amazonian Corporalities." *Journal of the Royal Anthropological Institute* 11 (3): 445–64.

Vilaça, Aparecida. 2010. *Strange Enemies: Indigenous Agency and Scenes of Encounters in Amazonia*. Durham, N.C.: Duke University Press.

Vilaça, Aparecida. 2016. *Praying and Preying: Christianity in Indigenous Amazonia*. Oakland: University of California Press.

Viveiros de Castro, Eduardo. 1996. "Images of Nature and Society in Amazonian Ethnology." *Annual Review of Anthropology* 25:179–200.

Viveiros de Castro, Eduardo. 1998. "Cosmological Deixis and Amerindian Perspectivism." *Journal of the Royal Anthropological Institute* 4 (3): 469–88.

Walker, Harry. 2012. "Demonic Trade: Debt, Materiality, and Agency in Amazonia." *Journal of the Royal Anthropological Institute* 18 (1): 140–59.

Walker, Harry. 2013. "Wild Things: Manufacturing Desire in the Urarina Moral Economy." *Journal of Latin American and Caribbean Anthropology* 18 (1): 51–66.

Walker, Harry. 2020. "Equality without Equivalence: An Anthropology of the Common." *Journal of the Royal Anthropological Institute* 26 (1): 146–66.

Werlang, Guilherme. 2006. "On Body and Soul." *Tipití* 4 (1): 103–27.

Whitaker, James Andrew. 2016. "In Search of the Soul in Amazonia." *Anthropos* 111 (1): 201–5.

Whitaker, James Andrew. 2021. "Sorcery and Well-Being: Bodily Transformation at Beckeranta." *Anthropology and Medicine* 28 (1): 78–93.

Whitaker, James Andrew. 2025. *The Shamanism of Eco-Tourism: History and Ontology among the Makushi in Guyana*. Cambridge: Cambridge University Press.

Yvinec, Cédric. 2014. "Temporal Dimensions of Selfhood: Theories of Person among the Suruí of Rondônia." *Journal of the Royal Anthropological Institute* 20 (1): 20–37.

CHAPTER 3

Indigenous Women in the Early Years of Brazilian Colonial Society

History and Uses of the Past

ELISA FRÜHAUF GARCIA

Relationships between Indigenous women and Iberian men were an essential part of the formative years of colonial society on the Brazilian coast by the beginning of the sixteenth century. Indeed, this statement is not new. Scholarship regarding the period has largely focused on these relations. They have been addressed since the first "nationalist" approaches at the beginning of the twentieth century, whose aim was to find the origins of modern countries in colonial society from a *mestizaje* perspective. For many generations of Latin American intellectuals, the mixing of people from African, American, and European backgrounds was the main standpoint for understanding the social history of their own countries or of those with an Iberian colonial past.[1] Nevertheless, in recent years, historiography on the formative period of colonial societies during the sixteenth and seventeenth centuries has shown how the presence of Indigenous women was much more than "sex and miscegenation." The alliances between them and European men structured the first contacts, essentially marking how the latter joined local societies and thrived in the Atlantic colonial world (Barr 2007; Sleeper-Smith 2001; Townsend 2004).

Members of the first European expeditions to the Atlantic coast of South America, for example, relied on alliances with Indigenous women and their relatives to survive and stand out among their peers. This was the case for Enrique Montes, a member of Juan Díaz de Solís's 1515 expedition to the River Plate. After spending some time on the southern coast of Brazil, he returned to Europe with Sebastián Caboto in 1528. On his journey back, Montes took with him "his concubines, two freed [*forras*] Indian women" (J. Prado 1939, 80). Shortly thereafter, when he returned to Brazil with Martim Afonso de Sousa's expedition, he had been promoted to "knight of the house, supplier of provisions to the armada, and informer of the River Plate." His "Indian" women, without whom he would hardly have achieved such recognition, were left in the Iberian Peninsula: one in Spain, another in Portugal (J. Prado 1939, 86).

Among the Iberians who frequented the Brazilian Atlantic coast, there were many other examples of men who had achieved some political capital as a result of their relationships with Indigenous women. This was the case for João Carvalho, one of Ferdinand Magellan's expedition pilots. He had lived on the Brazilian coast for four years, since he was abandoned there by the ship *Bretoa* in 1511, after being accused of stealing axes. When he returned to Europe, he left behind wives, relatives, and at least one son in Brazil. His previous experience on the South American Atlantic coast was one of the main reasons Magellan hired him. Carvalho was a valuable crew member because he was familiar with the region and spoke the language of the Indigenous peoples. He was, for example, quoted as an authority on the "customs" of Guanabara Bay inhabitants by Antonio Pigafetta.[2] Nevertheless, his main asset was the kinship network he had established. Hiring someone with former experience in the land was a successful strategy. The sailors were well received when the expedition arrived in Rio de Janeiro in 1519. As a sign of comradeship, the locals brought many gifts and goods to trade with the crew. When the expedition left, Carvalho took his son, known as *niñito* (little boy), with him, as well as two Indigenous women (Pereira 2018; J. Prado 1939, 64).

Although these narratives focus on male agents, they reveal the key roles played by women in the personal networks on which European empires depended in their formative years. This does not mean, however, that Indigenous women always played a central role in these relationships. Their male relatives were often represented as the protagonists, at least in the way the information was recorded. As a result, telling colonial history from a female perspective is challenging. Most Indigenous women, unlike their Iberian counterparts, did not have their names recorded in the sources. As Rebecca Jager has pointed out in relation to North America, European men often replaced Native women's names with generic terms such as "Indigenous woman" or "squaw," because of translation difficulties or cultural bias (Jager 2015, 4). The same happened on the Brazilian coast, where different categories were used to refer to Indigenous women instead of their names. For example, the mother of João Carvalho's aforementioned son was referred to by Herrera in the *Decadas* as "the woman of the land" (*mulher da terra*). On another occasion, she was referred to as "black" (*negra*) by a survivor of Magellan's expedition (Julio 2022, 41). This pattern in the colonial narratives produces, as Karen Vieira Powers (2002, 12) puts it, "androcentric histories." Although Native women were present, they were represented through an Iberian male prism.

Indigenous Women: Allies of Europeans in Overseas Territories?

As European groups settled overseas, the theme of the chief's daughter who "married" a European leader became a common narrative. Those narratives were incorporated into conventional and widely circulated stories about the making of colonial society. They were an important part of the history of the Americas but also material for some romanticized approaches. An unavoidable reference from North America is Pocahontas, whose agency was supposedly responsible for the English settlement at Jamestown. Although based on colonial records, her story has been transformed into a long-standing and well-known myth (Townsend 2004). Decades before Pocahontas, however, many similar cases occurred in Brazil (Metcalf 2007). The most famous is undoubtedly that of Catarina Paraguaçu, recently revisited by João Pacheco de Oliveira (2022). She stands out in Brazilian historiography for her union with the shipwrecked Diogo Álvares, who was better known as Caramuru, a nickname given to him by the Tupinambá people. What we know about the couple is a combination of historical data, which are found in administrative sources and colonial chronicles, and a series of reinterpretations produced in specific contexts with different purposes (Amado 2000; Treece 2013). Paraguaçu's political importance to the Portuguese empire was summarized crudely by Sebastião da Rocha Pita ([1730] 1878: 40–41), who described her as a "Lady of these heathens, [who] made them subject to the Portuguese yoke with less repugnance."

Many other areas in Brazil have their own "mythical foundational couple," such as Maria do Espírito Santo Arcoverde in Pernambuco. She supposedly saved the life of a Portuguese man, Jerônimo de Albuquerque, whose origin, unlike others, is well known. He was the brother of dona Brites de Albuquerque, who was the wife of Duarte Coelho. Thus, he was the brother-in-law of the Pernambuco donatory and had arrived there as part of his entourage. During a battle with a group of Indigenous people in the mid-1530s, Albuquerque was struck by an arrow and lost an eye. According to reports, this is how he got his nickname as "the crooked." In the narratives, the disability did not affect his "attractiveness." On the contrary, it reinforced his masculinity and value as a warrior. His masculine appeal was purportedly the reason he was saved from the anthropophagic ritual. The chief's daughter "fell in love" and pleaded with her father, the Arcoverde chief, for him to spare "the crooked." From then on, she and Albuquerque maintained a long marriage, which linked her people, the Tabajaras, to his people, the Portuguese (Hemming 1978, 164). The couple had eight children together. Known as the Adam of Pernambuco, he eventually had a total of thirty-five recognized direct descendants. In addition to those born from his relationship with Maria do Espírito Santo, he also had children with other Indigenous women, as well as in his later marriage to Felipa de Mello. Unlike Catarina Paraguaçu, Arcoverde would have been "replaced" by a woman from Portugal, which did not prevent her from standing out in local stories and traditions about first contacts. In part, this was because she saved Jerônimo de Albuquerque from death, symbolizing her alliance to the Portuguese people. But her fame is also linked to her eight children. Recognized by their father, they became a fundamental part of the local elite. Some even distinguished themselves in other spaces outside the local milieu. The most famous was Jerônimo de Albuquerque, his father's namesake and the famous conqueror of Maranhão (Meira 2017).

Even when local colonial narratives do not cover the full "plot" about the alliances between Indigenous women and European men, the main ingredient is there. We can see that in the case of a chief's daughter who, in the words of Frei Vicente do Salvador, "fell in love" with Vasco Fernandes de Lucena. The feeling was apparently mutual, since they had many children together. The man was also highly valued as a son-in-law by the chief, the father of the woman in question, and respected by the other Indigenous people. This relationship seems to have sealed the fate of the Portuguese during the siege of Olinda in the mid-sixteenth century, when they were surrounded by Indigenous people alongside their French allies. On that occasion, she acted with her female friends to help the besieged Portuguese by bringing them water and food to survive (Salvador [1627] 2010, 146). This also shows the importance of alliances and friendships among women during the colonial wars. Beyond the historiographical intentions to portray Indigenous women only from a gendered, romantic, or sexual perspective, these women did in fact have their own networks, which were essential on occasions like this. Apparently, this deed earned her a place on the 1758 list of "famous Indians" recognized for their participation in the "temporal and spiritual" conquest of Brazil. Once again, we have a woman's story without mentioning her name. She was simply described as an "Indian woman" who was an "instrument of victory" for the Portuguese against the French.[3]

The list of "famous Indians" also gives us an important element for understanding another reason those women were registered in the colonial records. The Portuguese male conquerors were not the only ones who thrived because of their relationships with Indigenous women. The same happened with the Catholic Church, especially some orders, such as the Jesuits and Benedictines. Catarina Paraguaçu, for instance, was the main benefactor of the Benedictines in Salvador. She was not only a local patron of the order but also featured in a sixteenth-century painting that represents the propagation of the Benedictines across the world. Located in the Basilica of the Virgin of the Consolation, in Turin, Italy, the painting depicts Catarina with a panache on her head, a pearl necklace, and a baby in her arms (Avila 2014, 170). The artwork dates back to the sixteenth century, which means that the importance of Catarina Paraguaçu for the establishment of the Catholic Church overseas might have been acknowledged when she was still alive.

Other Indigenous women were important locally, such as Maria Rosa, who was one of the richest women in Olinda in the sixteenth century. Although recovering information about her is not easy from the limited available documents, João Azevedo Fernandes (2003, 341) was able to trace fragments of her biography. She was close to the Jesuits and distinguished herself by helping them with confessions. In fact, she was so good at listening to the sins of the other Indigenous women that Father Antonio Pires thought she was a better confessor than he was.[4]

Looking back at that time, we know that another of the few Indigenous women whose biographies were registered was Bartira. She was later baptized with the Christian name Isabel Dias. The known narrative is that she was the daughter of Tibiriçá, who was the leading chief of the Tupiniquim people in São Paulo by the mid-sixteenth century. His support was crucial for the Portuguese settlement (Monteiro 1994, 210). As is well known, the European presence in that area was connected with the coast, where captive Indigenous people were traded from an island called Slaves Port (J. Prado 1939). As its name suggests, the place was a meeting point for Europeans from different origins who were involved in the slave trade (van Deusen 2015, 205).

In 1532, Martim Afonso de Sousa turned Slaves Port into São Vicente, which was the first Portuguese colonial village established in Brazil. This was only possible because of the support of the family formed by João Ramalho, Tibiriçá, and Bartira. The power of her family was remarkable in all of the crucial moments of colonial establishment in São Paulo. It was, for example, in her father's village that the Jesuits founded the first administrative building of the Society of Jesus in the region in 1554. At the time, the Portuguese were besieged by attacks from rival Indigenous groups, the result of both the conflicts later known as the Tamoio Confederation and divisions among the Tupiniquim themselves. Some of Tibiriçá's relatives, who had once been allies, switched sides and turned against the advances of colonial society. Faced with this situation, the Portuguese abandoned the village of Santo André in 1558 and moved to the outskirts of the Jesuit house. This gave rise to the village of São Paulo in 1560.

Bartira was an important character in this whole process, although she does not feature prominently in most narratives, not for lack of information, but because of the male-centric perspective so entrenched in our history. In addition to her personal accomplishments and family background, Bartira's role in São Paulo's colonial history was also linked to João Ramalho, who was her partner and a central figure for the Portuguese settling on the São Paulo plateau. He probably arrived there in the early 1510s. Very little is known about his former life in Portugal, but he was remarkably skillful in implicating himself in local customs. Married to various women, he had so many children that Tomé de Souza, Brazil's first governor-general, did not dare to attempt to count them.[5] Ramalho's cultural skills and large number of offspring made him the most powerful European man in São Paulo when the colonial society was established. According to Ulderich Schmidel ([1557] 1836, 57), Ramalho's village was a bandit cave, whose leader was none other than Ramalho himself. Despite his reputation as a "bandit," or perhaps because of it, Ramalho was able to gather five thousand Indigenous people in one day for a war while the king of Portugal was unable to gather even two thousand. Nevertheless, Bartira's place in the stories about her relatives is somewhat unclear. In fact, she is a character constructed according to convenience, by following the above-mentioned widespread narratives about "mythical foundational couples." Let us look more closely at her case.

In Search of Bartira in Colonial History

From the start, the documents commonly used by authors to tell Bartira's story are the Jesuit letters from their first years in Brazil. Nevertheless, none of them mentions her name. José de Anchieta used terms such as "mother brasílica" and "concubine brasílica" in passages that were later associated with her by Serafim Leite (1956, 2:114–15).[6] The same thing happened in another episode often mentioned in the historiography. It involves Bartira supposedly defending the priest Leonardo Nunes from Ramalho's threats. The incident is quite revealing about Indigenous women's agency. According to Pero Correa, an "indoctrinated" Indian woman "preached strong and with a big faith" in favor of Nunes and against the man who threatened him. The existence of a woman with such power speaking loudly and acting like a broker in an argument between men is remarkable. Yet, neither "Bartira" nor "João Ramalho" were mentioned in this document. It was, again, Leite (1956, 2:222) who added notes clarifying that Bartira was the woman in question. Nevertheless, the situation is unclear. Pero Correa did not mention any bond between the "indoctrinated Indian woman" and the men who threatened the priest, perhaps because he did not witness the episode but merely heard about it from two "Jesuit brothers" who were there.[7]

These letters show how Bartira's story is quite nebulous, especially since many authors were not interested in her or other women who were Ramalho's partners. He is often simply depicted as a man with many children, and not much attention is given to their mothers. The Indigenous women are represented as anonymous and homogenized. The main chroniclers from colonial times followed the same pattern. Actually, in the first narratives about colonial history, Ramalho was not mentioned either. In Pero de Magalhães Gandavo's ([1576] 2008, 103) writing, for example, neither Bartira nor Ramalho is quoted; São Paulo is depicted as merely a place where most residents "were born from Indian women from the land, and Portuguese men." In another part of the text, Gandavo ([1576] 2008, 49) refers to those mixed residents as "mamelucos."

By the early seventeenth century, however, Ramalho's existence is already registering in broader narratives about Brazil. From then on, the story of the establishment of colonial society in São Paulo began to be told by mentioning a specific Portuguese man, Ramalho, but not a specific woman. This was the case in Frei Vicente do Salvador's *History of Brazil*. According to Salvador ([1627] 2010, 171–72), Ramalho was "the father of many sons, akin with the best Indigenous people." Simão de Vasconcelos's ([1633] 1865, 75) approach was similar. He described Ramalho as living together with a woman to whom he was not married. Her name, however, was not mentioned.

The absence of Bartira was a constant in colonial historiography. This largely continued into the eighteenth century. Pedro Taques, for example, mentions only Isabel, the Christian name adopted by the daughter of "king Tibiriçá" after her baptism (Taques [1772] 2004, 75). The aristocratic approach to Indigenous allies continues in the work of Friar Gaspar da Madre de Deus. For him, Tibiriçá was "a king, or cacique," and João Ramalho had married the "daughter of the king." Friar Gaspar refers only to her Christian name, Isabel, later in a footnote, clarifying that she was the "princess of the Guaianases" (Madre de Deus 1797, 29–30). Nonetheless, these texts, both from the end of the eighteenth century, give us clues regarding the reason for the interest in Bartira. This approach is related to that of the genealogy of São Paulo inhabitants (Abud 2019).

After all, according to Taunay (1924, 113), João Ramalho was the "European patriarch of the people of São Paulo."

When Bartira appears in the broader narratives of colonial Brazil is still unclear. From the beginning of the nineteenth century, the best-known narratives followed the same colonial patterns mentioned above. According to Robert Southey ([1810–19] 1981, 65), for example, João Ramalho was "under the protection of the ruler [Tibiriçá] who gave him one of his daughters." Even the first Brazilian "national history" does not mention Bartira. Notably, Francisco Adolfo de Varnhagen ([1854] 1877, 125, 256) merely repeated the same narrative about João Ramalho; he depicted him as a man with a "large family" and with "countless sons and grandsons."

The reason Bartira was not included in the above narratives is not easy to understand. She and Ramalho had a relationship that was quite common in colonial society. The way European men allied to Indigenous peoples was by getting married according to the local customs, especially with women related to local Indigenous leaders. In doing so, they accessed Indigenous trade routes, including those related to slavery. This type of men, called *cunhamenas* in the Amazon region (Sommer 2011), was very common on the Atlantic coast during the sixteenth century. In some areas, slavery was their main business, as at the São Vicente port. During the establishment of colonial society on the São Paulo plateau, Manuel da Nóbrega, the first Jesuit provincial superior in Brazil, tried to promote Catholic marriage between Ramalho and Bartira, but that was not possible. Ramalho was already married in Portugal, although he had lived in Brazil for about forty years (Castelnau-L'Estoile 2019). Nevertheless, he and Bartira were recognized as a couple, and she was the only woman mentioned in his will. She was referred to there not as Bartira, but as the "Índia Isabel, whom he [Ramalho] called servant (*criada*)." And even though Ramalho had so many children that the first governor of Brazil did "not dare to count" them, the only ones identified in his will were the eight he had with her.[8]

Despite being largely nameless and thus marginalized in the archival record, Bartira demonstrates the importance of Indigenous women in Brazilian colonial society through their alliances with European men. Although colonial records highlight these women's importance for colonial purposes, it is clear that their alliances with the Portuguese also benefited their group when we look at their family trajectories. As Susan Sleeper-Smith (2001, 5) has pointed out in her study of the relationships between Indigenous women and French men in the Great Lakes region of North America, women who married fur traders used their position to "augment their own authority and that of their households." This was clearly the case with Bartira. All of her daughters with Ramalho were married to newcomers from Portugal. Most of their husbands held positions in colonial administration. As Silvana Alves de Godoy (2016) has shown, the most prominent families in São Paulo in the sixteenth and seventeenth centuries were Tibiriçá's descendants.

The importance of their descendants, however, was not limited to São Paulo. They also played a key role in the occupation of other areas at the time of the conquest. For example, they were essential to the construction of colonial society in Rio de Janeiro. This was the case for Tibiriçá's great-granddaughter and Bartira's granddaughter Marquesa Ferreira, who was one of the richest women in Guanabara at the end of the sixteenth century. As in other cases, her donations to the Benedictines and the Jesuits were fundamental for the development of their respective assets in the city of Rio de Janeiro and its surroundings, which were, respectively, the farms of Iguaçu and Santa Cruz. Marquesa Ferreira thus demonstrated her loyalty to colonial society, highlighting a profile that is still little studied in Brazilian historiography: the Indigenous women who integrated the local elites and were very skilled in movements that favored their groups (Julio 2022, 79).

The Uses of the Past: Celebrating the Sixteenth Century

Narratives in which Bartira and other Indigenous women are rarely mentioned, or even completely disregarded, are not specific to the colonial period. Historiographical and heritage narratives produced at key moments in the construction of regional and national identities also neglect or omit these women. For example, Bartira is mentioned only a few times in the historical monuments around São Paulo, although there are many references to her father, her partner, her descendants, and her people in sites of memory scattered throughout the city. Those monuments elaborate "historical narratives" using images and present a "visual memory"

of the history of São Paulo (Uhle 2013, 161). They are material representations of the consolidation of male-centered histories of the formation
of American colonial societies (see Powers 2002).

An important aspect of the monuments related to the settlement
narrative is their presence in various parts of the city, starting with the
inexorable Pátio do Colégio. Located where the first Jesuit building was
constructed, right at the top of the village headed by Tibiriçá, the building
as we know it today was reconstructed in the context of the celebrations
of the fourth centenary of the foundation of São Paulo (Canado 2021).[9]
In the Patio do Colégio, amid various relics, the exhibition focuses on the
conversion and the figures of Anchieta and Tibiriçá.

The case of José de Anchieta returns us to the imperial dimensions of
this chapter's topic. In the room dedicated to Anchieta, on the wall to
the right of his femur, we see a copy of his baptism record. The document
does not mention his mother's name. Instead, he is presented as the son
of "Joan de Anchieta and his wife." Although it is a reproduction of the
original document, the name of Anchieta's mother is well known, and
his background is more connected to the events that took place on the
São Paulo plateau than is commonly believed. Anchieta was a Canarian
from Tenerife, one of the last islands of the archipelago to be conquered
by the Spaniards (in 1496). He was born almost three decades later, the
son of the aforementioned Basque father and Mencia Diaz de Clavijo y
Llarena. According to more hagiographic versions, his mother belonged
to the "Canarian aristocracy." That is a euphemism, however, that indicates Indigenous ancestry. His mother was born in the context of the first
relations between the Spaniards and the Guanches. Anchieta was born
and spent his early years in a Canarian society that was very similar to
the one he would find years later in São Paulo.

The only mention of Bartira at Pátio do Colégio is related to Anchieta. It
is a sculpture in the garden that shows her being evangelized by him. This
artwork was transferred there from Rio de Janeiro in 1997, on the fourth
centenary of Anchieta's death. This means that the only mention of Bartira
in the Pátio do Colégio is relatively recent and was not included in the
original projects. It is not clear whether this is a sign of a new era in which
the androcentric perspective is being challenged by many social actors.

Another site of memory worth mentioning is the Tibiriçá Crypt in the
Sé Cathedral, which was inaugurated in 1954 during the celebrations of

the four hundredth anniversary of the founding of São Paulo. A sculpture there by José Cucé has Tibiriçá in the center, surrounded by other Indigenous people, representing the first inhabitants of São Paulo and symbolizing their hard work and the wealth of the region. No women are represented in the scene, which is surprising considering their important place in agricultural production by the time of Tibiriçá. Women's prominence in agricultural was registered by the first chroniclers (see O'Leary 2023), and later, when colonial society was already implemented in São Paulo, women formed the majority of captives, and many worked in agriculture (Monteiro 1994, 42).

The Museu do Ipiranga is another important site of relevant memory. Recently reopened in 2022, the museum houses a well-known exhibition created by Afonso Taunay in the lobby of the monumental axis. The exhibition was designed to show the history of Brazil from the perspective of São Paulo (Brefe 2005). Next to the main door are paintings of the characters considered central to the early period of the São Paulo saga, depicted in historical portraits from the early 1930s. These include *Dom João III* (1932), *Martim Afonso de Souza* (1932), *João Ramalho e filho* (1934), and *Cacique Tibiriçá e neto* (1934), all painted by José Wasth Rodrigues (Nascimento 2019). The aim here is not to analyze these paintings, which has been done by other scholars, but rather to point out the absence of Bartira and Indigenous women in general. This is a good example of how Indigenous women have been neglected in narratives of Brazilian history. Often only male protagonists are mentioned or portrayed, creating a scenario in which women are not present in the most important moments of our past. They were never placed among the decision makers.

Representations that omit women are widespread in the museum context. This is true of another well-known painting, *A fundação de São Vicente* (The foundation of São Vicente), painted by Benedito Calixto in 1900. It was painted before the main events mentioned so far, which are all related to the fourth centenary of the foundation of São Paulo. The artwork is important because of the painter's relevance in shaping historical moments. And it repeats the familiar pattern of omitting Indigenous women. Well-known men related to the founding of São Vicente are depicted in the painting: Martim Afonso de Souza, Tibiriçá and his brother Caiuby, and others who are always mentioned in the narratives about that period. The painting also shows groups of Indigenous people: some of them are definitely allies, others maybe not, but all of the figures are men. João Ramalho has a central place in the picture. He was painted "with his family," but no more details are given about them (Alves 2003, 217).

The above examples, however, are not meant to imply that no other references to the figure of Bartira appear in urban São Paulo. She was represented in a sculpture by João Batista Ferri in 1936. This work, called *Bartira*, represents a "bronze" Indian and was originally located in the Biacica Chapel. Although listed by the Department of Historical Heritage of the city of São Paulo in 1994, it is currently missing.[10]

Bartira is also represented in the Monumento à Fundação de São Paulo (Monument to the Foundation of São Paulo) by Luis Morrone. The monument was inaugurated in 1963, but it has its origins in the discussions concerning the fourth centenary. On that occasion, the Portuguese community organized itself around the figure of the Jesuit Manuel da Nóbrega as the founder of São Paulo, opposing him to Anchieta, who was seen as having a Spanish background (Uhle 2013). The monument, which is currently located in front of the Palácio Nove de Julho (9th of July Palace), depicts Bartira holding a baby in her arms, surrounded by Tibiriçá and João Ramalho. Nóbrega is also represented, of course, as is José de Anchieta, one Indigenous boy, Manuel de Paiva, and Martim Afonso de Sousa. As Ana Rita Uhle (2013, 259) points out, the posture chosen to compose Bartira represents a long visual tradition of identifying Indigenous women as mothers, as in the painting of Catarina Paraguaçu at the Basilica of the Virgin of the Consolation in Turin. Morrone's monument also aims to convey a message of reconciliation by representing miscegenation between an Indigenous woman and a Portuguese man, along with, of course, their child.[11]

Other depictions of Bartira appear in public spaces in São Paulo, such as on a street located in the Perdizes neighborhood, which is close to other streets also named for Indigenous people, as well as a João Ramalho street. The area has been targeted by urban political interventions, such as when Greenpeace led the placement of plaques in these spaces to mark the precarious situation of Indigenous peoples in the country.[12] The action is part of global movements for social justice that target spaces celebrating colonialism in the urban landscape. In these movements, Indigenous women have been chosen as the people who can represent well the debates from an intersection between gender and colonialism. In these discussions, Bartira has not been forgotten.

Beyond academia, postcolonial discussions have acquired considerable importance in recent decades in debates about public space, memory, and identity. Such discussions have been driven by social movements that target statues representing subjects currently associated with colonial atrocities (McClymont 2021). In Brazil, some of the preferred targets were precisely those related to the *bandeirantes* in São Paulo, such as the statue of Borba Gato and the Monumento das Bandeiras. Targeted twice, in 2013 and 2016, both were brought back into public debate in 2020, when the topic spread as a result of the global movements following the murder of George Floyd in the United States (Freitas 2021).

Postcolonial debates concerning public spaces highlight the subjects considered inappropriate for tributes while pointing out those who should occupy these spaces. Indigenous women are often presented as figures who could symbolize and embody the demands of the dissatisfied. One of the best-known cases is in Argentina, where a statue of Christopher Columbus was replaced in 2015 by a statue of Juana Azurduy, an Indigenous woman who was a leader in the independence of the River Plate from the Spanish Crown. Indeed, movements of such magnitude clearly thrive when supported by established political powers. In this case, the left-wing governments of Cristina Fernández de Kirchner and Evo Morales, from Argentina and Bolivia, politically and economically embraced the undertaking (Jiménez Frei 2019).

In Brazil, not only have statues and urban spaces been subjects of discussions and political actions, but Indigenous women have been brought to the center of the debates. There is a renewed interest in the few such figures known in our historical culture, and Bartira is one of them. She was, for example, one of the twenty-seven women chosen by the Federal Senate to be "honored" in the virtual exhibition *Heroínas Negras e Indígenas do Brasil* (Black and Indigenous heroines of Brazil), which was inaugurated on July 23, 2020.[13] On that occasion, the Federal Senate also posted a series of tweets about these women. For Bartira, however, the "tribute" did nothing more than reproduce a traditional view, favoring a positive perspective on colonization. When disseminated without further contextualization, such ideas can sometimes end up reinforcing outdated conceptions about Indigenous women, such as subservience, which seem opposed to those that the Federal Senate was seeking to promote.

Nonetheless, this is undeniably a time when profiles such as Bartira's draw the attention of those who want to know more about the political role of Indigenous women in Brazilian history. Despite much research still needing to be done, it is significant that some sectors of society demand the effective inclusion of these women in historical narratives and sites of memory. This signals their disagreement with the androcentric approaches that previously prevailed. It is undoubtedly a sign of new approaches in our historiography and in the public debate. Such new approaches are confronting the colonial memory that remains represented in views about the "birth" of Brazil, to use the expression of João Pacheco de Oliveira (2016).

Nevertheless, the current approach is also notably problematic in its views on Indigenous women. The manifestos of the social movements mentioned above have generated discussions about whether Indigenous identities have been reified. Such reification does not fit with the complex trajectory of alliances, negotiations, and conflicts with colonial powers that characterized these figures in the past (Gallinari 2020). Besides that, as discussed in this chapter, Indigenous women from the sixteenth century were depicted (or often not depicted) through different representations and perspectives. Because they were never the focus of the historical records, the most we can get are fragments of their lives. Even so, these fragments were recorded precisely because they were somehow connected to the establishment of colonial society. Looking at this past with contemporary eyes and focusing on someone who fits the profile of today's standards might add another layer to these women's stories beyond the ways in which their trajectories have already been used by various historical agendas since the sixteenth century.

Perhaps we should accept the limits of what we can know about these women's pasts and try to understand their choices on their own terms. As Camilla Townsend (2006) has said about Malinche, there is no such thing as a traditional biography of her; it is impossible because the data are insufficient. We do have enough information, however, to understand her time and the historical changes that she experienced. The same can be said about Bartira. We can understand her world and how global processes, such as colonialism, slavery, and both local and Atlantic alliances, affected the limitations and possibilities of her life.

Notes

1. For a general approach of the subject in Latin America, see Powers (2002). For Brazil, see Vainfas (1999), Prado (1928), and Freyre (1933).
2. "Pigafetta's Account of Magellan's Voyage," in Stanley (1874, 45).
3. Instituto de Estudos Brasileiros (IEB), Universidade de São Paulo, *Índios famosos em armas, que neste Estado do Brasil concorrerão para a sua conquista temporal, e spiritual*, códice 5.6, A8.
4. "Carta do Padre Antonio Pires aos Padres e Irmãos de Coimbra. Pernambuco, 04 de junho de 1552," in Leite (1956, 1:326).
5. "Carta de Tomé de Sousa ao rei. Salvador, 1° de junho de 1553," in Malheiros Dias and Vasconcellos (1921–24, 3:365).
6. "Carta do Ir. José de Anchieta ao P. Inácio de Loyola, São Paulo de Piratininga, [1 de setembro] de 1554," in Leite (1956, 2:114–115).
7. "Carta do Ir. Pero Correia ao P. Belchior Nunes Barreto: [São Vicente] 8 de junho de 1551," in Leite (1956, 1:222).
8. Will of João Ramalho, in Instituto Histórico e Geográfico de São Paulo (1904, 564). The original document was lost, so the available version is presented as a copy, without guaranteed authenticity. The case was the subject of historiographic and political conflicts by the end of the nineteenth and the beginning of the twentieth centuries (Capelato and Ferretti 1999).
9. For more on the anniversary, see Lofego (2004).
10. "São Paulo—Escultura *Bartira*," *Ipatrimônio*, accessed August 26, 2023, https:// www.ipatrimonio.org/sao-paulo-escultura-bartira/#!/map=38329&loc=-23 .48824799999998,-46.404574,17.
11. According to Uhle (2013, 193), an Indigenous woman represented in a similar way, as an "Indian mother, in reference to Bartira," was included by Brecheret in the Monument to the Bandeiras.
12. "Greenpeace faz intervenção em placas de ruas com nomes indígenas," *Veja São Paulo*, October 3, 2013, https://vejasp.abril.com.br/cidades/greenpeace-faz -intervencao-em-placas-de-ruas/.
13. "Mostra virtual apresenta mulheres que lutaram pela igualdade na história do país," *Senadonotícias*, July 24, 2020, https://www12.senado.leg.br/noticias /materias/2020/07/24/mostra-virtual-apresenta-mulheres-que-lutaram-pela -igualdade-na-historia-do-pais.

References

Abud, Kátia. 2019. *O sangue intimorato e as nobilíssimas tradições: A construção de um símbolo paulista, o bandeirante*. Cuiabá: Editora da Universidade Federal de Mato Grosso.

Alves, Caled Faria. 2003. *Benedito Calixto e a construção do imaginário republicano*. Bauru, SP: Editora da Universidade do Sagrado Coração.

Amado, Janaína. 2000. "Diogo Álvares, o Caramuru, e a fundação mítica do Brasil." *Estudos Históricos* 14 (25): 3–39.

Avila, Christovão de. 2014. *Brasões de armas: Armorial Histórico da Casa da Torre de Garcia D'Ávila*. Rio de Janeiro: Hexis.

Barr, Juliana. 2007. *Peace Came in the Form of a Woman: Indians and Spaniards in the Texas Borderlands*. Chapel Hill: University of North Carolina Press.

Brefe, Ana Cláudia Fonseca. 2005. *O museu paulista: Affonso de Taunay e a memória nacional, 1917–1945*. São Paulo: Editora da Universidade Estadual Paulista.

Canado, Roberto dos Santos, Jr. 2021. "Um monumento 'colonial' para uma cidade moderna: O conjunto jesuítico do Pátio do Colégio nas comemorações do IV Centenário de São Paulo." *Revista de pesquisa em arquitetura e urbanismo* 19:1–16.

Capelato, Maria Helena Rolim, and Danilo J. Zioni Ferretti. 1999. "João Ramalho e as origens da nação: Os paulistas na comemoração do IV centenário da descoberta do Brasil." *Tempo* 4 (8): 67–87.

Castelnau-L'Estoile, Charlotte de. 2019. *Un catholicisme colonial: Le mariage des Indiens et des esclaves au Brésil, XVIe–XVIIIe siècle*. Paris: Presses Universitaires de France.

Fernandes, João Azevedo. 2003. *De cunhã a mameluca: A mulher Tupinambá e o nascimento do Brasil*. João Pessoa, Brazil: Editora Universidade Federal da Paraíba.

Fernández-Armesto, Felipe. 1982. *The Canary Islands after the Conquest: the Making of a Colonial Society In the Early Sixteenth Century*. Oxford: Oxford University Press.

Freitas, André Luiz Ranucci. 2021. "Quebra das estátuas: possibilidades de uma (re) escrita decolonial e pública da história." Master's thesis, Universidade Federal Fluminense.

Freyre, Gilberto. 1933. *Casa-grande e senzala*. Rio de Janeiro: Maia and Schmidt.

Gallinari, Luciano. 2020. "Christopher Columbus and the Confederate Generals versus Native Peoples? The Struggle of Memories amid Removal, Replacement and Resignification of Their Monuments." *RiMe: Rivista dell'Istituto di Storia dell'Europa Mediterranea* 7 (2): 53–111.

Gandavo, Pero de Magalhães. (1576) 2008. *Tratado da terra do Brasil: História da província Santa Cruz, a que vulgarmente chamamos Brasil*. Brasília: Senado Federal, Conselho Editorial.

Ghosh, Durba. 2006. *Sex and the Family in Colonial India: The Making of Empire*. Cambridge: Cambridge University Press.

Godoy, Silvana Alves de. 2016. "Mestiçagem, guerras de conquista e governo dos índios: A vila de São Paulo na construção da monarquia portuguesa na América (Séculos XVI e XVII)." PhD diss., Universidade Federal do Rio de Janeiro.

Hemming, John. 1978. *Red Gold: The Conquest of the Brazilian Indians.* Cambridge, Mass.: Harvard University Press.

Instituto Histórico e Geográfico de São Paulo. 1904. *Revista do Instituto Histórico e Geográfico de São Paulo.* Vol. 9. São Paulo: Instituto Histórico e Geográfico de São Paulo.

Jager, Rebecca K. 2015. *Malinche, Pocahontas, and Sacagawea: Indian Women as Cultural Intermediaries and National Symbols.* Norman: University of Oklahoma Press.

Jiménez Frei, Cheryl. 2019. "Columbus, Juana and the Politics of the Plaza: Battles over Monuments, Memory and Identity in Buenos Aires." *Journal of Latin American Studies* 51 (3): 607–38.

Julio, Suelen Siqueira. 2022. *Gentias da terra: Gênero e etnia no Rio de Janeiro colonial.* Doctoral thesis, Universidade Federal Fluminense.

Leite, Serafim. 1956. *Cartas dos primeiros jesuítas do Brasil.* Vols. 1 and 2. São Paulo: Comissão do IV Centenário da Cidade de São Paulo.

Lofego, Silvio Luiz. 2004. *IV Centenário da Cidade de São Paulo: Uma cidade entre o passado e o futuro.* São Paulo: Annablume.

Madre de Deus, Gaspar da. 1797. *Memórias para a história da capitania de São Vicente, hoje chamada São Paulo.* Lisbon: Tipografia da Academia Real de Ciências.

Malheiros Dias, Carlos, and Ernesto Vasconcellos, eds. 1921–24. *História da colonização portuguesa do Brasil: Edição monumental comemorativa do primeiro centenário da independência do Brasil.* 3 vols. Porto: Litografia Nacional.

McClymont, Katie, ed. 2021. "The Fall of Statues? Contested Heritage, Public Space and Urban Planning." *Planning Theory and Practice* 22 (5): 767–95.

Meira, Jean Paul Gouveia. 2017. "'Merecedores de toda honra': A trajetória da família indígena Arcoverde nos espaços de poder do Império Ultramarino Português (1636–1706)." *Revista de História* 6 (1–2): 20–31.

Metcalf, Alida. 2007. "Women as Go-Betweens? Patterns in Sixteenth-Century Brazil." In *Gender, Race and Religion in the Colonization of the Americas,* edited by Nora E. Jaffary, chapter 2. Aldershot: Ashgate.

Monteiro, John M. 1994. *Negros da terra: Índios e bandeirantes nas origens de São Paulo.* São Paulo: Companhia das Letras.

Nascimento, Ana Paula. 2019. "Entre a fricção e a serenidade, a caminho do interior: os painéis de Wasth Rodrigues no peristilo do Museu Paulista." *Anais do Museu Paulista: História e Cultura Material* 27:1–58.

O'Leary, Jessica. 2023. "The Uprooting of Indigenous Women's Horticultural Practices in Brazil, 1500–1650." *Past and Present* 262 (1): 45–83.

Oliveira Filho, João Pacheco de. 2016. *O nascimento do Brasil e outros ensaios: "Pacificação," regime tutelar e formação de alteridades.* Rio de Janeiro: Contracapa.

Oliveira Filho, João Pacheco de. 2022. "Catarina Paraguaçu, senhora do Brasil: Três alegorias para uma nação." *Memórias Insurgentes* 1 (1): 24–59.

Otte, Thomas G. 2018. *The Age of Anniversaries: The Cult of Commemoration, 1895–1925*. London: Routledge.

Pereira, Paulo. 2018. "Brasil en la ruta de la primera vuelta al mundo: la estancia de la flota de Magallanes en Río de Janeiro." In *Actas del Congresso Internacional de Historia "Primus Circumdedisti Me"*, 165–78. Valladolid: Ministério de Defensa.

Petrone, Pasquale. 1995. *Aldeamentos paulistas*. São Paulo: Editora da Universidade de São Paulo.

Pita, Sebastião da Rocha. (1730) 1878. *História da América portuguesa*. Salvador: Imprensa Econômica.

Powers, Karen Vieira. 2002. "Conquering Discourses of 'Sexual Conquest': Of Women, Language, and Mestizaje." *Colonial Latin American Review* 11 (1): 7–32.

Prado, João Francisco de Almeida. 1939. *Primeiros povoadores do Brasil, 1500–1530*. São Paulo: Companhia Editora Nacional.

Prado, Paulo. 1928. *Retrato do Brasil: Ensaio sobre a tristeza brasileira*. São Paulo: Duprat-Mayença.

Salvador, Vicente do. (1627) 2010. *História do Brasil*. Brasília: Senado Federal, Conselho Editorial.

Schmidel, Ulderich. (1557) 1836. *Viaje al Río de la Plata y Paraguay*. Buenos Aires: Imprenta del Estado.

Sleeper-Smith, Susan. 2001. *Indian Women and French Men: Rethinking Cultural Encounter in the Western Great Lakes*. Amherst: University of Massachusetts Press.

Sommer, Barbara A. 2011. "Adquirindo e defendendo os privilégios concedidos pela coroa no norte do Brasil." In *Raízes do privilégio: Mobilidade social no mundo ibérico do Antigo Regime*, edited by Rodrigo Monteiro, Bruno Feitler, Daniela Calainho, and Jorge Flores. Rio de Janeiro: Record.

Southey, Robert. [1810–19] 1981. *História do Brasil*. São Paulo: Editora da Universidade de São Paulo.

Stanley, Henry, ed. 1874. *The First Voyage Round the World*. London: Hakluyt Society.

Stoler, Ann Laura. 2010. *Carnal Knowledge and Imperial Power: Race and the Intimate in Colonial Rule*. Berkeley: University of California Press.

Taques de Almeida Pais Leme, Pedro. (1772) 2004. *História da capitania de São Vicente*. Brasília: Senado Federal, Conselho Editorial.

Taunay, Afonso D'Escragnolle. 1924. *História geral das bandeiras paulistas*. Vol. 1. São Paulo: Typ. Ideal, H. L. Canton.

Townsend, Camilla. 2004. *Pocahontas and the Powhatan Dilemma: An American Portrait*. New York: Hill and Wang.

Townsend, Camilla. 2006. *Malintzin's Choices: An Indian Woman in the Conquest of Mexico*. Albuquerque: University of New Mexico Press.

Treece, David. 2013. "Caramuru, o mito: Conquista e conciliação." *Teresa: Revista de Literatura Brasileira*, no. 12–13, 307–44.

Uhle, Ana Rita. 2013. "Monumentos celebrativos: Aproximações entre arte e história (1925–1963)." PhD diss., Universidade Estadual de Campinas.

Vainfas, Ronaldo. 1999. "Colonização, miscigenação e questão racial: Notas sobre equívocos e tabus da historiografia brasileira." *Tempo* 4 (8): 7–22.

van Deusen, Nancy E. 2015. *Global Indios: The Indigenous Struggle for Justice in Sixteenth-Century Spain*. Durham, N.C.: Duke University Press.

Varnhagen, Francisco Adolfo de. 1877. *História geral do Brasil antes da sua separação e independência de Portugal*. Rio de Janeiro: E. and H. Laemmert.

Vasconcelos, Simão de. (1633) 1865. *Chronica da Companhia de Jesus do Estado do Brasil e do que obraram seus filhos nesta parte do Novo Mundo*. Lisbon: Editor A. J. Fernandes Lopes.

CHAPTER 4

"Outsiders"

Contributions Toward an Ethnographic
Theory of Acculturation

MARTA AMOROSO
(TRANSLATED BY DAVID RODGERS)

Os estrangeiros 'bons' também são 'criados' e 'fabricados' com comida durante o processo de torna-los mais 'the same' (o mesmo) e menos 'outros.' Porém, já que em muitos casos não podem devolver o gesto, raramente viram parentes próximos de um Kaxinauá. O fazer comer entre as pessoas de uma geração deve ser mútuo.

—CECILIA MCCALLUM, "ALTERIDADE E
SOCIABILIDADE KAXINAUÁ"

What do the partnerships of the Mura of Central Amazonia teach us about the politics of regard (Kelly and Matos 2019)? In this chapter, I examine the land regularization process for the Cunhã-Sapucaia Indigenous Territory (TICS), in which I acted as the consulting anthropologist (Amoroso 2000b). The process included the reflections of Mura people on what they call "our system," an expression used to speak about the meaningfulness of their relations. I show how the Mura classify the Pirahã, Apurinã, and Munduruku, who are part of the network of relations in many Mura villages and thus enter into the composition of what they call "our system." In terms of partnerships, I explore how crucial decisions made during the land regularization process actualized past alliances and partnerships constructed in the context of the logging and commercial fishing industries. The Mura participated in these activities along with migrant settlers and immigrant bosses, the so-called outsiders (*gente de fora*). I also show that, for these outsiders, a "politics of regard" is mobilized to establish broader social relations through the construction of kinship. Pursuing this aim, my analysis extends Peter Gow's (1991, 1997, 2003, 2006a, 2006b, 2010, 2014, 2015) proposal for an ethnographic theory of acculturation. Here the concept of "ethnographic theory"—taken from Goldman (2015)—emphasizes anthropological practice as an exercise in cultural translation. In Gow's critique, "acculturation," a concept associated with North American cultural anthropology, evokes the anthropological studies produced at Columbia University, which emphasized cultural change arising from contact (Wagley and Galvão 1949), as well as those conducted in Brazil—specifically, in Amazonia and Bahia—during the interwar period. In the sense proposed by Gow, however, the concept of acculturation acquires a new ethnographic contextualization, more focused on local dynamics, and represents a stimulating theoretical challenge for Amerindian studies. Drawing from ethnographic research in the central and southwestern regions of Amazonia (Bonilla 2005; Gow 1991; Suarez 2019), I reflect on how the flexible network of sociality among the Mura extends to relations with "outside" partners in a selective politics of acculturation, the "Murification" of strangers (Amoroso 1992; Fileno 2018).

The Mura contrast "outsiders" with the category "ancients/elders" (*os antigos*), which designates the founding couples of the Mura villages. Here I identify kinship narratives of a "mixed people," in which the Munduruku, Apurinã, and Pirahã all participate. "Outsiders," in turn, also applies to the non-Indigenous outsiders encountered in the proximities of the TICS region in the context of extractivist activities prior to demarcation, who were gradually absorbed into the Mura kinship network. The land regularization of the TICS thus reveals the principles of an Indigenous theory of alterity. My interest here is in accompanying the conditions under which the regime of relations with outsiders is actualized, setting out from McCallum's (1998) suggestion that these relations are constituted by the fabrication of similar bodies through the practices of conviviality and commensality.

Toward an Ethnographic Theory of Acculturation on the Lower Madeira River

In Gow's (1991) doctoral research on the Piro (Yine) people of the lower Urubamba, published as *Of Mixed Blood: Kinship and History in Peru-*

vian Amazonia, he for the first time used the formula that consolidated him in the field of Amazonian ethnology. In this work, he "subordinated history to culture and historiography to ethnography" (Viveiros de Castro 1993, 182), proposing that the history of the mixed people of the Lower Urubamba is one of kinship. The theme of acculturation emerges as a central dimension, which was explored again at diverse moments of the ethnologist's career (see Gow 2011, 2015), always accompanied by a critique of the U.S. culturalist appropriation of the concept. The latter approach was subsequently adopted by Brazilian anthropology and indigenism, where the concept came to signal processes of cultural change and disfigurement. Instead, Gow proposes a return to the German ethnological tradition and research on Amazonian Indigenous peoples from the first decades of the twentieth century, especially Walter Krickeberg's (1885–1962) ethnography on the multiethnic system of the Upper Xingu, to show that acculturation was originally formulated as a concept to describe the "ensembles," a term Gow (2010) takes from Lévi-Strauss (1971), constituted by Amerindian societies and cultures in exchange networks. In terms of a methodology for analyzing Amazonian Indigenous societies in their different contact situations, Gow emphasizes the adoption of a classic ethnographic model, which situates their social and cultural experience in a dialogue informed by ethnology.

Gow was particularly interested in understanding the logic of the regional nexuses connecting, for instance, the Piro-speaking peoples of the Ucayali-Urubamba, Manu, Piedras, Purus, and Juruá Rivers, which in turn were linked to a complex long-distance exchange system of considerable time depth. This covered a vast area of Southwest Amazonia and the Peruvian Andes to the north and south. His focus is thus on the conditions for the construction of cultural and linguistic borders, an aspect he calls "sills." He also recalls the lessons of Joanna Overing and the "late eternal master" Claude Lévi-Strauss by proposing to analyze what people say, which cultural anthropology does so well, but without avoiding the relationship between those speaking and those listening, a dimension also well explored by anthropology.

Ethnographic studies of the Mura of Central Amazonia were undertaken relatively late, toward the end of the twentieth century, as part of the regularization of the Mura people's lands—a process still not concluded (Amoroso 2000a, 2000b; Moreira Santos 2009; Romano 1998). The ethnographic documentation generated at the time was marked by the demands of Mura Indigenous associations fighting to win back their traditionally occupied lands. In the most recent demographic census, the Mura of Amazonia numbered more than fifteen thousand people, half of whom declared that they lived outside officially demarcated Indigenous lands (ILs) (IBGE 2012, 89) in localities situated in urban centers. These collectives' identification with the lower Madeira region, spanning from the creeks and lakes of the Autazes delta to the basin of the Mamoré River, has been documented since the beginning of the eighteenth century (Amoroso 1992). Meanwhile, the presence of the Mura in urban spaces was recorded by the Indian Protection and Rural Workers Localization Service (SPI), a government agency responsible for Indigenous affairs in the first decades of the twentieth century, and has been interpreted (Romano 1998) as an effect of the policies that territorialized their spaces of circulation.[1] This moment coincided with the early activities of the SPI, which mediated the extractivist activities of settlers on the lands traditionally occupied by the Mura, as well as controlling the Indigenous workforce and the commercialization of produce. The TICS, where I conducted my research, was homologated in 2000 and extends continuously over 460,000 hectares, the entire area covered by primary forest, with the Mura villages distributed along 110 kilometers of the Preto do Igapó-Açu River.

What patterns can be apprehended in Mura relationships? The expression "kin by regard" (*parente por consideração*) was collected among the kinship terms of the Mura and foregrounded in a study by Fernando Augusto Fileno (2018) on kinship and corporeality, which describes the preeminence of care-based performances in the construction of kinship relations. "Kin by regard" is thus an Indigenous Mura expression used in exchanges established between *turmas*—that is, groups of extended families that reside in neighboring houses. The latter is a residence pattern that corresponds to the internal divisions of the villages. The Mura also comprehend relations with "outsiders" as an extension of kinship by regard.

José Antonio Kelly and Marcos de Almeida Matos (2019) propose formulating certain relations in terms of a "politics of regard." Employing this term, the authors—inspired by Marilyn Strathern's concept of "regard," which they translate as *consideração* (consideration) in Portuguese and explain as "caring for," "thinking of someone," and "looking"—

describe forms of collective action and organization in lowland South America that combine relations between people (involving someone who acts and someone who is the cause of action) in performances that mobilize the exchange of care, words, food, and things. In the cases highlighted here, the politics of regard involves at least two levels of relations. The first centers on the fabrication and actualization of kinship among the Mura, while the second foregrounds the diverse forms of Indigenous political agency that involve local partnerships with "outsiders." A third level would also extend to shamanism, invoking the shamanic grammar of relations between the Mura and more-than-humans, the auxiliary spirits of the shamans, a plane this chapter merely touches on. Mura shamans, both male and female, are effectively masters in diplomacy with the nonhuman entities who share spacetime with villagers in relations mediated by shamanic communication.

Following and extending Gow's critical revision of the concept of acculturation, therefore, we could say that the Mura affirm themselves as a "mixed people," where kinship can encompass social relations with other Indigenous peoples from the region, just as the network also opens up to external allies and partners, as well as encompassing broader social relations with individuals possessing no prior kinship relation.

Outsiders

The *Relatório da Situação Fundiária* (Land ownership report) of the TICS, the largest Mura land in central Amazonia, notes the demographically small presence of non-Indigenous residents (Amoroso 2000b). One of the hypotheses put forward for the quantitatively limited presence of non-Indigenous people in the Preto do Igapó-Açu River channel was that although the Mura sought to bring together non-Indigenous people and other Indigenous people living there through kinship, doubts remained over whether certain houses—some connected by kinship with the Mura—would assert themselves as Mura and remain in the new Indigenous Land regime. Few land titles had been issued by federal and state agencies in the area claimed by the Mura, which the National Foundation for Indigenous Peoples (FUNAI) identified as a fact favorable to Mura demands.[2] Nonetheless, the report concealed a wide-ranging controversy that had erupted among Mura families during the land regularization process—a controversy that revolved around the status of people's relations with kin, with non-Indigenous commercial partners, and with individuals and families from other Indigenous groups.

I highlight the emblematic case of Fortunato Hazan, in which we can discern the ethics of Mura sociality mobilized in relations with "outsiders," where the controversy revolves around commercial partners from the period of extractivism preceding land demarcation. These partners from past commercial relationships have now—after official recognition of the Indigenous Land—become kin through "kinship by regard." Seven of the sixteen identified cases of non-Indigenous families compensated by the Brazilian national government and removed from the Mura territory relate to properties owned by the heirs of Fortunato Hazan, a resident of the Autaz Mirim region who ran extractivist activities on the Preto do Igapó-Açu River. Fortunato was the son of Ambrósio Hazan, a Moroccan Jew who had settled in Itacoatiara, Amazonas, in the 1940s. The latter had worked in diverse commercial ventures. His son Fortunato arrived in Autaz Mirim after the death of his father, curtailing his medical training in Belém, Pará, although this did not prevent him from working as a doctor in the Autaz Mirim region.

Fortunato Hazan took over the family business, which consisted of selling extractivist products like animal hides, latex (*balata* and *sorva*), and timber, a production chain based on the labor of Mura families from the Preto do Igapó-Açu River working in the *aviamento* system.[3] He inherited some of his properties from his father, a personal patrimony expanded by obtaining traditional lands from the Mura as payment for debts owed to him as their boss (*patrão*). The Mura provide many different versions of the magnified figure of Fortunato Hazan, signaling the various types of partnerships constructed by the Indigenous population with the *patrão*, as Miguel Aparício Suarez (2019) shows in his monograph on the Banawa, an Arawá-speaking people inhabiting the Purus River region in Amazonas State, Brazil.

Fortunato Hazan is remembered as a skilled doctor who practiced medicine and delivered babies. He also distributed allopathic remedies, donated by the Borba municipal government or purchased in Manaus and then sold to the Indigenous population. Over his eight-decade-long life, he married numerous times and had dozens of children. According to one of his descendants, whom I interviewed, he had around twenty-eight children. One of my Mura interlocutors, who was married to a woman from the Fortunato kin network, claimed that the *patrão*'s offspring numbered more than eighty children, dispersed across the region traditionally occupied by the Mura. The magnified attributes of this *patrão* of the Mura extend to his business activities along the Preto do Igapó-Açu and Autaz Mirim Rivers. These activities involved his capacity to sell merchandise, move capital in the banking network, maintain a fleet of commercial boats, and so on. And, of course, he was situated within the kinship network in which the Mura collectives participated on the lower Madeira River.

A Mura leader, the late Manoel Tiago Marques (1915–2022), provides a narrative describing how Fortunato Hazan's trajectory interweaves with those of the Mura families in relations that go beyond trade partnerships. Manoel Tiago tells us about the strategic actions taken by Fortunato Hazan in support of the Mura in response to the SPI's attempts to exploit their Brazil nut forests in the first decade of the twentieth century. The federal agency's officers had leased the Mura Brazil nut forests to private interests, alleging that the area had been abandoned by the Indigenous population. Manoel Tiago remembers taking part in the mobilization of Indigenous leaders to safeguard the traditional Brazil nut groves for the Mura and recalls an epic scene of Fortunato Hazan's boat carrying leaders from the Mura villages, the *peiara*, to seek justice from the governmental authorities in Borba and Manaus.[4]

This memorable episode assured Fortunato Hazan, who is seen as the *bom patrão*, or "good boss" (see Bonilla 2005), exclusive access to selling the produce of Mura families. Manoel Tiago was later confirmed as the agent responsible for organizing Indigenous labor in the extractive activities on the Preto do Igapó-Açu River.[5] As a result, the Mura villages began to open up to relations with workers from Fortunato Hazan's *aviamento* network, mediated by Manoel Tiago, an "outsider" married to a Mura woman from Sapucaia village to whom the Mura delegated the organization of work fronts involving Mura families. The conditions were thus created for reclassifying these "outsiders" as potential affines.

The Hazan case illustrates how the "politics of regard" is mobilized in the fight to maintain the territories traditionally occupied by Mura families. These efforts are heavily disputed by the region's non-Indigenous population. The Mura were subjected to the *aviamento* regime by the *regatões* (Truzzi and Leal 2014). In this system small river traders advance consumer goods and work instruments to the Indigenous population, who repay these debts by supplying extractive or agricultural produce. The Mura of the Madeira River frequently paid the debts by handing over Indigenous plots of land to the *regatões*.[6] These processes could in some cases be reversed with official Indigenous Land demarcation. The current presence of the Mura in lands on the Igapó-Açu River reveals how the preeminence of Indigenous inhabitants' ethics of sociality operates through the construction of kinship with "outsiders." In the local sphere, this serves as a powerful mechanism for controlling territoriality, which is associated with the territorial care of the ancients/elders, despite all of the pressures to abandon their area that the Mura were subjected to over the twentieth century.

The second case focused on a Pirahã family who reached the Mura village of Sapucaia over land routes just at the moment when the FUNAI work team, which I was coordinating, was conducting the identification work for the Indigenous land (Amoroso 2000a, 2000b).[7] The arrival of the Pirahã in an area traditionally occupied by the Mura signaled the new arrivals' interest in settling in one locality after years living isolated—a practice that FUNAI associates with "Indigenous people in voluntary isolation"—having migrated from the municipality of Humaitá (Rondônia State, Brazil), at the confluence of the Maici and Marmelos Rivers.[8]

The late D. Maria Dias da Silva, a Pirahã woman, was a village founder and a resident of the TICS since the period of demarcation. She identified herself as Mura-Pirahã and was recognized as such by the Mura. Her name is associated with the Fé em Deus village on the outer limits of the TICS. In 1997, D. Maria arrived at the Sapucaia village of the Mura after decades of living in the forest, where she had married, given birth to children, and raised them while constantly on the move, first accompanying her uncles, later her husband and children, and finally living alone with her still-young children. This was when she asked to settle in the Mura villages and when I first met her. The Pirahã moved within the strip of forest that extends across the Amapá River region, which is today the Amapá River Sustainable Development Reserve, until they reached Sapucaia village, which is located south of the TICS.

Rumors had emerged among the Mura in 1997 about the alleged aggressiveness of the "forest woman" who ferociously defended her children. These revealed the hostility shown toward the Pirahã when they first arrived. Later, though, one of D. Maria's children was invited by the Mura to accompany me, along with other inhabitants of the villages, to identify the section of the territory under study that coincided with the trail taken by her family. These data were included in the field research that provided the basis of the Detailed Identification Report for the TICS. Years later, I found D. Maria and her children, now married to Mura spouses, living in Fé em Deus village, which had been officially included within the borders of the TICS since that date. The residents of Piranha village, where I stayed on research trips, thus maintained relations with the Pirahã, although they kept a certain distance. Marking this distance, they said, "The Pirahã speak differently; they arrived in Sapucaia coming from the Amapá River; they lived in the forest." They also emphasized alleged hostility and strangeness concerning the arrival of the Pirahã woman, who kept her children with her even after they had married and started families, thus creating a village around herself. Some narratives explicate differences associated with the Pirahã in terms of their supposedly exotic customs. According to the Mura, the Pirahã are extremely meticulous in their care of objects, zealous of the goods and merchandise they introduced or had introduced into their lives in the Mura villages, and conserve and repair everything obsessively. At some point, however, the Pirahã were located in the category of "outsiders." Despite the differences, and perhaps precisely because of them, the possibilities of constructing kinship with the Pirahã through affinization, which initially occurred by capturing women from the Pirahã group, were always considered by the Mura. Marriages between the Mura and Pirahã established the conditions for living together. Although the differences never ceased to exist, Mura and Pirahã people maintained the mutual attention and care given to kin through relations of affinity.

Another noteworthy aspect of Mura sociability pertaining to the Pirahã has implications for the management of Mura territoriality, highlighting the regional nexuses of sociality mobilized in maintaining and expanding the traditionally occupied area. With the Pirahã, the Mura actualize their "forest science" (*ciência mateira*, according to Cangussu 2021), which refers to the knowledge involved in the mobility practiced on forest trails, revealing extensive networks of sociality on the lower Madeira. The Pirahã of Fé em Deus village enable a reflection on Indigenous peoples living in voluntary isolation that goes beyond the more usual approach based on anecdotes told by neighbors (Gow 2017, 2018). In this instance, we have first-person accounts from the Pirahã themselves concerning their decision to live in voluntary isolation. These narratives show us how their engagement with the Mura took place in extremely difficult circumstances, for example, after D. Maria had lost her husband and (as she recollected) remained alone in the forest with her sons and daughters. One of D. Maria's sons remarked in an interview given in 2016 about the decision made by their parents to live in voluntary isolation, spending part of their life "hiding in the forest." He recalled that in those circumstances, they made use of uncultivated plants to make foods, such as palm fruits and a kind of tuber, also known to the Mura as *manhafã*, which the Pirahã identify as the *cararoá* potato:

> We began in the forest, on the Amapá River. My father roamed unmarried and became attached; he fell in love with my mother. My mother roamed with her uncles. The two of them wandered far, hiding away, when they realized just how difficult it was. They lived upriver on the Escondido, and so they started getting to know each other; they had children and slowly made their way downriver. They made *cararoá* potato flour; it was their food. The potato grows from a vine; it's beautiful, bright yellow. They made açaí palmheart flour, babassu flour; that's what they did. They were Pirahã. After that they started mingling. Today we eat other kinds [of food]; we eat manioc flour.[9]

The extent of the relations network mobilized by the Mura thus includes the Pirahã as a possibility. These relations provide access to a highly developed knowledge about the forest in regions uninhabited by the Mura, through which the Pirahã sometimes trekked in their travels. This was demonstrated in the fieldwork that formed the basis for the TICS identification report. In this research, we were assisted by one of D. Maria's sons.

Piranha village, where my ethnographic research is based, also elicited narratives of those who identify themselves as the "ancients/elders." The histories of the ancients/elders on the birth of this Mura village have been a topic in my previous work (Amoroso 2013, 2016, 2018, 2020), but I return to them in the next section to highlight the limits of anthropology's ethnicity-based approach and to qualify the complex processes involved in the composition of collective life in which the history of Mura kinship is embedded. Among the Mura, a village is formed around a central couple, who draw in their married sons and daughters to live close to them, constituting an ideally autonomous and self-sufficient unit. I call attention to the moral aspect of this social pattern, drawing from Amazonian ethnology's reflections on Tupi-speaking peoples, which show us how the collective emerges from the chief couple (T. S. Lima 2005). For the Mura, the Indigenous concept of *peiara* qualifies the action of the couple who lead the group and from whose intentionality the collective emerges.

"Our System": History, Memory, and Kinship

A site initially formed around the domestic group of a couple, Piranha became a village in the 1970s with the construction of the dwellings of their married sons and daughters near the original house. The history of its foundation raises the topic of the shamanic system, the *pajelança* practiced by the Mura. The event defining the origin of Piranha village was the discovery by a shaman and his auxiliary spirit of a portal allowing access to the subaquatic plane of the *encantados* and the anaconda. In shamanic voyages accompanied by the shaman, the founder of the first house at the site learned about the presence of the anaconda who inhabits the Preto do Igapó-Açu River just downstream of the current village. The referent is in the rock formations that become exposed during the summer. The appearance of a serpent with the head of a piranha gave the locality its name. This entity from the *encante*, which translates as the "enchantment" and refers to a magical city under the river (see also Harris 2014; and Whitaker 2020), is one of many anacondas identified at strategic points within the TICS. Other such serpents known by the residents are located at Cunhã, on the Forno and Tapagem Rivers, and in Sapucaia. These are sites traditionally inhabited by the Mura of the Igapó-Açu. Today, they are the centers of villages.

The Mura inscribe memories of episodes like those involving the snake-piranha into the landscape.[10] These are places frequented in shamanic voyages and visited in dreams. Ethnography provides access to local understandings concerning the *caboclos do centro* and the *caboclos do fundo*, who (persuaded to act through the diplomacy of the shamans) obtain from the cannibal anaconda knowledge used to treat diseases, such as those caused by *assombramento* (a "haunting" involving the capture of the person's *sombra*, or shadow), complications arising from sorcery, or the punishments inflicted on the Mura by the "mothers" or "owners" of animals. The *encantados* are feared as threatening entities, and engagements with them involve extremely dangerous relations. Sometimes they are described as having the appearance of white men and women, who are well-dressed and keen to seduce the Mura (see Harris 2014; L. M. Lima 2015; Slater 1994; and Whitaker 2020).

I asked my hostess, a resident of Cacaia, what her parents' home had been like during this period. This was a time when the couple's adult children were establishing their own houses with their sons and daughters. I was immediately drawn into a discussion on the values of kinship, which was a topic of particular interest to her, and on a theory that informs other aspects of the relationship between the elders/ancients and the outsiders on the Preto do Igapó-Açu River. My interlocutor initially differentiated the trajectory of her sisters from her own. This differentiation was based on diverse "ethological" markers, in the sense attributed to the concept of "ethos" by Bateson (1936), which emphasizes a knowledge focused on spheres of behavior. As my interlocutor suggested, the dwellings of her sisters, which were built around the founding couple of Piranha village, illustrate the heterogeneity of the different relational modes, which are taken to be akin to what she calls a "river system." She used this expression as a kind of improvised translation of the anthropological concept of culture. She suggested that I check with her sisters about what their life trajectories were like before I formulate something about the river system with her. The goal was to better understand the way of life of the elder/ancient residents and how this knowledge is constantly actualized vis-à-vis outsiders. According to her, the actualization of this knowledge constructs a gradient of situations in which people are more or less informed and guided by the values of kinship.

In this intercultural dialogue, my host contrasted (1) the houses whose residents had not heard the advice and did not practice the knowledge of the elders, and who consequently constructed an erratic life trajectory that was distant from kin and "involved in *bandidagem* [criminality], in *putaria* [whoring]," with (2) the houses with residents (like herself) whose life values were similar to those valued by the elders. These values included a life guided by respect and by a knowledge passed down intergenerationally in advice given to sons and daughters, "at night, far from the television." As my interlocutor explained, the fact that most children of the founding couple maintain their homes today at the heart of Piranha village, living nearby and sharing the life of the community, does not signify that their trajectories are deemed similar. This helps us understand the complexity of the notion of "belonging" that is mobilized in this dialogue, as well as the aspects of subjectivity that are implied in the concept of acculturation.

"Upriver there is a rock that looks like a church; my grandmother lives there," interjected the thirteen-year-old daughter of my host, who was taking part in our dialogue on this occasion. I asked where a particular elder is buried, and they quickly replied, somewhat put out, that this elder lies in one of the cemeteries in the Indigenous land, alongside her husband. This was before retorting that we were not talking about this but about the presence of the elders/ancients in the traditional territory of the Mura. As they explained to me, we were discussing "our system" and the multiple temporalities that are implied within it. In contrast with the tombs of the dead, this involves the sites inhabited by the elders/ancients and their postmortem dwelling places in the landscape traditionally occupied by the Mura. The women of that house then taught me that this particular late elder today occupies a rocky outcrop that emerges in the dry season when the level of the Matupiri River drops. The Mura lament that this river was left out of the demarcated area of the TICS. "It's a church-like rock in the headwaters of the [Matupiri] river. It's there that my grandma lives," the girl told me, her mother adding that "everything has a beginning; everything has an end."

With the definition of a "river system," in Mura women's highly effective translation of the concept of culture, as deployed by anthropologists, we can note the implication of the temporality of life trajectories. This encompasses the memory of the living, the elders/ancients, and the ancestors, as well as a self-reflection concerning the values of the culture. According to the women from Cacaia, sharing community life also illustrates the practice of ways of life more or less like a river system. This practice involves respect for the teachings of the elders/ancients and shared memories of kinship. Our conversation then turned to the Mura school, with its culturally appropriate educational curriculum. My older interlocutor recalled that this exercise of translating the values of respect for the knowledge of elders is practiced by her with some of the school's teachers, her nephews among them, who have spent long periods learning from her through the oral practice of counseling.

From her house in Cacaia, my interlocutor pointed toward the distant urban center of Piranha village, where most of her five brothers live, and stated adamantly, "They are all outsiders." Piranha, a village that administratively covers other localities along the Preto do Igapó-Açu River, including Cacaia, has become increasingly modernized over the years. Today, it is "a little town, all lit up, it looks like Borba," as another inhabitant of the TICS told me. Its main road is tarmacked, and its facilities include a collective water cistern, a central motor generating electricity, and posts supplying electrical power to the dwellings, as well as buildings that house various services, such as a primary healthcare center, community centers, a school, and a sports center. These urban facilities were all acquired only after the Mura fought hard with municipal, state, and federal government administrations. Profits from the commercial exchanges, involving partnerships between Mura villages and tourist companies, which have operated for more than two decades in the TICS, are also converted into infrastructural improvements in the villages.

Alliances and Partnerships

Reflecting on Mura alliances and partnerships from an ethnographic perspective, as Peter Gow's work invites us to do, yields some surprising revelations. First, the Mura formulate their self-identification as a mixed people. In other words, TICS houses may show marriages between Mura men and women with other Indigenous groups in the region, such as the Munduruku, Apurinã, and Pirahã. This was the case in the first house in Piranha village, which was the result of the marriage of a Munduruku man, born in the Quatá Laranjal Indigenous Land, and a "legitimate" Mura woman from the Igapó-Açu River, born in Cunhã village.

Peter Gow (2014) focused on relations between Indigenous peoples in the lower Urubamba River, highlighting the differences that define and redefine collectives in the Indigenous Amazon. His analysis sought to understand the social dynamics of the Indigenous Amazon, but not in terms of the relations between linguistic and ethnic totalities, delimited by borders. The latter is a type of approach in cultural anthropology that is recognizable in relation to the notion of "ethnographic areas" (Galvão 1960). Instead, Gow proposed to make comparisons that consider the sets as composed of myriad Indigenous collectives that relate to each other while maintaining their differences. We have seen that the Mura construction of kinship with the Pirahã or the Munduruku does not erase the distinctions.

In partnerships with non-Indigenous people, however, the Mura use the Indigenous concept of "relative by consideration" to build matrimonial partnerships with nonrelatives. The process of bringing foreigners closer to Mura villages involves sharing a way of life and values guided by the memory of kinship.[11]

To further develop the Mura theory of acculturation, it is useful to return once again to Gow's proposal and his reading of the classic essay by Anne-Christine Taylor (1996) on the notion of acculturation among the Achuar. For Taylor, the Achuar person, in his or her individuality, is a repertoire of different states of being. She suggests, therefore, that anthropology needs to pay attention to the modulations involved in the lived experience of culture. What matters here is not the contrast between losing and keeping culture. Instead, it is the individual feeling of no longer being compelled to define one's "self" in relation to experiencing the entire range of states predicated in Achuar conceptualizations of personhood. The Achuar, Taylor suggests, enter and leave their culture, as well as move easily toward other cultures, but this movement does not imply a loss of their own culture.

This was what my interlocutor from Cacaia was telling us when she contrasted the "elders/ancients" with the "outsiders." She was highlighting the fact that only some residents of the TICS have access to (and proficiency in) Mura knowledge about the construction of personhood. This knowledge involves the commensality and advice through which mothers shape the bodies of their daughters, to, for example, control their first menarche. In the same way, they share with their sons and daughters an entire repertoire based on the ethics of respect, which applies to all phases of life. Hence, in an extended family, only some sons and daughters, like my interlocutor from Cacaia, consider themselves (and are considered) particularly skilled in speaking on behalf of their culture, or "our system."

My goal has been to show the strength of the alliances in Mura villages with Indigenous collectives from the region of the lower Madeira River in Brazil, an ensemble that encompasses the Pirahã, Munduruku, and Apurinã, among others. These partnership relations, in turn, reveal the conditions for the construction of relationships with outsiders, in commercial partnerships involving the participation of settlers and bosses in the *aviamento* system. These partnerships included individuals and groups who, engaged by the Mura through a "politics of regard" (Kelly and Matos 2019), stayed in the villages and were incorporated into the kinship network.

Notes

Epigraph: McCallum 1998. "'Good' strangers are also 'raised' and 'fabricated' with food during the process of making them more 'the same' and less 'other.' However, since in many cases they cannot return the gesture, they rarely turn into close kin of a Kaxinauá. The act of feeding among people from the same generation must be mutual."

This study was financed in part by the Coordenação de Aperfeiçoamento de Pessoal de Nível Superior (CAPES), Brazil.

1.   Translator's note (TN): SPI in Portuguese is Serviço de Proteção aos Índios e Localização de Trabalhadores Rurais.

2.   TN: In Portuguese, Fundação Nacional dos Povos Indígenas (previously Fundação Nacional dos Índios).

3.   On the involvement of immigrants in the *aviamento* (debt bondage) system on the Madeira River in Amazonas State, Brazil, and the activities of the *regatões*, or river traders, see Leal and Truzzi (2014).

4.   A Tupian term, *peiara* is also written *piwara* in the ethnological literature, translated as "the one who clears the path" (Wagley and Galvão 1949). In the context of the Mura Indigenous organizations, *peara* is used to identify political action of the leaders (OPIM 2009).

5.   In an interview granted to me in 1999, Ambrósio Hazan, one of Fortunato's heirs, reaffirmed this connection: "Tiago Marques de Sapucaia was in charge of organizing the work of the Indians and selling the Brazil nuts."

6.   Interview with Raimundo Moreira Coutinho, Toti, in Catuaba, November 24, 1999.

7.   Pirahã refers to people speaking the Mura-Pirahã language, inhabitants of the municipality of Humaitá (AM), the southernmost region of the hydrographic

basin of the Madeira River, at the confluence of the Maici and Marmelos Rivers. On the relations between the Mura and Pirahã, see Marco Antonio Gonçalves (1993, 2001).

8. On the categories of contact used in Brazilian Indigenism and in reference to Indigenous peoples living in voluntary isolation, see Ricardo and Gongora (2019), Gow (2011, 2015, 2018), and Vaz (2019).

9. Interview with José Dias da Silva, Fé em Deus village, TICS, 2016. Concerning the giant potato, *Casimirella* sp., which the Mura call *manhafã*, see Santos (2020) and Amoroso (2020).

10. This is similar to the "eco-cosmologies" of the upper Río Negro, the geographical aspects of the many sagas of the Cobra Grande (Giant Serpent) in Amazonia (see Kawa 2016). More recently, places have returned as a central focus of research concerning the processes for recognizing a region's intangible cultural heritage (Andrello 2012). The notion of eco-cosmology (Århem [1996] 2001, 214–37) was used in this context to describe the inscriptions in landscapes of relations of predation and reciprocity between the Makuna and entities of the cosmos, as mediated by the shaman.

11. On the networks of collectives in the Purus-Madeira interfluvial region and their relations with extractivist fronts, see Suarez (2019).

References

Amoroso, Marta R. 1992. "Corsários no caminho fluvial: Os Mura do rio Madeira." In *História dos índios no Brasil*, edited by Manuela Carneiro da Cunha, 297–310. São Paulo: Companhia das Letras/Secretaria Municipal da Cultura/FAPESP.

Amoroso, Marta R. 2000a. "Os Mura tentam recuperar terras loteadas e reduzidas no passado." In *Povos indígenas no Brasil, 1996–2000*, edited by Carlos Alberto Ricardo, 465–68. São Paulo: Instituto Socioambiental.

Amoroso, Marta R. 2000b. *Relatório circunstanciado de identificação e delimitação da T. I. Cunha-Sapucaia*. Brasília: FUNAI.

Amoroso, Marta R. 2013. "O nascimento da aldeia Mura: Sentidos e modos de habitar a beira." In *Paisagens ameríndias: Lugares, circuitos e modos de vida na Amazônia*, edited by Marta R. Amoroso and Gilton Mendes dos Santos, 93–117. São Paulo: Terceiro Nome.

Amoroso, Marta R. 2016. "Impasses do ambientalismo no Baixo Madeira: O caso Mura." In *Antropologia da ciência e da tecnologia: Dobras reflexivas*, edited by Claudia Fonseca, Fabíola Rohden, Paula Sandrine Machado, and Heloísa Salvatti Paim, 235–58. Porto Alegre: Sulina.

Amoroso, Marta R. 2018. "Transformations of Mura Territoriality in the Amazon." *History of Anthropology Newsletter* 42 (December 31). http://histanthro.org/notes/mura-territoriality/.

Amoroso, Marta R. 2020. "A descoberta do *manhafã*: Seguindo as trilhas da floresta com os Mura." In *Vozes vegetais: Diversidade, resistências e histórias da floresta*, edited by Joana Cabral de Oliveira, Marta R. Amoroso, Ana Gabriela Morim de Lima, Karen Shiratori, Stelio Marras, and Laure Emperaire, 167–86. São Paulo: Ubu.

Andrello, Geraldo. 2012. "Histórias tariano e tukano: Política e ritual no rio Uapés." *Revista de Antropologia* 55 (1): 291–330.

Århem, Kaj. (1996) 2001. "La red cósmica de la alimentación: La interconexión de humanos y naturaleza en el noroeste de la Amazonia." In *Naturaleza y sociedad: Perspectivas antropológicas*, edited by Philippe Descola and Gísli Pálsson, 214–37. Mexico City: Siglo Veintiuno Editores.

Bateson, Gregory. 1936. *Naven: A Survey of the Problems Suggested by a Composite Picture of the Culture of a New Guinea Tribe Drawn from Three Points of View.* Stanford, Calif.: Stanford University Press.

Bonilla, Oiara. 2005. "O bom patrão e o inimigo voraz: Predação e comércio na cosmologia Paumari." *Mana* 11 (1): 41–66.

Cangussu, Daniel R. 2021. "Manual indigenista mateiro: Princípios de botânica e arqueologia aplicados ao monitoramento e proteção dos territórios dos povos indígenas isolados na Amazônia." Master's thesis, Instituto Nacional de Pesquisas da Amazônia (INPA).

Fileno, Fernando Augusto. 2018. *No seio do rio: Linhas que casam, que curam e que dançam, parentesco e corporalidade entre os Mura do Igapó-Açu.* São Paulo: Alameda Editorial.

Galvão, Eduardo. 1960 "Áreas culturais indígenas do Brasil, 1900–1959." *Boletim do Museu Paraense Emílio Goeldi* 8:1–41.

Goldman, Marcio. 2015. "'Quinhentos anos de contato': Por uma teoría etnográfica da (contra) mestiçagem." *Mana* 21 (3): 641–59.

Gonçalves, Marco Antonio. 1993. *O significado do nome: Cosmologia e nominação entre os pirahã.* Rio de Janeiro: Sette Letras.

Gonçalves, Marco Antonio. 2001. *O mundo inacabado: Ação e criação em uma cosmologia amazônica.* Rio de Janeiro: Editora da UFRJ.

Gow, Peter. 1991. *Of Mixed Blood: Kinship and History in Peruvian Amazonia.* Oxford: Clarendon.

Gow, Peter. 1997. "O parentesco como consciência humana: O caso dos Piro." *Mana* 3 (2): 39–65.

Gow, Peter. 2001. *An Amazonian Myth and its History.* Oxford: Oxford University Press.

Gow, Peter. 2003. "Ex-cocama: Identidades em transformação na Amazônia peruana." *Mana* 9 (1): 57–79.

Gow, Peter. 2006a. "Canção Purús: Nacionalização e tribalização no sudoeste da Amazônia." *Revista de Antropologia* 49 (1): 431–64.

Gow, Peter. 2006b. "Da Etnografia à História: 'Introdução' e 'Conclusão' de *Of Mixed Blood: Kinship and History in Peruvian Amazonia.*" *Cadernos de Campo* 15 (14–15): 197–226. https://revistas.usp.br/cadernosdecampo/issue/view/3211.

Gow, Peter. 2010. "Um cline mítico na América do Sul Ocidental: Explorando um conjunto levistraussiano." *Tellus* 10 (18): 11–38.

Gow, Peter. 2011. "'Me deixa em paz!' Um relato etnográfico preliminar sobre o isol-amento voluntário dos Mashco." *Revista de Antropologia* 54 (1): 11–46.

Gow, Peter. 2014. "Lévi-Strauss's 'Double Twist' and Controlled Comparison: Transformational Relations between Neighbouring Societies." *Anthropology of This Century* 10 (May). http://aotcpress.com/articles/lvistrausss-double-twist -controlled-comparison-transformational-relations-neighbouring/.

Gow, Peter. 2015. "Steps towards an Ethnographic Theory of Acculturation." *Etnogra-fia: Praktyki, Teorie, Doświadczenia* 1:34–39.

Gow, Peter. 2018. "'Who Are These Wild Indians': On the Foreign Policies of Some Voluntarily Isolated Peoples in Amazonia." *Tipití* 16 (1): 6–20.

Harris, Mark. 2014. "Enchanted Entities and Disenchanted Lives along the Amazon Rivers, Brazil." In *The Social Life of Spirits,* edited by Ruy Blanes and Diana Espírito Santo, 108–25. Chicago: University of Chicago Press.

IBGE (Instituto Brasileiro de Geografia e Estatística). 2012. *Censo Brasileiro de 2010.* Rio de Janeiro: IBGE.

Kawa, Nicholas C. 2016. *Amazonia in the Anthropocene: People, Soils, Plants, Forests.* Austin: University of Texas Press.

Kelly, José Antonio, and Marcos de Almeida Matos. 2019. "Política da consideração: Ação e influência nas terras baixas da América do Sul." *Mana* 25 (2): 391–426. http://dx.doi.org/10.1590/1678-49442019v25n2p391.

Lévi-Strauss, Claude. 1971. *L'homme nu.* Paris: Plon.

Lima, Leandro Mahalem de. 2015. "No Arapiuns, entre verdadeiros e -*ranas*: Sobre as espaços, as lógicas, as organizações e os movimentos dos espaços do político." PhD diss., Universidade de São Paulo.

Lima, Tânia Stolze. 2005. *Um peixe olhou para mim: O povo Yudjá e a perspectiva.* São Paulo: Editora UNESP.

McCallum, Cecilia. 1998. "Alteridade e sociabilidade Kaxinauá: Perspectivas de uma antropologia da vida diária." *Revista Brasileira de Ciências Sociais* 13 (38): n.p.

Moreira Santos, Ana Flávia. 2009. *Conflitos fundiários, territorialização e disputas classificatórias: Autazes (AM), primeiras décadas do século XX.* PhD diss., Uni-versidade Federal do Rio de Janeiro/Museu Nacional.

OPIM (Organização dos Professores Indígenas Mura). 2009. *Yandé Anama Mura.* Documentação Audiovisual e Recuperação do Patrimônio Imaterial dos Pajés e Pearas. Mura: Autazes AM.

Ricardo, Fany, and Majoí Fávero Gongora, eds. 2019. *Cercos e resistências: Povos indígenas isolados na Amazônia brasileira.* São Paulo: Instituto Socioambiental.

Romano, Adriana Athila. 1998. "Índios de verdade: territorialidade, história e dif-erença entre os Mura da Amazônia Meridional." Master's thesis, Universidade Federal do Rio de Janeiro.

Santos, Gilton Mendes dos. 2020. "Transformar as plantas, cultivar os corpos." In *Vozes vegetais: Diversidade, resistências e histórias da floresta,* edited by Joana Cabral de Oliveira, Marta R. Amoroso, Ana Gabriela Morim de Lima, Karen Shi-ratori, Stelio Marras, and Laure Emperaire, 140–53. São Paulo: Ubu.

Slater, Candace. 1994. *Dance of the Dolphin: Transformation and Disenchantment in the Amazonian Imagination*. Chicago: University of Chicago Press.

Suarez, Miguel Aparício. 2019. "A relação banawá: Socialidade e transformação nos Arawá do Purus." PhD diss., Universidade Federal do Rio de Janeiro/Museu Nacional.

Taylor, Anne-Christine. 1996. "The Soul's Body and Its States: An Amazonian Perspective on the Nature of Being Human." *Journal of the Royal Anthropological Institute* 2 (2): 201–15.

Truzzi, Oswaldo, and Davi A. Leal. 2014. "De caixeiros a seringalistas: Portugueses comerciantes no rio Madeira." Paper presented at the ABEP XIX Encontro Nacional de Estudos Populacionais, São Pedro, November 24–28.

Vaz, Antenor. 2019. "Povos indígenas em isolamento e contato inicial na Amazonia: As armadilhas do desenvolvimento." *Tipití* 16 (1): 125–45.

Viveiros de Castro, Eduardo. 1993. "Review of *Of Mixed Blood: Kinship and History in Peruvian Amazonia*, by Peter Gow." *Man* 28 (1): 182–83.

Wagley, Charles, and Eduardo Galvão. 1949. *The Tenetehara Indians of Brazil: A Culture in Transition*. New York: Columbia University Press.

Whitaker, James Andrew. 2020. "Water Mamas among the Makushi." *Folklore* 131 (1): 34–54.

CHAPTER 5

Friends and Enemies

Reflections on the Sindagua Wars of Barbacoas,
Colombia, c. 1597–1635

KRIS LANE

This chapter examines the battle for Barbacoas, a lowland tropical region located along Colombia's rugged Pacific coast, named for the stilt houses of its inhabitants. Beginning at the turn of the seventeenth century, long after highland conquest, Spanish settlers and their Indigenous allies pushed into this region in successive waves in search of human captives and gold dust. Viewed by outsiders as a "resource frontier" much like the upper Amazon just over the Andes mountains to the east, the Province of Barbacoas was inhabited by various Indigenous peoples whose histories we scarcely know. Most, including a group called Sindaguas in Spanish records, were all but exterminated in the quest for gold, to be replaced by enslaved Africans and their descendants. Yet the story of the Sindaguas, famed headhunter-bandits, reminds us that colonial-era alliances and partnerships went both ways, and that symbols of power like the human head also found new currency amid mutual predation and social incorporation.

For the early colonial period in what became known as Spanish America, the story most often told is one of armed European invaders defeating Indigenous peoples unlucky enough to live on or near precious metals deposits. Such tales of violent conquest are punctuated by rare triumphs or reversals, epitomized by the successful ousting of Spanish interlopers by the ancestral Shuar of southeast Ecuador sometime around the year 1600. This foiled conquest tale from the edge of Amazonia, in which gold-hungry foreigners were rewarded with mouthfuls of molten metal amid mass rebellion, was recounted by ethnographer Michael Harner in his popular ethnography *The Jívaro: People of the Sacred Waterfalls* (1972). Harner lifted the story from the pages of Jesuit Juan de Velasco's 1789 *History of the Kingdom of Quito*, but it was already accepted as fact by most Ecuadorians.

Perhaps sensing echoes of anticolonial, anti-gold-mining struggles of Indigenous Chileans (the ancestral Mapuche) from about the same time as the so-called Shuar revolt, anthropologists Philippe Descola (1994, 1996) and Anne-Christine Taylor (1994; Taylor and Landázuri 1994) were more circumspect in addressing how exactly the Spanish were driven out of this gold-rich region of the western Amazon (to which prospectors returned in droves in the 1980s after consulting historical records). The Shuar, Achuar, and select neighbors must have allied through partnerships to drive away the gold seekers, but how, given their famously atomistic social organization? Presumably it helped to be famed as incorrigible headhunters, even cannibals (Newson 1996; Karsten 1935). Sindagua resistance on the Pacific side of the Andes would echo this tale of mutual alliances against "settler-extractivists" a few decades later, from the 1610s to the 1630s.

On the Spanish side of the Shuar story, Indigenous allies (and captives) had enabled a small number of foreign interlopers to penetrate the rainforest, locate gold deposits, find means of subsistence, and otherwise navigate and extract. Everywhere Spanish conquistadors and other foreigners went in the Americas, they assumed that Indigenous peoples knew where to find precious metals deposits, how they might be exploited, and in some cases, as in highland Bolivia, even how complex ores were refined. Profound Indigenous geographical, geological, and metallurgical knowledge systems and technologies were evident in material culture. Plunder was proof (TePaske 2010; Whitehead 1990).

Helping the interlopers was almost as dangerous as fighting them. Early revelations of mines quickly led to mass abuses, which in turn convinced some Indigenous groups to hide their geological knowledge. Spanish officials and other commentators complained bitterly of this kind of resistance, which took several forms (Platt and Quisbert 2007). In sum, Indigenous peoples all over the Spanish- and Portuguese-claimed Americas were severely challenged by European gold lust, sometimes siding with the invaders in hopes of political advantage and sometimes forming new alliances with neighbors (mostly other Indigenous groups) to resist mining incursions—or simply dissimulating about the location of mineral deposits. Before examining the particulars of the Sindagua wars of early seventeenth-century Colombia, it is worth noting a shift in the historiography of European conquest in the Americas, keeping South America's equatorial lowlands in mind as a final "resource frontier," an imaginary yet also genuine El Dorado. How have colonial-era Indigenous alliances been reframed?

Your Conquest or Mine? The New Conquest History and the Endless Frontier

Stories of crushing loss and plunder, if not "total conquest," are much more common than the heroic Ecuadorian/Shuar exception or its Chilean/Mapuche analog, yet massive revision of conquest narratives has emerged in recent decades, particularly in Mexico and Central America, but lately extending to South America, including Amazonia. These "corrections" have been driven largely by recognition of super-numerous Indigenous allies whose aims only partly aligned with those of foreign interlopers (Mikecz 2020; Powers 2005; Restall 2012, 2021).

Public discourse remains fixated on the Black Legend of unique Spanish greed and cruelty, tempered by Jared Diamond–style (1997) environmental determinism, but the archive-based historiography of the Spanish conquests in America has shifted toward recognition of Indigenous allies as fundamentally necessary, even paramount. Indeed, for Mexico and Central America, European invaders like Hernando Cortés and Pedro de Alvarado have been demoted to second-rank status, in some revisions acting as mere tools of wily Tlaxcallans and other enemies of the Aztecs or Colhua-Mexica (Brian, Benton, and García Loaeza 2015; Restall 2018; Townsend 2019). "Co-conquistadors" prevailed in Yucatán and Guatemala as well, pursuing their own agendas to the chagrin of so many (or so few) Spaniards (Asselbergs 2004; Matthew 2012; Matthew and Oudijk 2007; Restall 1999).

The conquest narratives of the Incas and Muisca of Colombia have not been so radically revised, but historians north and south increasingly emphasize Spanish interlopers' absolute dependence on Indigenous allies, such as the Cañari and Chachapoyas of Ecuador-Peru, plus drafted or enslaved Central Americans (Lovell 2022; Mikecz 2024). In Colombia, these allies included circum-Caribbean Indigenous captives forced to march up the mountains. Spanish chroniclers such as Juan de Castellanos (1589) and Pedro Simón (1627) had a way of writing such people, usually referred to as *indios* amigos, out of their heroic narratives or mentioning them only in passing, prompting "New Conquest" historians to read between the lines in search of alternate, "friendly Indian" perspectives (Gamboa 2010).

In the Andes, unlike in Mesoamerica, a tradition of Indigenous counternarratives (or co-conquistador testimonies) never fully materialized, but scholars of Indigenous elites have revisited the mostly Spanish-language archival record for clues. Andean elites in seventeenth-century Ecuador, for example, toggled between claiming direct descent from the "great" Incas and tracing genealogies of ancient resistance to the Inca "tyrant," depending on the politics of their own time (Powers 1995; Guengerich and Ochoa 2021). Whether their ancestors were "co-conquistadors" or more traditionally aligned "native lords" who deserved recognition as such, midcolonial Indigenous caciques and *kurakas* went out of their way to prove their historical role as faithful allies (McEnroe 2020; Garrett 2005).

Other ways of flipping conquest narratives suggest that Indigenous groups used the Spanish as their allies rather than the other way around. In a major revision of the conquest of the Incas, Andeanist R. Alan Covey (2020) spotlights weakness and division among Atahualpa's ranks at the time of Francisco Pizarro's fateful 1532 march to Cajamarca. Internal divisions have long stood out as a significant factor in the precipitous fall of Inca Peru, but Covey argues that the gaping aperture provided by civil war (combined with the Inca Atahualpa's irascible temperament) did more than just help Pizarro and his tiny cohort of isolated Spaniards. It enabled Indigenous nobles (including top women; see also Garcia's chapter in this volume) unhappy with Atahualpa's politics to muscle in and pursue their own goals, much as their peers had in Mesoamerica.

On the other side, murderous Spanish clan rivalries, plus the survival of the Inca "rump empire" at Vilcabamba, seemed to drive home the point: the Pizarro brothers did not oversee a Spanish conquest of the Inca empire, but rather they initiated, unwittingly, a locally driven breakup of a fragile, overextended web of fictive kin ties called Tawantinsuyu. The new image is of a small number of foreigners playing the role of wedge (or scissors), only to be forsaken by their own king, as regicides and rebels to be cut down by another pseudo-emperor, Charles V. What followed Inca collapse and clan wars was a Spanish "reconquest of Peru," led by a mix of bureaucrats, civilian militias, and missionaries, that lasted many decades beyond the 1541 death of Francisco Pizarro. In this long, drawn-out process, Indigenous allies were everywhere key. Even outspoken Indigenous critics of the colonial order, such as Felipe Guamán Poma de Ayala, writing nearly a century after Atahualpa's capture, might be seen in this light (Adorno 1986). Guamán Poma, like many contemporaries (de la Puente 2018), never considered himself a conquered subject; he was an autonomous, if beleaguered, native lord, frank and assertive.

Things were not so different in New Granada, which was "another Peru," as some of its principal narrators claimed (Francis 2007), where Spanish and German conquistador factions fought each other as much as anyone else, although they never hesitated to throttle powerful Indigenous caciques when terror suited their needs. In this part of the Andes, no empire was conquered. The "New Kingdom" of Granada was a fiction cut from whole cloth. Everywhere one looked, Indigenous peoples still had the run of the land, especially the region's many "hot country" gold-mining frontiers (Muñoz 2024; Caillavet and Pachón 1996). Meanwhile, a new mestizo elite gained purchase in the highlands, developing its own historical sensibilities (Dcardorff 2023; Rappaport 2014).

Be this as it may, Spaniards made off with considerable South American gold, and they would continue to search for and extract more— thanks to Indigenous auxiliaries and enslaved Africans—beyond the old boundaries of Tawantinsuyu and well outside the domain of the highland farmers of northeastern Colombia (Bryant 2014). This long-term extractive project, as in the silver mines of northern Mexico beyond the old Aztec frontier, would require a more subtle, intimate blend of aggression and alliance with Indigenous peoples, most of them never having regarded themselves as subjects of foreign sovereigns.

Mining the unconquered margins of Mexico included state-sponsored colonization of "wild frontiers" by conquest-era Indigenous allies like the

Tlaxcallans, a pattern repeated elsewhere in Spanish-claimed America. Other intrepid invaders included Roman Catholic priests, usually Franciscans and later Jesuits, but also Mercedarians, Dominicans, and others, often styling themselves as brakes on settler excesses (see also chapters by Loureiro Dias and Whitaker in this volume). Frontiers remained divided, however, as settler-colonists frequently resented the missionaries, regarding them as unfair competitors for scarce export commodities and Indigenous "hands."

Brazilian historiography has made a similar turn toward emphasizing Indigenous and other forms of local agency in the face of intruders searching for mineral, botanical, and "spiritual" wealth. Heather Roller (2021) emphasizes persistent Indigenous control of not just Amazonia but also the vast Paraguay River basin throughout colonial times. To this we might add much of present-day Uruguay, where Indigenous-controlled spaces persisted through the eighteenth century (Erbig 2020). Hal Langfur (2006, 2014, 2023) and others have documented Indigenous persistence elsewhere amid late colonial Brazil's gold and diamond rushes in Minas Gerais, Goiás, and Mato Grosso, as well as in Amazonia. Whereas much of the prior historical research conducted in this area emphasizes resistance over cross-cultural alliances, Mary Karasch (2016) found considerable evidence of mutual dependency in gold-rush era Goiás. Cross-cultural alliances were also significant in the nearby Guianas (Whitaker 2025; see also Whitaker's chapter in this volume). Taken together, one might now speak not only of endless "co-conquests" but also of an endless Indigenous American frontier (Levin Rojo and Radding 2019).[1]

In all these revisionist views of conquest and extraction in regions claimed by Iberians, we acknowledge more evidence of Indigenous absorption of successive waves of imperial claims making, missionary activity, and settler colonialism. Even so, "conquest" dynamics were always greatly accelerated and typically violent on mining frontiers. Gold, silver, and precious stones had a way of concentrating the mind in a way that endless prairies, scrub forests, and marshlands did not. Greed was at play, to be sure, but throughout early modern times and beyond, American precious metals were the fuel of empires worldwide, and not only western European ones. Silver and gold shipped from North, Central, and

South America drove imperial expansion throughout Eurasia. Mughal India is a case in point (Chaudhuri 1978).

Thus, from the time of Columbus forward, controlling mines containing precious metals was a matter of state, which put Indigenous peoples inhabiting potential mining zones in an impossible bind. Such thinking did not disappear with independence, and today's "resource frontiers" also increasingly pit states against Indigenous groups (in South America and beyond), who are framed in public discourse as obstacles to progress if they do not comply with extraction-oriented policies (Gudynas 2015; Leal 2018). Seeing beyond Indigenous victimhood during resource booms requires careful reading of refractory sources, but as Gary Van Valen (2013) showed in his study of the rubber boom in nineteenth- and twentieth-century Bolivia, no latex would have been extracted without a complex interplay of alliances involving Indigenous groups.

Leaving behind "miraculous" tales of conquest to take a longer view of Indigenous survival, strategic alliances, and reconfigurations amid resource grabs can be instructive. In *Defiance and Deference in Mexico's Colonial North*, historian Susan Deeds (2003) tells the story of how Indigenous allies and enemies—often the same people at different times or in different configurations over the course of the seventeenth century—defined New Spain's northwest silver frontier. In this telling, the gradual creation of New Biscay was in every way a shared and hotly contested project, much like that of the New Kingdom of Granada in South America. Deeds's book is one of several archivally rooted histories that chronicle the slow, generation-by-generation advance of colonial settlement ultimately reliant on Indigenous agency. *Defiance and Deference* is not simply a story of conquest, enslavement, and despoliation, although Indigenous peoples clearly suffered tremendously in the name of silver (as well as other minerals).

A much starker story is told by historian Andrés Reséndez (2016) in a prize-winning book entitled *The Other Slavery*, a sharp reminder that, as in contemporary Brazil (Monteiro 2018), backland paramilitary sorties were as much slaving ventures as treasure-seeking ones. Captives—as laborers and fictive kin—were everywhere prized. Enemies could be transformed into allies, or they could be exterminated, depending on the will of the victors. The story of Colombia's Sindaguas falls somewhere between the tales told by Deeds and Reséndez, with slow penetration and settlement of a mining frontier punctuated by fierce mutual predation, slaving, and exile. Nothing would have happened without Indigenous alliances, some of which were long-standing.

More recent work by historians Dana Velasco Murillo (2016, 2021), Sean McEnroe (2012), and Laurent Corbeil (2018) explains how central Mexican Indigenous colonists like the Tlaxcallans made their own alliances with local conquered, or "reduced," peoples, such as the Guachichil in northern silver towns like Zacatecas and San Luis Potosí. Taking the story further, Daviken Studnicki-Gizbert (2022) narrates the long (but accelerating) process of social and environmental transformation in and around San Luis Potosí as silver, then gold mines, dove into the sacred Cerro de San Pedro. At play across the centuries were unstable, often interethnic alliances. The result of these colonizations and extractive enterprises is a giant Anthropocene hole in the ground, or a "Plantationocene" based on this history (see Whitaker 2020).

In the northernmost Andes, Spanish and Euro-American gold seekers faced a distinct reality. By the end of the sixteenth century, settlers controlled (albeit tentatively) a string of highland towns plus a few modest ports. "Conquered" Indigenous subjects lived mostly within a few days' walk of lofty townsites like Tunja, Bogotá, Popayán, and Pasto. Yet reputedly bellicose, unconquered peoples also abounded, even in some parts of the highlands and uncomfortably close to the king's highway, or camino real (Muñoz 2024; Montoya 2014).

Spanish-descended ranchers, hacienda owners, and traveling merchants feared the Pijao and Páez (Nasa) of Colombia's Cordillera Central, as did scores of Indigenous allies "reduced" to tribute payment and personal service at the conquest frontier. Meanwhile, some lowland Indigenous groups, such as the Carares, menaced travelers navigating the middle Magdalena River, New Granada's main transportation artery. Other groups effectively controlled the lower Cauca and parts of the upper Magdalena (Caillavet and Pachón 1996). Meanwhile, the ample Atrato River, the Chocó's Atlantic outlet, remained entirely in Indigenous hands until the eighteenth century, when gold prospectors flooded the region (Williams 2005).

Spanish and creole penetration of Colombia's wet Pacific coast remained tentative at the start of the seventeenth century, but the process took a sudden lurch, driven by a blend of gold lust and desire for new Indigenous subjects. At this time, circa 1600, the tiny Pacific port of Buenaventura was surrounded by unconquered groups, such as the Noanamáes, and the long stretch of lowland forest from Esmeraldas, Ecuador, to eastern Panama lay in the hands of mostly unknown Indigenous peoples or fugitive Africans (Beatty Medina 2006, 2012).

The circumscribed limits of Spanish dominion were notably starker on the other side of the Andes (Renard-Casevitz, Saignes, and Taylor 1988). The eastern llanos of New Granada's north and the vast and rugged Amazon watershed to the south were even less known to Spaniards and their descendants than the greater Chocó. This was not for lack of trying, as both the llanos and the Putumayo attracted cyclical hordes of El Dorado seekers and a handful of missionaries. The first recorded Jesuit in equatorial Amazonia's piedmont was Rafael Ferrer, sent east from Quito in 1599. Portuguese Jesuits soon worked from the other direction, moving upstream from São Luís do Maranhão (see Loureiro Dias's chapter in this volume). Quito-based Franciscans followed close on the heels of the Jesuits via Sucumbios, but the Amazon was vast, and entirely in Indigenous hands (Newson 1996). The northwest Pacific frontier of South America seemed closer to hand if no less "wild." Its main attractions were the same as they had always been: gold and "Indians."

To Pacific Shores

In 1599, the alleged year of the great Jívaro Revolt in upper Amazonia and the confirmed year of a major Mapuche uprising in Chile, a veteran of lowland sorties throughout what is now Colombia published a manual for "late-stage" conquistadors. Bernardo de Vargas Machuca's *Indian Militia and Description of the Indies* ([1599] 2008) was intended to school both immigrants and creoles in the ways of war—specifically "Indian" war. Fighting Indigenous insurgents meant creating an "Indian" or "Indies-appropriate" militia, something quite different to what soldiers knew from Europe or the Mediterranean, yet also distinct from the earlier conquistadors. There would be no great open-field battles or flanks of artillerymen squaring off against cavalry in the South American jungle. This was counterinsurgency, a.k.a. guerrilla or "little war," and *indios* amigos were essential, always more numerous than those paramilitary fighters calling themselves Spaniards.

To conquer what remained of "the Indies," by which Vargas Machuca meant areas in rainforests, cloud forests, wetlands, and *páramos*, one had to learn from both Indigenous allies and enemies. Indeed, one had to rely on them for pointers and warnings at every turn, as European knowledge and tactics were mostly inappropriate, even counterproductive. To fight "Indian Wars," one had to fight—and think, Vargas Machuca insisted— like an "Indian." Failure to do so was fatal, if not by dart, then by snakebite.

Also at this time, the final years of the sixteenth century, Quito's top crown officials made peace with the Maroons of Esmeraldas, offering to leave them alone if they promised not to ally with foreign corsairs, the likes of Francis Drake and his cousin Richard Hawkins (who visited Esmeraldas in 1594 shortly before his capture). The Esmeraldas Maroons, whose famous 1599 portrait proved they had ready access to gold (De-Boer 1996), were to remain exempt from draft labor and tribute payment in exchange for declaring fealty to King Philip III and accepting the presence of a lone Mercedarian missionary (Beatty Medina 2012; Lane 2002; Rumazo González 1948–49).

In theory, the Esmeraldas Maroons were model "resource frontier" allies, which is why Quito's audiencia president had them painted—in effect as allied "Indian" chieftains. The portrait, executed by an Indigenous artist (Webster 2017), suggests accord, but records say the Pacific coast Maroons were divided, and only one clan lived under the authority of the central figure in the painting, don Francisco de Arobe. The Maroons' history of shifting alliances and enmities in their long struggle to remain autonomous is nothing if not head spinning, filled with false promises, side switching, and dissimulation, but always reliant on Indigenous— plus a few European—allies (Lane 2002: Rueda 2001).

What is generally forgotten is that the audiencia, or high court, of Quito also made an alliance with a group of Indigenous neighbors of the Esmeraldas Maroons known as the Barbacoans. Though not a formal treaty, the accord appears in Quito treasury records from 1598 (ANE Real Hacienda caja 36). Like the father and sons in the Maroon painting, the Barbacoas representatives were given iron and steel weapons and tools, along with luxury textiles, in exchange for promises not to attack Spanish subjects at sea or on land and not to ally with foreign pirates.

In the case of Las Barbacoas, a name given to an Indigenous "nation" but also to a long stretch of coast running from roughly the Ecuador-Colombia border near Tumaco to the port of Buenaventura, west of Cali, Spanish authorities extracted an extra promise. The Barbacoans were not to mistreat shipwreck victims stranded along the Pacific coast but rather to succor them and deliver them to multilingual Indigenous allies of the Spanish in the highlands near Tulcán. The most feared enemy here was the sea. Indeed, this treacherous sandbar-filled passage of the Pacific coast from Gorgona to Atacames had produced the Maroons of Esmeraldas, descendants of so many castaways on their way to Peru from Panama.

The Province of Las Barbacoas, like that of Esmeraldas—and for that matter, the greater Chocó region as a whole—was fabled for its "rivers of gold." Alluvial deposits of gold and platinum are still heavily exploited there today. Spanish settlers and their descendants, plus a growing number of enslaved and free people of African descent, were by this time—again, the turn of the seventeenth century—consolidating control of familiar highland microclimates, where they could grow wheat and raise sheep, as well as process sugar and raise cattle, but they were running out of sources of foreign exchange. Highland or inter-Andean gold mines outside Pasto and Popayán were numerous but inconstant, demanding more labor and other inputs over time (Calero 1997; West 1952). Some mines were also chronic targets of lowland Indigenous raiders and therefore expensive to defend.

Investments in cattle ranching and sugar production were lucrative for some, but southwest Colombia lacked the textile-making workforce and pre-Columbian population base of highland Ecuador or Colombia's northeastern savannas. A manufacturing future seemed unlikely. Low population density coupled with rugged, wet terrain and daunting distances meant that nothing could sustain the colonial enterprise better or more immediately than the expansion of precious metals mining frontiers. Only gold justified the distances and other logistical obstacles presented by the northern Andes. As Vargas Machuca noted, going for the gold meant gearing up for long dangerous slogs in the equatorial jungles and cloud forests that spilled down on either side of the great cordilleras. The real road to El Dorado was treacherous, and reversals—ambush, betrayal, mantraps, poison darts, beheadings—were to be expected.

Other push factors drove expansion into Colombia's wet Pacific low-lands circa 1600. At least two generations had passed since highland conquest, and encomiendas granted to the first conquerors and their immediate offspring were reverting to the Crown. Disease epidemics, including a devastating one in the late 1580s (Alchon 2003, 76–78), had also ravaged highland Indigenous populations, wiping out tribute in-come and shrinking markets for imported goods. The project of expand-ing gold-mining frontiers also promised access to more Indigenous peo-ples through revival of the encomienda system, a trade-off the Spanish Crown accepted despite moral qualms. Hardy colonists of the sort Vargas Machuca sought to mold could win honor, new subjects, and perhaps a fortune in gold.

As with the initial highland conquest, penetrating "hot country" (*tie-rra caliente*) could not be done from scratch, or "alone." Extracting newly conquered, or "reduced," peoples' labor plus forest resources would re-quire heavy reliance on remaining Andean highlanders (to provide food, supplies, and carriage) as well as dependence on newfound Indigenous allies inhabiting the rainforest world below (Lane 2000). Put another way, not everyone living in the Pacific coastal lowlands (or upper Ama-zonia, for those headed the other way) could be treated as an enemy, even if identifying certain groups to be conquered was absolutely required to win an encomienda.

As in the first phase of conquest, nothing could be accomplished with-out a host of Indigenous friends, but none of this "neoconquest" aggres-sion could be legally justified without identifying incorrigible Indigenous enemies. The difference now, after the 1598 death of Philip II, was that the language of conquest was out of fashion, replaced by terms familiar to modern observers of the Amazon. "Pacification" was the new "conquest," which enabled Spanish subjects and their Indigenous allies to engage in paramilitary "punishments," or *castigos*, aimed at subduing alleged reb-els. As in previous times, Indigenous peoples on all sides continued to follow their own agendas despite the desires of their self-styled overlords, secular and religious.

From the highland settler-colonist perspective, then, the only way to "develop" (i.e., create or perpetuate family dynasties) from here was to exploit lowland gold deposits, on both the Pacific and Amazonian sides of the Andes, and to conquer and incorporate the peoples that lived among them. Nothing else would do, and time was of the essence, lest the highland towns strung across the Andes between Bogotá and Quito shrivel to insignificance. Highland-based Catholic missionaries echoed this urgency, anxious to "harvest" lowland souls.

The same was thought true of the even smaller towns between Cali and Santa Fe de Antioquia, for whom the Chocó proper remained the promised land (Williams 2005). It all sounds a bit like a midcolonial version of the "extractivist dilemma," a do-or-die proposal, no time to waste (Gudynas 2015). The problem, as it had been since the time of Pizarro, was that lowland Indigenous peoples in this region were not easily befriended, much less persuaded to mine gold to benefit outsiders. Given the region's compact geography and coastwise traffic (quite unlike the continental vastness of Amazonia), it is impossible to think of them as "uncontacted" or in any way naive.

Going for the Gold

Beginning in the year 1600, highland Hispanic towns near the Ecuador-Colombia border suffered a spate of attacks. Many of the victims were not Spaniards or their descendants but rather Indigenous allies and, occasionally, enslaved Africans. Highland Indigenous leaders near Tulcán had brokered the circa 1599 peace deal with the Barbacoans to their west, but who exactly Las Barbacoas were remained unclear. The Arawakan name had been imported from the Caribbean by the conquistadors back in the 1520s to refer to tidewater stilt houses, so we can only wonder what these riparian peoples called themselves. Feared as cannibals, the Barbacoans had kept their promise to deliver shipwreck victims to the Spanish after a well-documented wreck in 1600. The truce was apparently broken not by Las Barbacoas, but by highland Spanish subjects itching for a fight (Lane 2002).

Indeed, the "official" tide turned from peace making to warmongering in the same year, when a new audiencia president took office in Quito. The governor of Popayán Province, who claimed jurisdiction over the unconquered Barbacoas district, had already argued against Quito's appeasements. Echoing restless settler elites, the governor called for violent conquest and, in the case of the Esmeraldas Maroons, reenslavement.

Other commentators pointed to the Barbacoas district's violent past, dismissing the current truce as a sham. Lowland raiders from somewhere in the province had attacked gold-mining camps along the Patía River gorge north of Pasto in the 1580s, and outlying ranches and farms were just as exposed (AGI Quito 16: 27).

Meanwhile, Quito audiencia president Miguel de Ibarra called for a new road linking the northern Ecuadorian highlands to the coast to ease trade with Panama, which was an old dream. Autonomous Maroons and "Barbacoans" were not just obstacles in Ibarra's view, but also wasted sources of labor. Resulting incursions, including armed attempts to extract tribute from Indigenous inhabitants of the lower Mira River valley and to plant gold-mining colonies of enslaved Africans (mostly from Upper Guinea and Greater Congo) in the heart of Barbacoas, prompted violent reprisals.

By 1607, Indigenous payback included the ritual taking and display of dozens of "friendly Indian" and African (including Maroon) heads. Or so said horrified witnesses, who also suspected cannibalism. In the first instance, the headhunters were labeled Malabas, an Indigenous group said to inhabit the border between what is today coastal Colombia and Ecuador (near Tumaco). Were they Barbacoans, or did Las Barbacoas refer to some other group farther north or upriver? Belligerent highlanders would soon try to find out.

In 1610, a new Popayán governor, don Francisco Sarmiento de Soto-mayor, sponsored a heavily armed sortie into Barbacoas Province led by a self-financed, Cali-based militiaman, Captain Francisco Ramírez de la Serna (AGI Quito 16: 38). Styled in official documents as a justified reprisal, or *castigo* (punishment), for criminal acts including murder, larceny, and even piracy, the 1610 Ramírez expedition was essentially a slaving raid (Romero 2018).

Spanish America's frontier militia expeditions were not unlike Brazilian *bandeiras*, replete with military sound and fury but largely composed of Indigenous allies and with the principal aim of collecting and selling captured "enemies" as booty. Indigenous allies were typically allotted a share of the material plunder. None of this was legal, but long-standing prohibitions on Indigenous enslavement could be circumvented by claiming "just war," as happened with the Pijao and Paeces of Colombia and the Mapuche of Chile (Berger 2023; Muñoz 2024). Again, in the absence of missionaries or other advocates, frontier-dwelling Indigenous peoples were on their own (see Loureiro Dias's and Whitaker's chapters in this volume).

In the case of the 1610 coastal entrada, or sortie, that set out from Cali, Capt. Ramírez was reticent in naming names or counting allies, but he relied heavily on a wide array of Indigenous informants, guides, interpreters, paddlers, porters, hunters, foragers, cooks, healers, and archers as he sought to "punish" an allegedly incorrigible backland cacique, or chieftain, he called Mamadagi, head of the so-called Pil people. It was important (for legal cover) to have a clearly named enemy: a rebel cacique plus a "tribe," or "nation." Also targeted were groups labeled Paripasos, Timbas, and Cacahambres (or Cacachames).

In addition to fighting men, creole captains such as Ramírez relied on interpreters to communicate with Indigenous friends as well as enemies. How much was mutually understood in these rainforest exchanges remains unclear, but as with the early conquistadors' experiences, one imagines only a tiny number of multilingual interlocutors (à la Malintzin; Townsend 2006) fathomed each side's intentions, even as they proved powerless to prevent sudden violent outbursts.

Even so, Ramírez knew exactly what he wanted: gold, slaves (*piezas*), and official recognition for self-funded Crown service. He also knew how to stake a narrative and therefore legal claim. Led by expert Indigenous friends, Ramírez and his team attacked—unprovoked—several river-dwelling Native groups above the tideline between Buenaventura and the Patía River. Along the way, he and his allies apprehended or killed Indigenous leaders and took dozens of captives of all sexes and ages from every "rebel" village. The cacique Mamadagi was among those captured, according to Ramírez. Everywhere he and his men went, they panned for gold.

On what may have been the Iscuandé River, his southernmost target, Ramírez described a raid on stilt houses belonging to the Indigenous Pil. The raid yielded numerous captives plus useful information for the next campaign. Upriver on the Patía and neighboring waterways, he was told, lay great villages occupied by "Las Barbacoas." To boot, all the rivers in the region were reputedly "extremely rich in gold and abundant with foodstuffs and very healthy." Ramírez and his allies produced a map (see figure 5.1) that suggests a fairly clear if schematic understanding of the Pacific coastal lowlands between Buenaventura and Esmeraldas.

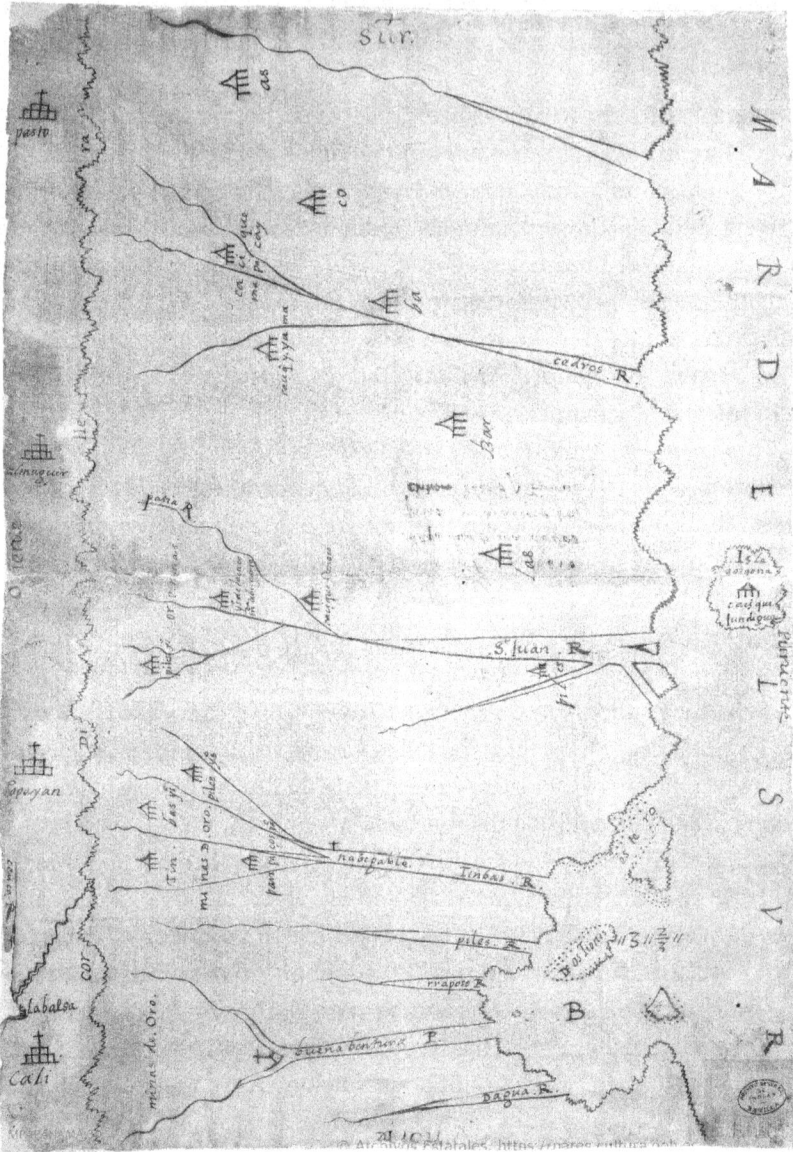

FIGURE 5.1 Pacific coastal lowlands between Buenaventura and Esmeraldas. *The Province of Las Barbacoas, c. 1610*, Courtesy of Archivo General de Indias, Mapas y Planos Panamá 30.

With captives and gold dust, Capt. Ramírez returned to Cali by way of the port of Buenaventura, which he found threatened by the belligerent Noanamáes. He makes no mention of the Indigenous paddlers and other allies who had made his own long-distance locomotion possible, but this is standard in Spanish colonial paramilitary narratives going back to the time of the conquistadors. The heroic captain, or caudillo, as prescribed by Vargas Machuca, was the man out front, the one making all the important decisions. It was only a minor embarrassment for Ramírez that the swift Noanamáes easily outpaddled his tired allies and disappeared in the Pacific surf. All told, this "Indian Militia" relied on Indigenous people, yet they were not named nor credited when an operation met with success. Ramírez's report to Popayán's governor also omitted mention of Indigenous rebels called Sindaguas, although his description of the enemy "Piles" came close (AGI Quito 16: 38).

Ramírez made clear, using the revised language of the day, that he had engaged not in conquest but in "just punishment" of rebellious subjects of the king of Spain. According to this narrative, everything was above board, and this was not an unprovoked slaving raid. Rather, justice had supposedly been served. Chief Mamadagi and his ilk had allegedly committed both common and heinous crimes, to be repaid with forced labor. The captive "Piles" and others were "delinquents," "highwaymen," and "idlers," now put to work on sugar plantations near Cali. Ramírez promised they would be indoctrinated in the Roman Catholic faith.

In subsequent years, a sequence of similar paramilitary entradas or reprisals set out from Quito and Ibarra, south of the old Inca border at Rumichaca, and also from Pasto and Popayán. None produced a narrative as thorough as Ramírez's, but the raids went out almost annually through the 1620s, repeatedly penetrating the Barbacoas lowlands from different angles. According to governors' reports and other letters, each self-organizing militia returned to the highlands with dozens or even hundreds of captives, and all their caudillos talked up untapped "rivers of gold." Have we any idea who the objects of these repeated aggressions were? Or how they thought of themselves? Not really, but a fragment of an origin myth was collected from "Barbacoan" inhabitants near the mouths of the Micay and Patía Rivers and recounted by Mercedarian friar Miguel Cabello Balboa, circa 1583:

They discuss and recount their origins very differently one [group] from another, but all conform in saying their primary ancestors came down from the highlands and mountain chains, which, in effect, is true. Those of the San Juan and Patía Rivers say their first parents emerged from an earthen jar, because the moon placed two eggs there and with the heat of the sun man was born of them; from a male and a female that came out of there went multiplying the rest, and they went down from the cold country to search for salt, and to save themselves the work of coming and going they remained on the coast, its perpetual residents; they say there will come a final day, that some great hills must fall, with them below; they have sanctuaries or secret shrines where they offer gold and bead wealth [*chaquira*] to the sun and moon, and to their dead grandparents, whom they believe walk among them wandering, aiding the good and punishing the bad. (Cabello Balboa [1583] 2001, 45–46, translation by Kris Lane)

Enter the Sindaguas

Amid this relentless guerrilla pincer movement, an Indigenous "nation" called by the Spanish Sindaguas burst onto the scene (or into the archival record). Were they a new people? An old one? A blend? It is hard to say, but the Mercedarian friar just quoted had mentioned in the same 1583 report a notorious cannibal group called Hondaguas (or Handaguas) said to inhabit some part of the Barbacoas interior (Cabello Balboa [1583] 2001, 41). Even so, only in the 1620s did Spanish officials identify the most belligerent of all Pacific lowlanders as Sindaguas (Lehmann 1949). Famed headhunters, the Sindaguas were something like the Pacific coast equivalent of the Shuar, and some commentators said as much, calling them "Jíbaros."

It was the Sindaguas, said Popayán governor Juan Bermúdez de Castro in 1629, that had been on the warpath for decades, responsible for a series of murderous attacks far from their isolated homeland (AGI Quito 16: 49). They marched up the Patía gorge in troops to raid villages, mines, ranches, and cane fields all along the river and its isolated Pasto-area tributaries. The Sindaguas were not alone. They, too, had allies or friends. Sindagua warriors from the uplands had been joined by coast dwellers in destroying early mining camps on or near the Telembí River, as well as in sacking the Spanish basecamp on that river at Santa María del Puerto (i.e., modern Barbacoas, Colombia) in 1620. This was a particularly memorable event for certain settler-colonists.

Worse still, the Sindaguas and their compatriots were now taking to the sea, attacking Spanish vessels along the Pacific coast. According to some angry Spaniards, the Barbacoas district's worst Indigenous rebels, like their Dutch contemporaries, had become ruthless corsairs. Also like the Dutch, who in 1624 (only five years earlier) had sacked Guayaquil and suddenly become a proximate maritime threat, the Sindaguas were recruiting allies. To stimulate struggling miners in New Granada to bring their enslaved workers to Barbacoas, King Philip IV had by decree reduced taxes on brute gold production (from 1/10 to 1/15; AGI Quito 16: 57). The pressure to conquer the Sindaguas and to extract gold was intense.

Governor Bermúdez's claims proved premature, but his successor, don Lorenzo de Villaquirán, kept up the "extractive" pressure. There was more evidence of potential profit in Barbacoas thanks to a Panama-based slave owner who had installed a small alluvial mining colony on the Telpí River near a newly founded Pacific port, Santa Bárbara de la Isla del Gallo (just north of Tumaco). In the meantime, an Italian and Swiss Jesuit pair, Francisco Rugi and Juan de Henebra, went with paramilitary escort from Quito to Santa María del Puerto to establish a mission, arriving in February 1632 (Barnuevo [1643] 1960). Rugi, who had recently failed in a similar endeavor among the Jívaro or Shuar east of Loja (1630–31), later reported from the port of Tumaco that he had baptized 1,900 Indigenous people (ANE Popayán caja 14, no. 36).

In 1634, the year after his appointment, Governor Villaquirán recruited the son of a Pasto-based encomendero whose father had been killed (allegedly by the Sindaguas) at Santa María del Puerto in the 1620 raid. Goaded on by his "very manly" mother, doña Brígida, Francisco de Prado y Zúñiga, aged twenty-six, organized a punitive sortie, or *castigo*, made up of fifty-four "Spaniards" (*españoles*) and 220 "friendly Indians." Prado's Indigenous allies were most likely archers, whereas the troop's "Spaniards" carried harquebuses, muskets, and lances. The latter also wore quilted cotton armor to protect against poisoned darts. The far more numerous Indigenous "friends," most of them no doubt barefoot and without armor of any kind, hauled supplies plus a portable prison, wooden stocks, and two dozen iron collars strung together in two chains of twelve (AGI Quito 16: 63; Ponce Leiva 1991–92). The principal objective of this sortie, like so many before it, was clear.

The Prado y Zúniga expedition left Pasto in September 1634, and by December their leader reported early victories from "the headwaters of the Iscuandé River, Province of this Sindagua." Prado had split his forces into two groups, each with twenty-four highland creole soldiers and one hundred Indigenous allies. Paddling or marching up and down different waterways, these units captured or killed several alleged Sindagua headmen and freed captives said to have been taken during raids on the highland village of Sacampús, below Pasto on the Guáitara River (AGI Quito 16: 63). Most of the captives were Quechua speakers, or they understood Quechua when questioned by interpreters.

Also found during the expedition, according to Prado y Zúniga, were the smoked heads of three captives, who were victims of the highland raids. More prosaically, the soldiers discovered a cache of textiles, horseshoes, shawl pins, and the apparent remains of a religious statue looted from Pasto-area settlements.

Another raid on a Sindagua village in October 1634 led to the killing of a leader (the Spanish use the term cacique, although we do not know if such men accepted or used this title) and several "warrior" (*guerrero*) allies, plus capture of the headman's several wives and many children. In his narrative, Prado was careful to emphasize the "manly" valor of his opponents even as he denounced their heinous or atrocious crimes, polygyny, and supposed sins against nature. It was necessary, as Cali's Capt. Ramírez had shown, to play up spirited resistance in order to claim proper credit as a neoconquistador, a worthy encomendero. To attribute guilt, Prado also inventoried more items said to have been stolen from the ranches and sugarcane fields below Pasto, and he ordered the three severed heads buried with Christian solemnity.

Early success against the Sindaguas was temporarily halted by an Indigenous informant-turned-spy's alleged betrayal, which led to a dramatic ambush, described by Prado y Zúniga as follows:

> On the ninth of the said month [of October 1634], upon going out to reconnoiter the land in search of the enemy the said field marshal [Prado y Zúniga] with a great force of soldiers and friends [i.e., Indigenous allies], having left the camp with all the captives well provisioned, some three

leagues up on the banks of the Patía River the enemy ambushed us from a great, steep hill in the shape of a harpoon where they had built a great platform of stones and cut a great deal of forest so as to fire down upon our camp, and from there they shot a great quantity of darts upon the outer ramparts, where the said field marshal and certain soldiers demonstrated well their valor, retiring only after their cotton armor was filled with darts, which hung from them. One soldier came out with a wound through the thigh and one Indian friend had one in the arm, but neither [injury] was life-threatening. Thus were we forced to return again to basecamp. (AGI Quito 16: 63)

The invaders survived the ambush, but Prado claimed the Sindaguas had shouted "that before becoming friends of the Spaniards they would eat their wives and children" (AGI Quito 16: 63). He also said that the Sindaguas had repeatedly "made a joke of the Spaniards" in their easy command of the swift and treacherous Patía River. He ordered Indigenous allies to fashion a new fleet of canoes, no easy task in the best of circumstances.

Forced to walk, the soldiers found rainforest trails booby trapped or blocked by felled trees. The captain's party nevertheless managed to apprehend and kill another cacique (or headman) and several "warriors" in subsequent days, seizing forty captives. The vanguard then narrowly escaped another Sindagua ambush, in which warriors again descended on them, firing from cliffs. Farther upriver, according to Prado y Zúniga's reckoning, his men attacked and killed yet another Sindagua headman and several accompanying warriors. They also collected more captives, including "baptized" Indigenous persons who had been abducted near Pasto.

As the militia advanced farther upriver, Prado and his men crossed a kind of border. They found themselves facing off against Indigenous headmen and their followers, who claimed to have only recently become "very much related with the Sindaguas by marriage." This was evidence that the Sindaguas were expanding their kinship networks by exogamous marriage rather than only by raiding and taking captives from distant sites. At least, that is one way to read the testimony (à la Vilaça 2002). Combined with claims of Sindagua piracy, allies were apparently being recruited on all sides, upriver and down.

But for Prado y Zúñiga, the end of Sindagua history was near. By March 1635, he reported to Popayán's governor that he and his men had captured all but one Sindagua "cacique" and his small group of followers. Once this headman, called Piacha, was apprehended, there would remain in the Province of Barbacoas "no root of such an evil people as these have been" (AGI Quito 16: 63). Thanks to the efforts of Prado and his Indigenous friends, the "evil" Sindaguas would be annihilated. In the meantime, one wonders what scores Prado's allies were settling of their own accord, what information they were gathering, and what futures they imagined for themselves once the vengeful settlers' *castigo* was over. Whether or not they knew it, the future of Barbacoas would center on gold extraction and an influx of Africans (Lane 2000).

Exit the Sindaguas

Field Marshal Prado y Zúñiga's exuberant report to his superiors suggests that he believed he was engaged in a righteous police action that was also a sort of ethnic cleansing, an imperial excision. In this view, there was a rebellious tribe or nation called Sindaguas whose evil deeds, including (Prado claimed) headhunting and cannibalism, were inexcusable, and they had to be punished with a blend of summary execution and exile. Thus far, he seemed to have the law on his side. He was aware of orders not to commit "excesses."

But what happened on August 14, 1635, at the site Prado grandly dubbed Santiago del Sindagua, his upper Iscuandé River basecamp, was more than what *derecho indiano*, or "the law of the Indies," typically permitted. Perhaps bearing in mind the killing and mutilation of his own father in 1620 not far away at Santa María del Puerto, Prado y Zuñiga ordered a Catholic priest to baptize no fewer than eighty-four captive Sindagua warriors. Once christened, the men were lined up against posts and garroted in turn by eight "friendly Indians" made to serve as executioners.

Mutilation followed mass murder. Prado ordered the bodies of the sixteen Sindagua headmen deemed most culpable for past atrocities decapitated and quartered. Their body parts were displayed at various "crime sites," and their heads were taken to Santa María del Puerto's pier on the Telembí River, where they were displayed on tall pikes.

It was quite a show of private vengeance or royal justice, but how might these eighty-four throttlings and sixteen Sindagua heads (and all the posted body parts) have been interpreted? Were the headmen's heads still recognizable as individuals as they rotted in the humid heat? Or had they been smoked or otherwise conserved by the Indigenous "friends" who had been ordered to cut them off? Was this a strictly "Spanish" *castigo*? We do not know. The young militia captain must have assumed his intended lesson was clear (fear me, fear your distant king whose will I represent under his banner, fear my God), but for a people known for taking and smoking the heads of select captives (not all of them), and for having long experience with neighboring and invading settler-colonists (and occasional priests), we cannot know what they felt or understood when faced with this gory spectacle.

Presumably the lesson in terror was not intended for Sindagua warriors at all, as it seems that most of those captured had been slain. Survivors, the record suggests, were mostly women and children. What was to become of them? A plan to exile remaining Sindaguas to the highlands was ultimately scrapped in favor of keeping captives in or near the Spanish mining camp of Santa María del Puerto on the Telembí, where they provided household services for budding gold mine-owning elites like Prado y Zuñiga and his family. Individuals labeled Sindaguas subsequently fade from the documentary record of Barbacoas, appearing here and there into the early eighteenth century.

Indigenous Perspectives

The discussion presented so far has focused on the testimony of the Sindaguas' self-styled conqueror, who was a young Spanish creole, but his extravagant mass execution required that he follow legal conventions, including taking eyewitness testimony from alleged victims and captives. In these brief testimonies, many of them given by Indigenous allies or tributary subjects held captive among the Sindaguas for several years, we gain a rare glimpse into another world.

Captive deponents such as Beatriz Tanguana, who was a Quechua-speaking highlander captured on a sugar plantation below Pasto, and Felipe Pil, who had formerly been held by the Spanish in a gold-mining camp before being freed by the Sindaguas, hint at something more than alleged crime sprees and supposed "sins against nature" (AGI Quito 16: 67). The witnesses seem to suggest that their captors (or in Pil's case, liberators, as he is labeled a "Sindagua") were a composite group made up of scattered riparian clans, culturally similar neighbors, coastal fishing folk, and highland refugees. All of these people were fervently motivated to expand their domain at the gold-hungry colonizer-invader's expense.

The captives were betwixt and between, and some, like Beatriz Tanguana, claimed that they had been treated like slaves. In considering these accounts, we should keep in mind that they were asked leading questions and were under duress when interrogated. Further, Tanguana and other highlanders testified that their Sindagua captors used their less fortunate relatives' severed heads "for their witchcraft," and that they ate some portion of their butchered flesh immediately after their raids. For Prado y Zuñiga and his superiors, the testimonies verified what was already suspected: the Sindaguas were not only thieves and kidnappers but also cannibals and supposedly "sinners against nature." Who knew what sort of diabolical pacts they made using the human heads?

For us, these witness testimonies raise largely unanswerable questions. Why behead and eat the hapless Indigenous subjects of highland Spanish elites? And why keep others (women mostly) captive? And junior males like Felipe Pil? Why free him if only to belittle him (as seems to have occurred in Pil's case)? Were these various acts forms of predation (or "human hunting") carried out with the aim of "familiarization" and incorporation after a period of hazing, as seen in some Amazonian societies (Costa 2017; Fausto 2012)? As such, perhaps these acts were a means of creating new kin by "care" and "feeding," accompanied by subjection and humiliation. Was this a desperate form of "openness to the Other" in a time of crisis (Lévi-Strauss 1995; Viveiros de Castro 1992)? With this in mind, smoked heads and the treatment of select captives may have constituted material evidence of spiritual alliances with fellow victims of Spanish predation.

Testimonies collected and penned by Prado y Zuñiga and others are hardly troves of incidental ethnography, but they do seem to highlight

Sindagua political atomization, as well as provide evidence for the creation of new allies through marriage. As in the earlier Ramírez testimony
from 1610, which labeled dozens of headmen, or "caciques," among the
Piles and their neighbors, the Sindaguas of early 1630s Barbacoas seem to
have recognized no paramount chief. Instead, they allowed scores of men
of many ages (and at times, varying ethnic monikers) to oversee their
own communities and to lead their own war parties. It is hard to identify
anyone in charge of a larger project or grand strategy in these name-rich
testimonies. Perhaps we are just missing such information in the records
because the invaders missed it and never wrote it down.

A long time ago, historian Peter Marzahl (1970) surmised that the
Sindaguas (as rendered in these and other early seventeenth-century
testimonies) looked more like an ad hoc conglomeration of frontier out-
casts, isolates, and captives than a primordial or ancient "tribe" or even
federation. There was something new about them, it seemed, as if they
were improvising in the face of repeated attacks. In reading surviving
testimonies, I have tended to agree, influenced by work on "neo-tribes,"
or "new peoples" (Salomon and Schwartz 1999).

Heads and Hunters, Friends and Enemies

In a 2016 book, Colombian geographer Marta Herrera Ángel approached
the Sindaguas from a different angle. Herrera used most of the same
archival sources cited above and more to argue for "Barbacoan" cultural
survival. In my view, the so-called Sindaguas' future was dim after their
dramatic mid-1630s "punishment," even if a small number of refugees
with the Sindagua surname carried on under Spanish rule. Where I see
a dead end, however, Herrera sees ample evidence of survival, adaptation, and even a clear through line to the modern Awá Kwaiker or Awa
Pit of the Colombia-Ecuador border region (Herrera Ángel 2016; Cerón
Solarte 1986). *El conquistador conquistado*, as Herrera's title implies, is a
chronicle of resilience. Mine is a tale of defeat—effectively the erasure of
a new, effervescent, and improvisational Indigenous society.

In Herrera's telling, the so-called Sindaguas were not conquered by
"the Spanish," which was an unhelpful term by the 1630s, as she notes,
despite the self-ascription *español*. And they were not (simply) replaced

by enslaved Africans and their descendants, who are the region's majority population today. Many Awá speakers and adjacent Indigenous groups suffered greatly, Herrera admits, as most were forced to serve colonial intruders. In the end, however, the peoples of the lowlands conquered the conquistadors and in effect absorbed them. African-descended miners and their families were likewise transformed, learning almost everything about survival in the Pacific-edge forest from Indigenous peoples.

Thus, as an uncanny case of mutual misunderstanding, the back-and-forth taking of heads from the early seventeenth-century neoconquest era fits a pattern of what Herrera (2016, 19) labels "cultural exchange, mestizaje, and hybridization." The late Neil Whitehead (2002) might have seen "the poetics of violence" at work here in the "tribal zone" (Ferguson and Whitehead 1992), but how such poetics was understood on the side of those silenced by the record, arguably the losing side, remains obscure.

What tugs at me most, as it did when I started this project more than thirty years ago in the archives of Quito and Popayán, as well as in several visits to the ravaged Barbacoas gold fields beginning in 1995, is the broader global context of extractive frontiers, of relentlessly "mining the margins" and what we might learn from colonial and neocolonial extraction's various historical iterations (Lane 1996). I acknowledge the central importance of diverse Indigenous agendas and thus unexpected and uneasy alliances, both temporary and long term, as well as strategies for what we might call cultural survival. What the Sindaguas show us, if nothing else, is an example of a group's refusal to capitulate despite repeated attacks and intense diplomatic (and possibly priestly) pressure.

Yet, as in the history of the primary conquest era, which refers to the first wave of armed incursions that toppled the Aztec-Mexica, Inca, Muisca, and other polities, it seems that the Spanish again extracted considerable amounts of gold at everybody else's expense (TePaske 2010). I have a hard time keeping my eyes on co-conquistadors, even if some Indigenous allies fashioned themselves as such in their petitions to the viceroys and kings of Spain across several centuries of colonial rule. I am more intrigued by what aims, what spiritual engines, what relations, and what hybrid cosmologies drove Indigenous rebels like the Sindaguas (see Harris 2010; Sweet 1992). For example, did they still see themselves as descendants of highland salt seekers who would one day return to the mountains?

The documentary record compiled and left behind by Spanish and Spanish-descended colonists suggests that a cultural community of some kind emerged in the lowland forests of what is today southwest Colombia only to be sacrificed en masse for gold. A remnant group of women and children appears to have survived and may have carried on or reconstituted some version of Sindagua identity, art, and history. If some portion of that shared memory persisted among the Awá Kwaiker, it remained their secret (Curnow and Liddicoat 1998; Obando Ordóñez 1992; Ehrenreich 1985). Perhaps that is as it should be.

What the people we know from the historical record as Sindaguas thought they were doing, or what they were capable of, or what roles they played in changing or steering their shared destiny, I do not know. But for a time, they (like the allied Shuar on the other side of the Andes) were on a mission. And like the Shuar, they made a name for themselves as fearsome headhunters and long-distance raiders par excellence. They gave resistance to the mineral-hungry colonial project a try, and with no apparent need of a charismatic leader like the later Juan Santos Atahualpa (Jones 2018) or Túpac Amaru (Walker 2014).

In the true and fabled story of the Sindaguas, I see much more than a historiographical tug-of-war about cultural survival versus extinction or about co-conquest versus military defeat. We may flip the script to suit our preferences, but too often the outcomes of such conflicts look familiar. In the case of gold mining in "Indian country," they look almost everywhere the same, although different in detail. One may be reminded of the Black Hills gold of South Dakota, which spawned the Battle of Little Bighorn and the crushing reprisals that followed, as well as the Ghost Dance. As in so much of Amazonia, for every head taken by one side, a hundred more were taken by the other—until the mines and waterways and mountain paths were secured so that "yellow metal" might flow unchecked into the wider world.

In this blood-soaked early stage of "resource frontier" expansion into the Pacific lowlands of northwest South America, highland and lowland Indigenous allies played vital roles. Some groups and individuals evidently had scores of their own to settle with the Sindaguas, and some must have found new opportunities to gain status or wealth in the emerging slave-based extractive regime that characterized the region for the next two centuries. One could call theirs a story of co-conquest, albeit one with a likely foreshortened future. Other veterans of these wars may have retreated into the forest, perhaps creating new agglomerations, as is so often seen in Amazonia. I am inclined to say that ghost histories befit certain patches of equatorial South America, as suggested by the Yanomami intellectual Davi Kopenawa (2013). In this telling, gold lust is a curse that thrusts diverse peoples into a maelstrom, yielding up stories that read more like parables than chronicles of heroism, shared glory, or resilience.

Note

1. Scholars such as Pekka Hämäläinen (2008, 2019, 2022) have gone a step fur-
    ther in treating expansionist groups like the Comanche and Lakota as nomadic
    empires.

References

Archival Sources

AGI (Archivo General de Indias), Seville, Spain, legajos Quito 16, 22, 23, 25
ANE (Archivo Nacional del Ecuador), Quito, sections Popayán and Real Hacienda

Published Sources

Adorno, Rolena. 1986. *Guaman Poma: Writing and Resistance in Colonial Peru*. Aus-
    tin: University of Texas Press.
Alchon, Suzanne A. 2003. *A Pest in the Land: New World Epidemics in a Global
    Perspective*. Albuquerque: University of New Mexico Press.
Asselbergs, Florine. 2004. *Conquered Conquistadors: The Lienzo de Quauhquechol-
    lan: A Nahua Vision of the Conquest of Guatemala*. Niwot: University Press of
    Colorado.
Barnuevo, Rodrigo. (1643) 1960. "Relación apologética del antiguo como del nuevo
    descubrimiento del río Amazonas según los misioneros de la Compañía de Jesús."
    In *Historiadores y cronistas de las misiones*, edited by Julio Tobar Donoso, 313–19.
    Quito: Biblioteca Ecuatoriana Minima.
Beatty Medina, Charles. 2006. "Caught between Rivals: The Spanish-African Maroon
    Competition for Captive Indian Labor in the Region of Esmeraldas during the
    Late Sixteenth and Early Seventeenth Centuries." *Americas* 63 (1): 112–36.
Beatty Medina, Charles. 2012. "Between the Cross and the Sword: Religious Conquest
    and Maroon Legitimacy in Colonial Esmeraldas." In *Africans to Spanish America:
    Expanding the Diaspora*, edited by Sherwin K. Bryant, Rachel S. O'Toole, and Ben
    Vinson III, 95–113. Urbana: University of Illinois Press.

Berger, Eugene. 2023. *This Incurable Evil: Mapuche Resistance to Spanish Enslavement, 1598–1687*. Tuscaloosa: University of Alabama Press.

Brian, Amber, Bradley Benton, and Pablo García Loaeza, eds. 2015. *The Native Conquistador: Alva Ixtlilxochitl's Account of the Conquest of New Spain*. University Park, Pa.: Penn State University Press.

Bryant, Sherwin K. 2014. *Rivers of Gold, Lives of Bondage: Governing through Slavery in Colonial Quito*. Chapel Hill: University of North Carolina Press.

Cabello Balboa, Miguel. (1583) 2001. *Descripción de la Provincia de las Esmeraldas*. Edited by José Alcina Franch. Madrid: CSIC.

Caillavet, Chantal, and Ximena Pachón, eds. 1996. *Frontera y poblamiento: Estudios de historia y antropología de Colombia y Ecuador*. Bogotá: IFEA/SINCHI/Universidad de los Andes.

Calero, Luis F. 1997. *Chiefdoms Under Siege: Spain's Rule and Native Adaptation in the Southern Colombian Andes, 1535–1700*. Albuquerque: University of New Mexico Press.

Castellanos, Juan de. 1589. *Elegías de varones ilustres de Indias*. Madrid: Viuda de Alfonso Gómez.

Cerón Solarte, Benhur. 1986. *Los awa-kwaiker: Un grupo indígena de la selva pluvial del Pacífico Nariñense y el Nor-Occidente Ecuatoriano*. Quito: Abya-Yala.

Chaudhuri, K. N. 1978. *The Trading World of Asia and the East India Company, 1660–1760*. Cambridge: Cambridge University Press.

Corbeil, Laurent. 2018. *The Motions Beneath: Indigenous Migrants on the Urban Frontier of New Spain*. Tucson: University of Arizona Press.

Costa, Luiz. 2017. *The Owners of Kinship: Asymmetrical Relationships in Indigenous Amazonia*. Chicago: HAU Books.

Covey, R. Alan. 2020. *Inca Apocalypse: The Spanish Conquest and the Transformation of the Andean World*. New York: Oxford University Press.

Curnow, Timothy Jowan, and Anthony J. Liddicoat. 1998. "The Barbacoan Languages of Colombia and Ecuador." *Anthropological Linguistics* 40 (3): 384–408.

Deardorff, Max. 2023. *A Tale of Two Granadas: Custom, Community, and Citizenship in the Spanish Empire, 1568–1668*. New York: Cambridge University Press.

DeBoer, Warren R. 1996. *Traces behind the Esmeraldas Shore: Prehistory of the Santiago-Cayapas Region, Ecuador*. Tuscaloosa: University of Alabama Press.

Deeds, Susan M. 2003. *Defiance and Deference in Mexico's Colonial North: Indians under Spanish Rule in Nueva Vizcaya*. Austin: University of Texas Press.

de la Puente Luna, José Carlos. 2018. *Andean Cosmopolitans: Seeking Justice and Reward at the Spanish Royal Court*. Austin: University of Texas Press.

Descola, Philippe. 1994. *In the Society of Nature: A Native Ecology in Amazonia*. New York: Cambridge University Press.

Descola, Philippe. 1996. *The Spears of Twilight: Life and Death in the Amazon Jungle*. Translated by Janet Lloyd. New York: New Press.

Diamond, Jared. 1997. *Guns, Germs, and Steel: The Fates of Human Societies*. New York: Norton.

Ehrenreich, Jeffrey, ed. 1985. *Political Anthropology of Ecuador: Perspectives from Indigenous Cultures*. Albany: Society for Latin American Anthropology/SUNY.

Erbig, Jeffrey Alan, Jr. 2020. *Where Caciques and Mapmakers Met: Border Making in Eighteenth-Century South America*. Chapel Hill: University of North Carolina Press.

Fausto, Carlos. 2012. *Warfare and Shamanism in Amazonia*. Translated by David Rodgers. New York: Cambridge University Press.

Ferguson, R. Brian, and Neil L. Whitehead, eds. 1992. *War in the Tribal Zone: Expanding States and Indigenous Warfare*. Santa Fe, N.Mex.: School of American Research.

Francis, J. Michael. 2007. *Invading Colombia: Spanish Accounts of the Gonzalo Jiménez de Quesada Expedition of Conquest*. University Park, Pa.: Penn State University Press.

Gamboa Mendoza, Jorge Augusto. 2010. *El cacicazgo muisca en los años posteriores a la Conquista: Del sihipkua al cacique colonial, 1537–1575*. Bogotá: ICANH.

Garrett, David T. 2005. *Shadows of Empire: The Indian Nobility of Cusco, 1750–1825*. New York: Cambridge University Press.

Gudynas, Eduardo. 2015. *Extractivismos: Ecología, economía y política de un modo de entender el desarrollo y la Naturaleza*. Cochabamba: CEDIB.

Guengerich, Sara V., and Margarita R. Ochoa. 2021. *Cacicas: The Indigenous Women Leaders of Spanish America, 1492–1825*. Norman: University of Oklahoma Press.

Hämäläinen, Pekka. 2022. *Indigenous Continent: The Epic Contest for North America*. New York: Norton.

Hämäläinen, Pekka. 2019. *Lakota America. A New History of Indigenous Power*. New Haven, Conn.: Yale University Press.

Hämäläinen, Pekka. 2008. *Comanche Empire*. New Haven, CT: Yale University Press.

Harner, Michael. 1972. *The Jívaro: People of the Sacred Waterfalls*. New York: Natural History Press.

Harris, Mark. 2010. *Rebellion on the Amazon: The Cabanagem, Race, and Popular Culture in the North of Brazil, 1798–1840*. Cambridge: Cambridge University Press.

Herrera Ángel, Marta. 2016. *El conquistador conquistado: Awás, Cuayquer y Sindagua en el Pacífico colombiano, Siglos XVI–XVIII*. Bogotá: Universidad de los Andes.

Jones, Cameron D. 2018. *In Service of Two Masters: The Missionaries of Ocopa, Indigenous Resistance, and Spanish Governance in Bourbon Peru*. Stanford, Calif.: Stanford University Press.

Karasch, Mary C. 2016. *Before Brasília: Frontier Life in Central Brazil*. Albuquerque: University of New Mexico Press.

Karsten, Rafael. 1935. *The Head-Hunters of Western Amazonas: The Life and Culture of the Jibaro Indians of Eastern Ecuador and Peru*. Helsinki: Societas Scientiarum Fennica.

Kopenawa, Davi. 2013. *The Falling Sky: Words of a Yanomami Shaman*. Edited by Bruce Albert, translated by Nicholas Elliott and Alison Dundy. Cambridge, Mass.: Belknap/Harvard University Press.

Lane, Kris. 1996. "Mining the Margins: Precious Metals Extraction and Forced Labor Regimes in the Audiencia of Quito, 1534–1821." PhD diss., University of Minnesota.

Lane, Kris. 2000. "The Transition from *Encomienda* to Slavery in Seventeenth-Century Barbacoas (Colombia)." *Slavery and Abolition* 21 (1): 73–95.

Lane, Kris. 2002. *Quito 1599: City and Colony in Transition.* Albuquerque: University of New Mexico Press.

Langfur, Hal. 2006. *The Forbidden Lands: Colonial Identity, Frontier Violence, and the Persistence of Brazil's Eastern Indians, 1750–1830.* Stanford, Calif.: Stanford University Press.

Langfur, Hal, ed. 2014. *Native Brazil: Beyond the Convert and the Cannibal.* Albuquerque: University of New Mexico Press.

Langfur, Hal. 2023. *Adrift on an Inland Sea: Misinformation and the Limits of Empire in the Brazilian Backlands.* Stanford, Calif.: Stanford University Press.

Leal, Claudia. 2018. *Landscapes of Freedom: Building a Postemancipation Society in the Rainforests of Western Colombia.* Tucson: University of Arizona Press.

Lehmann, Henri. 1949. "Les Indiens Sindagua (Colombie)." *Journal de la Société des Américanistes* 38:67–89.

Lévi-Strauss, Claude. 1995. *The Story of Lynx.* Translated Catherine Tihanyi. Chicago: University of Chicago Press.

Levin Rojo, Danna A., and Cynthia Radding, eds. 2019. *The Oxford Handbook of Borderlands of the Iberian World.* New York: Oxford University Press.

Lovell, W. George. 2022. *Death in the Snow: Pedro de Alvarado and the Illusive Conquest of Peru.* Montréal: McGill-Queen's University Press.

Marzahl, Peter. 1970. "The Cabildo of Popayán in the Seventeenth Century: The Emergence of a Creole Elite." PhD diss., University of Wisconsin, Madison.

Matthew, Laura E. 2012. *Memories of Conquest: Becoming Mexicano in Colonial Guatemala.* Chapel Hill: University of North Carolina Press.

Matthew, Laura E., and Michel R. Oudijk, eds. 2007. *Indian Conquistadors: Indigenous Allies in the Conquest of Mesoamerica.* Norman: University of Oklahoma Press.

McEnroe, Sean F. 2012. *From Colony to Nationhood in Mexico: Laying the Foundations, 1560–1840.* New York: Cambridge University Press.

McEnroe, Sean F. 2020. *A Troubled Marriage: Indigenous Elites of the Colonial Americas.* Albuquerque: University of New Mexico Press.

Mikecz, Jeremy M. 2020. "Beyond Cajamarca: A Spatial Narrative Reimagining of the Encounter in Peru, 1532–1533." *Hispanic American Historical Review* 100 (2): 195–232.

Mikecz, Jeremy M. 2025. *Mapping Conquest: A Spatial History of the Spanish Invasion of Indigenous Peru (ca. 1528–1537).* New York: Cambridge University Press.

Monteiro, John M. 2018. *Blacks of the Land: Indian Slavery, Settler Society, and the Portuguese Colonial Enterprise in South America.* Edited and translated by James Woodard and Barbara Weinstein. New York: Cambridge University Press.

Montoya, Juan Davíd. 2014. "'Las más remotas tierras del mundo': Historia de la frontera del Pacífico, 1573–1687." PhD diss., Universidad Pablo Olavide.

Muñoz, Santiago. 2025. *The New Kingdom of Granada: The Making and Unmaking of Spain's Atlantic Empire*. Durham, N.C.: Duke University Press.

Murillo, Dana Velasco. 2016. *Urban Indians in a Silver City: Zacatecas, Mexico, 1546–1810*. Stanford, Calif.: Stanford University Press.

Murillo, Dana Velasco. 2021. "'To Search and Claim': Indigenous Prospectors, Silver Mining, and Legal Practices in Spanish America, 1530–1600." *Colonial Latin American Review* 30 (4): 498–519.

Newson, Linda A. 1996. "Between Orellana and Acuña: A Lost Century in the History of the North-West Amazon." *Bulletin de l'Institut Français d'Études Andines* 25 (2): 203–31.

Obando Ordóñez, Pablo. 1992. "Awa-Kwaiker: An Outline Grammar of a Colombian/Ecuadorian Language, with a Cultural Sketch." PhD diss., University of Texas at Austin.

Platt, Tristan, and Pablo Quisbert. 2007. "Knowing Silence and Merging Horizons: The Case of the Great Potosí Cover-Up." In *Ways of Knowing: Anthropological Approaches to Crafting Experience and Knowledge*, edited by Mark Harris, 113–38. New York: Bergahn.

Ponce Leiva, Pilar, ed. 1991–92. *Relaciones histórico-geográficas de la Audiencia de Quito*. 2 vols. Madrid: CSIC.

Powers, Karen Vieira. 1995. *Andean Journeys: Migration, Ethnogenesis, and the State in Colonial Quito*. Albuquerque: University of New Mexico Press.

Powers, Karen Vieira. 2005. *Women in the Crucible of Conquest: The Gendered Genesis of Spanish-American Society, 1500–1600*. Albuquerque: University of New Mexico Press.

Rappaport, Joanne. 2014. *The Disappearing Mestizo: Configuring Difference in the Colonial New Kingdom of Granada*. Durham, N.C.: Duke University Press.

Renard-Casevitz, France-Marie, Thierry Saignes, and Anne-Christine Taylor. 1988. *Al este de los Andes*. 2 vols. Lima: IFEA.

Reséndez, Andrés. 2016. *The Other Slavery: The Uncovered Story of Indian Enslavement in America*. New York: Houghton Mifflin.

Restall, Matthew. 1999. *Maya Conquistador*. Boston: Beacon.

Restall, Matthew. 2012. "The New Conquest History." *History Compass* 10 (2): 151–60.

Restall, Matthew. 2018. *When Montezuma Met Cortés: The True History of the Meeting that Changed History*. New York: Ecco.

Restall, Matthew. 2021. *Seven Myths of the Spanish Conquest*. 2nd ed. New York: Oxford University Press.

Roller, Heather F. 2021. *Contact Strategies: Histories of Native Autonomy in Brazil*. Stanford, Calif.: Stanford University Press.

Romero Vergara, Mario Diego. 2018. *Poblamiento y sociedad en el Pacífico colombiano, siglos XVI al XVIII*. 2nd ed. Cali, Colombia: Universidad del Valle.

Rueda Novoa, Rocío. 2001. *Zambaje y autonomía: Historia de la gente Negra de la Provincia de Esmeraldas, siglos XVI-XVIII.* Quito: Abya-Yala.

Rumazo González, José, ed. 1948–49. *Documentos para la historia de la Audiencia de Quito.* 8 vols. Madrid: Afrodisio Aguado.

Salomon, Frank, and Stuart B. Schwartz, eds. 1999. *The Cambridge History of the Native Peoples of the Americas*, vol. 3, *South America.* New York: Cambridge University Press.

Schwartz, Stuart B. 2015. "Denounced by Lévi-Strauss." *Americas* 59 (1): 1–8.

Schwartz, Stuart B., and Frank Salomon. 1999. "New Peoples and New Kinds of People: Adaptation, Readjustment, and Ethnogenesis in South American Indigenous Societies (Colonial Era)." In *The Cambridge History of the Native Peoples of the Americas*, vol. 3, part 2, *South America*, edited by Frank Salomon and Stuart B. Schwartz, 443–501. New York: Cambridge University Press.

Simón, Pedro. 1627. *Primera parte de las noticias historiales de las conquistas de Tierra Firme en las Indias Occidentales.* Cuenca, Spain: D. de la Yglesia.

Studnicki-Gizbert, Daviken. 2022. *The Three Deaths of Cerro de San Pedro: Four Centuries of Extractivism in a Small Mexican Mining Town.* Chapel Hill: University of North Carolina Press.

Sweet, David. 1992. "Native Resistance in Eighteenth-Century Amazonia: The 'Abominable Muras' in War and Peace." *Radical History Review* 1992 (53): 49–80.

Taylor, Anne-Christine. 1994. "Les bons ennemis et les mauvais parents: Le traitement symbolique de l'alliance dans les rituels de chasse aux têtes des Jivaros de l'Equateur." In *Les complexités de l'alliance*, vol. 4, edited by E. Copet-Rougier and F. Héritier-Augé, 73–105. Paris: Archives Contemporaines.

Taylor, Anne-Christine, and Cristóbal Landázuri, eds. 1994. *Conquista de la región Jívaro, 1550–1650.* Quito: MARKA/IFEA.

TePaske, John J. 2010. *A New World of Gold and Silver.* Edited by Kendall Brown. Leiden: Brill.

Townsend, Camilla. 2006. *Malintzin's Choices: An Indian Woman in the Conquest of Mexico.* Albuquerque: University of New Mexico Press.

Townsend, Camilla. 2019. *Fifth Sun: A New History of the Aztecs.* New York: Oxford University Press.

Van Valen, Gary. 2013. *Indigenous Agency in the Amazon: The Mojos in Liberal and Rubber-Boom Bolivia, 1842–1932.* Tucson: University of Arizona Press.

Vargas Machuca, Bernardo de. (1599) 2008. *The Indian Militia and Description of the Indies.* Edited by Kris Lane, translated by Timothy F. Johnson. Durham, N.C.: Duke University Press.

Vilaça, Aparecida. 2002. "Making Kin out of Others." *Journal of the Royal Anthropological Institute* 8 (2): 347–65.

Viveiros de Castro, Eduardo. 1992. *From the Enemy's Point of View: Humanity and Divinity in an Amazonian Society.* Translated by Catherine V. Howard. Chicago: University of Chicago Press.

Walker, Charles F. 2014. *The Tupac Amaru Rebellion*. Cambridge, Mass.: Belknap.

Webster, Susan V. 2017. *Lettered Artists and the Languages of Empire: Painters and the Profession in Early Colonial Quito*. Austin: University of Texas Press.

West, Robert C. 1952. *Colonial Placer Mining in Colombia*. Baton Rouge: Louisiana State University Press.

Whitaker, James Andrew. 2020. "Strategic Alliance and the Plantationocene among the Makushi in Guyana." *Social Anthropology* 28 (4): 881–96.

Whitaker, James Andrew. 2025. *The Shamanism of Eco-Tourism: History and Ontology among the Makushi in Guyana*. Cambridge: Cambridge University Press.

Whitehead, Neil L. 2002. *Dark Shamans: Kanaimà and the Poetics of Violent Death*. Durham, N.C.: Duke University Press.

Whitehead, Neil L. 1990. "The Mazaruni Pectoral: A Golden Artefact Discovered in Guyana and the Historical Sources Concerning Native Metallurgy in the Caribbean, Orinoco and Northern Amazonia." *Archaeology and Anthropology* 7:19–38.

Williams, Caroline. 2005. *Between Resistance and Adaptation: Indigenous Peoples and the Colonisation of the Chocó, 1510–1753*. Liverpool: Liverpool University Press.

CHAPTER 6

Makushi Alliances in Guyana

Partnerships Against Predation

JAMES ANDREW WHITAKER

This chapter examines historically documented relations formed by Makushi groups in Guyana (formerly British Guiana) with European colonists and various Indigenous peoples (particularly "Carib" groups) in the context of slaving conducted against them during the nineteenth century. The Makushi are an Indigenous people in Brazil, Guyana, and Venezuela. Interactions between Makushi groups and Europeans have been documented since at least the 1740s. The chapter highlights Makushi initiative and intentionality in their relations with outsiders and builds on an emerging historiographical turn in the ethnohistory of lowland South America that emphasizes Indigenous agency in historical contexts (see Roller 2021; Van Valen 2013; and Whitaker 2025). Focused on ethnohistory and historical anthropology but also informed by my ethnographic fieldwork with Makushi groups in Guyana since 2012, this chapter shows how Makushi people took active roles in pursuing their interests during the colonial era in their relations with European and Indigenous others in both symmetric and asymmetric relational contexts.

Although the devastating results of European colonization in lowland South America are very clear (see Hemming 1978, 1987; and Taussig 1987), images of diminished agency have too often been cast on Indigenous Amazonians in the past in regional historiography. The resulting depiction has frequently been one of almost inevitable demise. Indigenous people, however, often took active and intentional roles in efforts not only to counter the European colonial front but also to co-opt, appropriate, and control relationships with colonial forces and vectors.[1] They additionally deployed diverse strategies for engaging with Indigenous neighbors, who were often managing their own relations with Europeans. This chapter presents two contrasting historical cases of such engagements involving Makushi groups in the context of slaving raids.

In recent years, a renewed historiographical turn that highlights Indigenous historical agency, strategy, and intentionality has emerged. Some ethnohistorians and historical anthropologists have begun to challenge historical depictions of Indigenous people in Amazonia by considering them more as historical actors and less as passive historical subjects. For example, Gary Van Valen's (2013) groundbreaking book *Indigenous Agency in the Amazon* highlights how historical Mojo groups in Bolivia actively and agentively engaged with missionaries, as well as with the European ideologies they encountered. In some cases, the Mojo even seem to have sought missionaries in their pursuit of local goals (Van Valen 2013, 13, 27). Mark Harris (2010) has also examined active historical Indigenous engagements with Europeans and their ideologies in Brazil. Barbara Sommer (2005) has analyzed historical Indigenous relations with *cunhamenas* with a focus on alliances. More recently, Heather Roller (2021) has written about Indigenous "contact strategies," which invert historical efforts by European colonists to "attract" Indigenous groups for "pacification" and settlement. She emphasizes what she calls "histories of native autonomy" and the agency of Indigenous groups in initiating and managing historical interactions with Europeans in Brazil.

This historiographical turn toward Indigenous agency has emerged concurrently with discussions in Amazonian ethnology over whether regional Indigenous social relations are better characterized as symmetric or asymmetric. The roots of this debate date back many decades to the work of Claude Lévi-Strauss (1949) and to later efforts to identify structural patterns in Indigenous social organization in Amazonia (see Overing 1981, 1989; and Rivière 1984). Its more recent articulation, however, is found in work by Carlos Fausto (2008, 2012) and Luiz Costa (2017), who suggest that asymmetry is a generalizable model for much of lowland South America. For Fausto (2008, 342), a new way of understanding asymmetry in Amazonia was needed because the prior emphasis on symmetry (particularly in contexts of exchange) in the regional ethnological literature complicated and obscured asymmetric relations (see Costa and Fausto 2010). Yet, while asymmetry characterizes many regional interactions, some Indigenous groups in lowland South America do orient more toward symmetric relations with others (see Descola 2013, 351–52). Although this sometimes takes the form of "friendship" relations, which often provide a foundation for symmetrically oriented partnerships across the region (see Killick 2009; Santos-Granero 2007; and Whitaker 2024), an emphasis on symmetry can also emerge in varied and complicated contexts of power.

The formation of both symmetric and asymmetric relations with others can evince agency and strategic intentionality on the part of Indigenous groups in Amazonia in different contexts. For example, some groups in the region explicitly reject identification with the dominant pole (i.e., predation) often associated with relations of asymmetry and identify as victims of others (see Rival 1998). In some other cases, groups seek to use a subordinate status to either "prey" on or "solicit" those in asymmetric positions above them (see Bonilla 2016; Penfield 2017; and Walker 2012). In contrast, Makushi groups have often sought to form symmetric relations when possible and to neutralize asymmetries when necessary (Whitaker 2025). Although similarities exist throughout the region in patterns of forming relations with others, the diversity of social organization and historical experiences across Amazonia casts doubt on overly broad generalizations of either asymmetric or symmetric relations as predominant.

For many Makushi, a preference for symmetric versus asymmetric relations with outsiders is linked to a history of being enslaved (Whitaker 2020, 2024). Their past experiences with slavery differ from those of some other groups in the Guianas who were historically involved in slaving (including against Makushi groups), for example, the Akawaio and Kariña (Whitaker 2016b), or who otherwise have experience having slaves or servants, such as the Trio (see Brightman 2016; and Grotti and Brightman 2016). Also, Makushi leadership is generally characterized by horizontal forms of political organization and strategies that emphasize persuasion and consensus building (see Santilli 1994). As is common across Amazonia, Makushi village leaders mostly lead through facilitation and conciliation rather than through exertions of authority or coercion. Unlike some groups, they often seek to extend such cooperative relations in their engagements with outsiders.[2]

Despite their preference for symmetric relations, Makushi groups have sometimes found themselves in asymmetric positions vis-à-vis outsiders in historical and contemporary contexts. This chapter considers historical cases of both symmetric and asymmetric relations. It examines a case of asymmetric relations between some Makushi groups and a Carib-led (probably Kariña) Indigenous polity, which they strategically manipulated, and a second case in which a Makushi group strategically sought to co-opt Anglican missionaries. In both cases, the focus of this chapter is on better understanding Makushi agency in strategically forming specific relations with others to curb slaving conducted against them. The chapter shows how Makushi people in the region have sometimes sought to make certain relations symmetric that were otherwise asymmetric, within specific contexts in the past and present.[3]

Early History of the Makushi

Although the Makushi likely had prior contact with Europeans, they first appear by name in historical documents in 1740 within the context of a slaving raid from Brazil, which under governmental orders explicitly targeted them and neighboring Wapisiana groups in the region of the Uraricoera River (QF 1903a, 99–100; see Whitaker 2016b, 75–76; and Williams 1932, 13–14). The attack was led by an Irishman named Belforte (written in the Portuguese documents as Lourenço Belforte), who was an experienced enslaver in the region (Hemming 1987, 30).[4] Although the location of Makushi groups is uncertain prior to this, such attacks seem to have contributed to eastward migration by some Makushi into Dutch colonial territory to avoid enslavement (Sommer 2005, 426). This choice by some Makushi people to move east provides an early example of agency in response to colonial pressures and sets the stage for subsequent interactions with Dutch and later British colonists.

During the 1750s and 1760s, the Makushi are mentioned in the writings of the Dutch colonial leader Laurens Storm van's Gravesande (see Whitaker 2016b, 77–78). The Dutch and Wapisiana (Arawakan-speaking neighbors of the Makushi) were in conflict in 1753 over the Wapisiana

killing three Dutch colonists and some Makushi and Carib persons who
had accompanied them, which seems to have led to a Dutch-supported
and Carib-led attack on the Wapisiana in the Essequibo region (The National Archives of the UK, CO 116/31, October 20, 1753; see C. A. Harris
and de Villiers 1911, 179, 302–3; and Whitehead 1988, 156). Makushi
people may have participated in the raid on the Wapisiana. By this time,
alliances between the Dutch and some Carib groups had been formed in
the region (Whitaker 2016a) and some Makushi groups appear to have
at least sometimes had cooperative relations with the Dutch. In 1765,
the Makushi and Wapisiana were in conflict, but a Dutch post-holder
was able to pass through after meeting with representatives ("owls")
from both groups (TNA CO 116/34, November 1765; see BGB 1898a,
120; and C. A. Harris and de Villiers 1911, 486–87).[5] In 1769, another
Dutch post-holder passed through the Makushi and Wapisiana territories, including reportedly near a site called Pirara, with interpreters
who knew Makushi and Wapisiana (C. A. Harris and de Villiers 1911,
616–17). These eighteenth-century Dutch references to the Makushi
suggest that they sometimes had cooperative relations with the Dutch,
despite the raids against them by other Indigenous groups (particularly
the Caribs and Akawaio) more closely allied with the Dutch colonial
regime (Whitaker 2017).

    During the 1770s, the Makushi are briefly mentioned in relation to
a Spanish expedition in the frontier between Brazil and the then Dutch
colonial territories (Humboldt and Bonpland 1881, 35). This and other
European expeditions worried the Portuguese and led them to build Fort
São Joaquim to consolidate and protect their imperial control over the
Rio Branco area. The Portuguese soon began efforts to attract Makushi
and other Indigenous groups to the fort, where they sought to convert
them to Christianity and to exploit their labor. Although exploitation and
conflicts with the Portuguese led to the departure of some Indigenous
groups, the Portuguese continued their policies of contact and attraction
to the fort. A Makushi "rebellion" in 1790, however, led to the expulsion
of many Indigenous people from the region (Farage 1991, 164–68; Hemming 1987, 31–37; Santilli 1994, 17; Whitaker 2025).

    Within the context of the different European colonial fronts, Makushi
relationships with colonial entities took different forms. While the Portuguese sought to settle them near Fort São Joaquim as laborers, which

was a common pattern in regional Portuguese and Spanish colonization, the Dutch took a different approach. In the Dutch colonies of Essequibo, Demerara, and Berbice, which became officially British in 1814 and were collectively renamed British Guiana in 1831, Indigenous leaders (called "captains" and "owls") were given special objects that represented "official" leadership status and formalized them as allies of the colonial government (Benjamin 1992, 8; Whitaker 2016a, 36, 41; Whitehead 1988, 169).[6] For example, the Dutch presented silver-topped canes with the insignia of the Dutch West India Company, special hats with silver plumes, and other objects to some Indigenous leaders in 1778 with stipulations that they maintain their settlements, provide requested support, and accept nominations from the Dutch colonial government for future Indigenous leadership positions (BGB 1898b, 122, 136, 187–88). Rather than create a nearby converted labor force, the Dutch mostly wanted to officialize and co-opt Indigenous leadership during the 1770s because of heightened concerns over plantation security. They sought to formalize existing Indigenous alliances as a force against rebellions and desertions by enslaved persons of African descent (Alston 2023; Benjamin 1992; Menezes 1973, 1977; Whitehead 1988).

There is limited evidence for Makushi-Dutch alliances during the late eighteenth century. This contrasts with several Dutch alliances with Carib, Akawaio, Arawak, and Warao leaders and groups (BGB 1898b, 187–88, 207). The colonial pattern of officialized leadership and formal alliances with Europeans, however, became a standard by which successive governments (colonial and postcolonial) sought to co-opt existing forms of Indigenous leadership (Benjamin 1992; Farage 1991; Santilli 1994). Such co-optation became the mechanism through which colonial partnerships with Indigenous groups were sought and formalized.

This mechanism largely continued under British colonial rule. Makushi efforts to strategically ally with the Europeans soon emerged and echoed reports from the previous century involving Indigenous groups. For example, evidence comes from a letter written by a British post-holder named Charles Edmonstone in 1816.[7] He writes: "I must, however, observe that the Macoushies [sic] are by far the most numerous tribe, and have never failed to send a part of their number with every expedition that has been under my direction. There were, in fact, in the expedition to Mahaicony, Indians from at least fourteen different tribes, and in the last expedition alluded to in your Excellency's letter, from ten" (BGB 1898d, 269). The letter indicates that some Makushi helped the British against uprisings and escape attempts by enslaved people. Edmonstone reportedly led at least fifteen expeditions during his time in Demerara between 1780 and 1817 (Alston 2023, 6–9; Menezes 1973, 70). British colonial officials kept lists of Indigenous leaders and the forces they could muster for these expeditions. For example, although the document provides minimal context, one such list from 1818 refers to a Makushi leader named Simary who resided in Essequibo and had over two hundred "family and friends at 15 days' journey" (BGB 1898c, 12). The sparse available references to the Makushi during this time point to some degree of Makushi-Anglo cooperation. On the Makushi side, this cooperation was likely aimed at trying to form partnerships with some measure of symmetry.

Asymmetric Relations in the Early Nineteenth Century

Although limited in scope, there is evidence that the leadership of some Makushi groups was partially folded into larger and hierarchical multiethnic Indigenous polity structures during the early nineteenth century. This evidence comes primarily from the writings of a British colonist, John Hancock, who led an expedition to the Makushi territory in late 1810, after a much mythologized visit to Georgetown by a Carib leader named Mahanarva (a.k.a. Manariwan). The latter was deeply involved in attacking and enslaving other Indigenous groups (including the Makushi) (Burnett 2000, 54–56; Farage 1991, 170–73; Whitaker 2016b, 86–93). From Mahanarva's residence near Pirara, according to the standard story, he brought with his entourage Makushi captives, which he intended to sell to the colonists as slaves. During his visit, he requested that the British continue the Dutch colonial policy of giving "presents" to allied Indigenous groups, which was initially granted by the new British authorities under the stipulations that he cease war and enslavement of other Indigenous peoples, such as the Makushi, and accept British rule (Farage 1991, 170–73; Harris and de Villiers 1911, 109–10; Menezes 1973, 1977). Although the British colonial government was reluctant to follow through when Mahanarva returned two years later, such payments do seem to have eventually resumed, although the British balked at agreeing to make them annual or obligatory (see Farage 1991, 172–73; Menezes 1973, 72–75; and Whitehead 1988, 170–71). Within the context of this unexpected visit and its aftermath, we get a sense of Makushi relations with the Europeans and their Indigenous neighbors at the time (see Whitaker 2025).

Hancock's subsequent journey to the interior in 1810 was undertaken partly as a response to Mahanarva's visit to Georgetown (Burnett 2000, 55). The purpose of Hancock's travel was to assess the danger posed by Mahanarva, to curtail enslavement of Indigenous groups, and to get a broader sense of Indigenous relations in the hinterlands of British Guiana (see Farage 1991, 171; and Hancock 1835, 46). Once he arrived in the interior region, Hancock called a large meeting of Indigenous leaders, which reportedly included fourteen Makushi "captains." While contemporary traditional village leaders are often called *toshaos*, "captain" is a term that recurs in colonial documents and refers mostly to Indigenous leaders recognized by the colonial regime. Traditional village leaders and captains were often probably the same person. During the Dutch regime, colonial authorities tried to keep careful watch, as well as a measure of control, over Indigenous leadership, but the transition to British rule had resulted in some slippage in European control. As such, Hancock's visit was likely spurred, to some degree, by motivations related to political and military intelligence.

Regarding political relations in the hinterlands, Hancock writes that the Indigenous leaders whom he met "unanimously agreed that Mahanarwa [*sic*] was not only *caqui* [supreme leader] of the Caribees [Caribs], but was acknowledged by themselves and by all the other tribes" (Hancock 1835, 26; see Whitaker 2016b, 88–89). Hancock reports being told by unnamed locals that the paramount leadership position "was either hereditary, or elected by an assemblage of their chiefs, and could only be deposed by a majority in a public council" (Hancock 1835, 26). This most likely refers to a type of war leader, which was sometimes called an "owl" in Dutch documents, that would emerge during times of duress among some Indigenous groups in the region and that was often central in alliances and partnerships with European colonial regimes (see Whitehead 1988, 59–60, 169–70; and Bolingbroke 1813, 99). This type of leader differed from traditional village leaders by (1) influence (and perhaps sometimes control) over larger polities, incorporating multiple villages, kinship networks, and even sometimes other ethnic groups (e.g., Makushi people in the case of Mahanarva's polity) and (2) access to more coercive forms of authority relative to the consensus-based authority of traditional village leaders (Whitaker 2016b, 88). This form of leadership seems to have been mostly a response to warfare conditions in which multiple groups needed to coordinate under a central heading. Since they sometimes incorporated different Indigenous groups, which could involve intergroup tensions, it is unclear how stable or permanent such large Indigenous polities were at the time. The inclusion of Makushi groups in an alliance centered on a Carib leader is perhaps surprising, considering that some Carib groups (including the one led by Mahanarva) were involved in slaving against Makushi people.

A significant difficulty here is that the term Carib is rather ambiguous within this context. As previous scholarship has shown (Drummond 1977; Farage 1991; Stone 2017; see also Harris and de Villiers 1911, 178), this term was frequently used in unclear and imprecise ways during the colonial era. Often the term was used merely to mark a perception among Europeans that a particular Indigenous group was bellicose, which was sometimes used to fabricate justifications for attacking, enslaving, or co-opting that group depending on the circumstances. Although it is unfortunately not possible to ascertain the exact ethnicity marked as "Carib" here, Mahanarva quite possibly may have led a Kariña group (Whitehead 1988). It is unclear whether Makushi people would have seen Caribs as an identifiable group of enemy enslavers or would have defined their enemies in a different and perhaps more narrow way. The central problem is that we do not know how Makushi people historically conceptualized the groups that are called Caribs in the archival record. In the present, however, some Makushi people refer to Caribs as their historical enemies. What is relatively clear is that Mahanarva was not Makushi, so he would have been an outsider to these groups. Nevertheless, Makushi people were reportedly part of the multiethnic polity that he led.

This raises another question concerning whether this was a forced arrangement, a result of British efforts to curtail Indigenous warfare, or a relational strategy (involving the manipulation of an asymmetric relationship to obtain benefits) among some Makushi groups at the time. The situation and its analysis are complicated by Hancock's later suggestion, in 1827, that the Makushi were somewhat "independent of the Caribs" and not entirely under their control (QF 1903b, 2). Did some Makushi groups willingly enter an alliance with a Carib polity under Mahanarva? If so, when and how did this alliance begin and end? Also, what was the character and form of the alliance and how did it affect Makushi relations with the Europeans?

By 1810, some Makushi leaders had apparently formed cooperative relations with Mahanarva, as well as with British colonists like Edmonstone (Whitaker 2016b, 337–38).[8] Some Makushi potentially aiding a Dutch-Carib allied raid in the 1750s also suggests that forms of cooperation may have dated back many decades in select cases despite Carib raids against Makushi groups in the region. The formation of such a partnership amid either ongoing or recurrent hostilities likely indicates division between different groups of Makushi people, which may have acted somewhat autonomously in terms of their relative alliances. In other words, it was not a simple matter of the Makushi being allied with the Caribs. Instead, a complex and multidimensional picture emerges of various Makushi groups holding shifting alliances and enmities with different Carib groups. Neither was necessarily characterized internally by an encompassing ethnic identity at the time. In terms of Mahanarva's multiethnic polity, shifting relations with Makushi groups may have been divided between those groups allied with the polity and those raided by it. Within this context, desires for strategic accommodation may have driven decision making and diplomacy among some Makushi leaders. Cooperation with an enemy (actual or potential) may have been preferable to risking enslavement or other forms of predation (Whitaker 2025). The situation might also suggest that some Makushi leaders were aiming for alliances of their own with the Europeans.

By temporarily accepting an asymmetric position vis-à-vis Mahanarva, some Makushi leaders may have saved their villages from attacks and their fellow villagers (as well as themselves) from being killed or taken captive and enslaved. In other words, some kind of Makushi-Carib cooperative relationship or partnership may have been intended to minimize raiding against Makushi villages. Such a strategy of intentionally positioning themselves in the subordinate position of an asymmetric relationship (e.g., under Mahanarva) resonates with several cases described ethnographically in recent years among other Indigenous groups in Amazonia, such as the Paumari (Bonilla 2016), Sanema (Penfield 2017), and Urarina (Walker 2012), of strategically accepting or even seeking subordinate positions in relation to other groups (Indigenous or non-Indigenous) to benefit in one way or another from the dominant group. Such benefits might include acquisition of material goods, protection, political or economic opportunities, specialized knowledge, marital exchanges, or other desiderata. In the case examined here, rather than seeking material or political-economic advantages, as reported in many such cases in Amazonia, Makushi groups were likely aiming for survival and perhaps some degree of protection by cooperating with the Carib-led polity under Mahanarva. Different benefits may have been sought in their cooperation with Edmonstone. Nonetheless, temporary Makushi acceptance of outside control, dominance, or "mastery" (Fausto 2012) contrasts with their broader efforts to form balanced and reciprocal relations with outsiders (Whitaker 2024). Subsequent interactions with Anglican missionaries evince Makushi efforts to curb predation while minimizing asymmetries with allies.

According to Hancock (1835, 46; QF 1903b, 2), the relationship between Makushi and Carib groups allegedly involved the "selling" of Makushi kin to the latter. He claims that Makushi men thus sent the widows and children of their deceased brothers into enslavement. Although the meaning of "selling" is ambiguous here, this suggests that Makushi-Carib cooperative relations may have facilitated a (perhaps partial) conversion of slaving raids into a slave trade along a relational nexus involving kinship (Whitaker 2025). This continued to be exploitative for Makushi groups, but by focusing on trading, it may have prevented the deaths generally associated with Carib raiding for *poitos*. The various historical and contemporary meanings of the term *poito*, which can refer both to "son-in-law" and to "slave," probably reflect regional transformations of affinal kinship, trade, and captivity at the time (Whitehead 1988, 2, 57; see Abbott 2009; Farage 1991).[9] In other words, the customary access of the father-in-law to the labor of his son-in-law during the period of "bride service" provided an idiom on which relations of enslavement could be built, although these relations were clearly different from bride-service practices. As reported in Hancock's account, however, the "selling" of sisters-in-law and nieces potentially involved a secondary transformation of kinship.[10] The first transformation marks a change in male captives' status from quasi-affines to enslaved people. The second transformation, which is less examined in the regional literature, may mark a change (whether prior or subsequent) in the position of female affines (Whitaker 2016b, 91–92). Despite reported recognition of Mahanarva's paramount leadership, some Makushi leaders complained to Hancock's expedition of being pressured to engage in slave trading (QF 1903b, 2). Hancock frames these complaints in relation to the Caribs in general, but they may have been more targeted toward particular groups (such as the polity controlled by Mahanarva). While the Makushi-Carib relationship may have been cooperative, it was still asymmetric and exploitative.

Although Makushi people were most likely under duress in their decisions to cooperate with Mahanarva, the incorporation of some Makushi groups into a Carib-dominated multiethnic polity, which was notably absent from the Makushi oral histories that I encountered during ethnographic fieldwork in Guyana, may nevertheless represent an early case (resonating with eighteenth-century reports that suggest Makushi-Dutch cooperation) of Makushi leaders forming strategic and pragmatic relations of cooperation with outsiders.[11] Although sparsely recorded, some evidence for likely cooperation between Makushi and Carib groups, within the context of engagements with Europeans, exists from the 1750s into the 1810s. These relations, however, seem to have waned by the mid-1820s. At that time, despite limited evidence, the Caribs were reportedly experiencing demographic decline. Many of their remaining groups had shifted closer to the Brazilian side of the frontier. For example, William Hilhouse (1825, 29) claims that "though, about twenty years ago [around 1805], they [the Caribs] could muster nearly a thousand fighting men, at this moment it would be difficult to collect fifty in the whole country below the falls. Those that remain have retired so far into the interior, that their services are entirely lost to us; but they still preserve a strong attachment to the Colony, and a very slight manifestation of kindness would soon induce them to return." This claim must be read within the broader context of Hilhouse's desire to turn regional Indigenous groups into a regimented colonial fighting force (Menezes 1973, 76–77). Nonetheless, smallpox, other epidemics, and casualties from wars had likely resulted in substantial demographic losses and migrations (Harris and de Villiers 1911, 181; Hilhouse 1825, 128; Whitaker 2016b, 99, 104). By 1841, the Carib population along the coast, as well as that of several other Indigenous groups in British Guiana, had reportedly declined dramatically (Schomburgk [1847] 1922, 54). This demographic decline, along with the diminishment of the coastal market for Indigenous slavery, which nevertheless continued in Brazil, may partly explain a disintegration of the multiethnic Carib-led polity in British Guiana led by Mahanarva. Hilhouse (1825, 37) suggests that the Makushi population had also declined by the mid-1820s, which may have variously resulted from epidemics, migration, and raiding by other Indigenous people (particularly Carib and Akawaio groups), who especially targeted the Makushi relative to other regional Indigenous groups (BGB 1898c, 27; see Whitaker 2025; and Whitehead 1988). Nevertheless, prior to these reports of severe demographic decline, Makushi groups appear to have strategically engaged in asymmetric relations with a Carib-led multiethnic polity.

Symmetry with Missionaries in the Mid-Nineteenth Century

From the 1830s to the 1850s, a generation after Makushi involvements with Mahanarva and Edmonstone, Makushi groups in and around a village called Pirara sought and formed new relations with Anglican missionaries (Farage 1991; Rivière 1995; Whitaker 2025). These relations involved strategic alliances that further connected them with the British colonial sphere. Like the above-mentioned cooperative (albeit coercive) relations between Makushi and Carib groups, these new relations also emerged against a backdrop of raiding that targeted Makushi people. Some evidence shows that slaving by Carib groups still occurred against the Makushi in British Guiana; and some of this evidence points to the Caribs from the Corentyne region in Dutch colonial territory (present-day Suriname) playing a significant role (BGB 1898c, 65; Rivière 2006, 167; Whitaker 2016b, 185–88). At the time, the relationship between slave trading (involving a sordid exchange of human beings for money or trade goods) and slave raiding (involving negative reciprocity through violent kidnappings) seems to have remained ambiguous (Rivière 2006, 207–8).[12] Planned raids might be converted into trading expeditions and perhaps vice-versa in some cases (Whitaker 2016b, 86–87).

There are also indications that British colonists, including colonial officials (particularly post-holders), were sometimes involved in illicit practices involving Indigenous slavery and kidnapping in British Guiana

(APS 1840, 28; BGB 1898d, 286–87; Schomburgk 1848, 88). This is an important point to keep in mind, since many of the British documents point to slaving from Brazil, which shared an undemarcated border with British Guiana at the time. Colonial interests and accusations of slaving sometimes overlapped. Nonetheless, despite the limitations of the available documents in clarifying the full scope and scale of regional slavery during the 1830s and 1840s, the main threat for Makushi groups around Pirara does seem to have come from raids from Brazil. Such raids resonate with those in which the Makushi first appeared in historical documents almost a century prior.

Against this backdrop of ongoing raiding and the threat of subsequent enslavement, Anglican missionaries entered the interior region from their operational bases near the coast of British Guiana. In 1833, John Armstrong, an Anglican missionary with the Church Missionary Society (CMS), traveled from his mission post at Bartica to the Makushi territory in the process of conducting evangelical visits to Indigenous villages in the interior region (BGB 1898c, 50).[13] From his interactions with Indigenous people during this visit, he learned of ongoing slaving raids from Brazil against Makushi villages. In response, he wrote a letter of protest to Brazilian officials; he also claimed that local Makushi people expressed desires for a resident missionary (CMS/C/W/O14, 23, 25; see Whitaker 2016b, 109–13; Whitaker 2020, 885–86).

There is some indication that Armstrong sought this kind of overture from local Indigenous groups (BGB 1898, 50; see Whitaker 2025). It is not altogether clear how much the missionaries knew about the situation in and around Pirara before this visit, since British colonists had previously made documented visits there. Also, the missionaries had visited nearer Indigenous villages and received visits at Bartica from various Indigenous groups. After Armstrong's journey to the Makushi in 1833, the two missionaries associated with the CMS at Bartica—Armstrong and Thomas Youd—recurrently report receiving visits from Makushi and neighboring Indigenous groups for many years afterward. The reasons for these visits may have ranged widely, from curiosity to desires for material goods or other resources (including various forms of outside knowledge). They may have also involved efforts to form relationships or to gauge the benefits and dangers posed by the Europeans, as well as spiritual interests or goals involving transformations (see Capredon, Ceriani

Cernadas, and Opas 2023; Grotti 2022; Halbmayer 2013; Vilaça 2010, 2016; and Whitaker 2021). Although the Makushi-Carib partnership led by Mahanarva had apparently disintegrated by this time, Mahanarva's grandson is mentioned as being involved in one such visit (CMS/C/W/O100, 35).[14] These visits came to a head in 1837, when Youd was visited at Bartica by a Makushi group that included the son-in-law of the Makushi leader at Pirara (Whitaker 2016b, 118–21). Youd was told that buildings and fields had been prepared there for his or another missionary's arrival (CMS/C/W/O100, 43).[15] According to Youd, the visitors clearly desired a resident missionary (Whitaker 2025).

After quite a bit of back-and-forth communication between Youd and the Church Missionary Society, he received permission to make an exploratory visit to the Makushi territory (Rivière 2006, 264). When he traveled to Pirara in 1838, however, he went ahead and started a new mission there (CMS/C/W/O100, 45), the first Anglican mission to the Makushi people (Whitaker 2025). According to his reports, Youd was well received by Makushi and other Indigenous people there, and the mission proceeded with church services and classes taught by Youd that focused on religious matters and the English language. Later, however, in 1838, there was a scare at Pirara that a slaving raid from Brazil was imminent. Makushi groups from across the region reportedly gathered in preparation to repel the attack. Although this raid never happened, these fears indicate the existence of rising tensions with Brazil in relation to Youd's mission. Youd came under pressure. His position at Pirara soon became untenable. The Brazilian authorities saw him as a threat, which was perhaps reasonable considering subsequent events. Some Makushi people reportedly declared that they would follow Youd wherever he relocated the mission after having taken the trouble to "fetch" him (CMS/C/W/O100, 46). This provides some evidence of their continued desire for an Anglican missionary presence (or perhaps their liking for Youd). Such evidence, however, comes primarily from the writings of Youd and his supporters. Within the context of ongoing tensions and disagreements with Brazil, Youd relocated the mission twice, first to Urwa in 1839, and second to Waraputa in 1840 (CMS/C/W/O100, 23, 28, 47; Whitaker 2020, 886).

The situation at Youd's missions in the interior region of British Guiana suggests that the desires of Makushi and sometimes other Indigenous groups for a missionary (and particularly a British one) were strategically aimed, at least in part, at curbing ongoing attacks against them, which were reportedly coming mostly from Brazil at the time. The transparency and thoroughness of the reports from Youd and previously from Armstrong are unclear, but one can certainly ascertain the interests of British colonialism within this context, as well as the self-interest of the missionaries and other colonial figures. Much of the evidence concerning the reported raiding comes through the writings of the missionaries and their supporters, particularly Robert Schomburgk. The existence of the raids (whether actually occurring in some cases or not) provided a rationale for a British presence and even an occupation (Whitaker 2025). This seems to have been a goal for Schomburgk, who was commissioned by the British government to demarcate the border between British Guiana and Brazil. Nonetheless, despite the Makushi case coming to the attention of the British government, general support from the British colonial governor, and a temporary British military occupation of Pirara (CMS/C/W/O100, 26, 46; Harris and de Villiers 1911, 114–15; Rivière 2006, 42; Whitaker 2016b, 168–69), there was seemingly limited British interest in the Makushi territory, which nevertheless became largely subject to what has been referred to as "absent-minded imperialism" (Rivière 1995).

Local Makushi groups continued to seek a British missionary presence even after Youd's death in 1842 (Whitaker 2025).[16] Similar to Youd's experience with the Pirara villagers, an unidentified Makushi group told John James Lohrer, who was also an Anglican missionary with the Church Missionary Society, during his visit to the interior region in the 1850s that they had prepared buildings and fields in preparation for a new missionary (CMS/C/W/O55, 6, 9). The Church Missionary Society, however, did not intend to develop a new mission in the contested border region (see Menezes 1977). From the 1830s to the 1850s, these Anglican missionaries and likely others were actively sought out by Makushi people, at least in part as a means of curbing certain threats of external predation, as well as maintaining access to outside goods, connections, specialized knowledge, and other resources and benefits (Whitaker 2016b, 107–57). This continued despite the missionaries' limited ability to reduce the threat of raids or to provide a significant source of material resources.

Similar to previous strategic Makushi relations with Edmonstone and some Carib groups, Makushi engagements with Anglican missionaries (which were characterized by the efforts of some Makushi people to befriend and attract missionaries to their villages) reveal agency and desires for symmetric balance in their relations with outsiders. Yet the primary goal here appears to have been to form strategic partnerships against external predation (Whitaker 2020). Decades later, according to geological surveyor Charles Barrington Brown (1876; Brown and Sawkins 1875), some Makushi groups still feared the possibility of raids and related attacks by outsiders. Various attempts to procure Anglican missionaries as strategic partners and colonial allies continued in British Guiana into the late nineteenth century (Im Thurn 1883, 79).

Makushi Strategic Partnerships and Amazonian Historiography

The documented pattern of Makushi groups forming cooperative and allied relations with certain outsiders to curb predation against their villages and communities, as well as for various other strategic purposes, evinces their historical agency and intentionality. Although threats of raiding often came from Brazil during the eighteenth and nineteenth centuries, they occurred within a broader historical context of predation, which variously included Brazilian soldiers, Dutch Indigenous proxies, Indigenous enemies, and rogue British colonists, among others. Reports concerning these overlapping vectors of predation were also complicated by European colonial rivalries, which sometimes led to accusations of enslavement and raiding being variously weaponized as imperialist or nationalist propaganda.

Frequently under conditions of duress, Makushi people and their leaders strategically sought and formed relationships with outside partners to further their interests. Material goods, knowledge, connections, and security were variously sought through these relationships. The tactics and methods involved were often flexible to accommodate changed conditions and constrained opportunities in the face of colonization and its attendant forces. The pattern that emerges, however, is one of deploying hospitality and initiating forms of exchange as a way of developing cooperative relationships with potentially useful outsiders (Whitaker 2024). Such practices are not limited to the Makushi, but Makushi groups strongly emerge in these accounts as active and flexible agents of history, not merely as passive subjects.

As described elsewhere in Amazonia, "contact strategies" and "Indigenous agency" are evident among the Makushi and other Indigenous peoples in the historical record of Guyana (see Roller 2021; and Van Valen 2013). What is remarkable in the historical cases discussed in this chapter is the flexibility of Makushi leaders and villages in striving to form cooperative relations centered on some measure of symmetry. Unlike some Indigenous groups in lowland South America, whose social relations are portrayed as permeated by asymmetry (see Costa 2017; and Fausto 2012), Makushi groups have often tried to negate asymmetric relations in the past and present. As still occurs today, the Makushi groups discussed in this chapter sought to form strategic partnerships while attempting to manipulate asymmetric relations to amplify symmetry whenever possible in various contexts. This can be seen in their past efforts to raise their standing in the Carib-led polity and in triangulated cooperation with British colonist Charles Edmonstone. It was echoed later in Makushi efforts to form allied relations with missionaries.

These past cases add to the growing historiographical turn in lowland South America toward a greater analytical emphasis on agency, intentionality, and strategy in past Indigenous encounters and relations with Europeans across the broader region. Although the sources used by historians for understanding such interactions are most often written by colonial Europeans, which has contributed in the past to an overemphasis among scholars on European agency and intentions, the goals and aspirations of Indigenous people, such as the Makushi in Guyana, become evident in the accounts that are narrated and described. Their voices can be heard through the historical record by way of ethnographic interpretations of ethnohistorical accounts. The use of R. G. Collingwood's historical "imagination"—an interpretive method that can be honed through active fieldwork with descendant communities of people documented in the historical record—can be useful in these circumstances as a way of fleshing out inchoate past accounts (Harris 2010, 2; Whitaker 2018). Ethnography and archival analyses come together within this context to discern and amplify Indigenous voices within documented histories.

Makushi groups emerge as active and intentional agents in various historical relations with colonists (e.g., Charles Edmonstone), missionaries (e.g., John Armstrong and Thomas Youd), and other Indigenous groups (e.g., Mahanarva's Carib-led polity) during the colonial era. Often striving for symmetric relations within asymmetric contexts, Makushi efforts to cultivate external partners contribute to a historiographical turn that provides a lens for understanding Indigenous people as historical actors who through strategy and initiative have sometimes overcome the predations to which they have been subjected by colonialism and its vectors.

Notes

Epigraph: I would like to thank the Cadbury Research Library: Special Collections, University of Birmingham, and the Church Mission Society for granting permission to publish material from the archives of the Church Mission Society.

1. Such an approach does not diminish the horrors of European colonization in the Americas, nor does it negate the victimization that Indigenous groups experienced as a result of colonization. Rather, it contributes to further recognition of the agency of Indigenous peoples within this history (see Salomon and Schwartz 1999; and Schwartz 2002).
2. See Farage (1991) and Santilli (1994) for discussions concerning Makushi leadership in situations involving interactions with outsiders in Brazil.
3. The Makushi history presented in this chapter (including colonial contact, the Makushi-Carib alliance, and Anglican missionization) is partly based on Whitaker (2016b) and has been variously discussed in subsequent work (Whitaker 2020, 2024). These themes are examined in greater detail in Whitaker (2025). This chapter's central aim is to comparatively examine two historical cases in relation to Makushi groups engaging with outsiders in symmetric and asymmetric contexts.
4. See Sommer (2005) for more on this and other such slaving expeditions in Brazil.
5. Dutch post-holders were colonial appointees and often traders positioned at key locations to promote Dutch security and economic interests (Whitehead 1988).
6. See Farage (1991) for more on relations (particularly involving leadership) between Indigenous groups and the Portuguese and Dutch during the eighteenth century.
7. During British colonial rule, after the Dutch, post-holders were colonial officials who largely managed trade, security, and other relations with local Indigenous groups in the interior zones.
8. See Farage (1991, 173) for reluctance on the part of the British colonial government to fulfill the terms of their agreements with Indigenous groups.

9. See Farage (1991, 111–17) for a broader treatment of the various uses of the term *poito* and cognate terms in the Guianas. Since marriage and subsequent affinal relations involving the term *poito* can indicate alliances, slave trading and efforts to form alliances through affinity may possibly be connected in some historical instances.

10. This selling may have involved some degree of exchange centered on manufactured goods (Farage 1991), as well as perhaps European misunderstandings of local marital practices and changes within these practices.

11. The oral histories that I collected during fieldwork visits to the Makushi village of Surama (2012–20) never included the theme of Makushi-Carib alliances. When I asked about this, my interlocutors insisted that Makushi and Carib groups were historically enemies and that Makushi groups never willingly submitted to Carib groups.

12. Yet, Robert Schomburgk (1848, 87–88) indicates that the "sale of females" (which Hancock described in his earlier writings) had declined significantly, although he mentions knowing of cases, including one seemingly involving a British official, "where females have been sold during our visits from 1835 to 1844, and carried to Demerara" (see also Sweet 1981).

13. Bartica is north of the Makushi territory and the broader Rupununi region.

14. In writing about this visit, Youd seems to refer to Mahanarva as "King Menerwa" and mentions his proficiency in speaking Dutch (CMS/C/W/O100, 35; see Whitaker 2016b, 114).

15. See Schomburgk (1839a, 165; see also Rivière 2006a: 256, 264) for a description of the preparations that the villagers at Pirara made for a resident missionary, as well as the population expansion in the village in the build-up to Youd's arrival. Schomburgk (1839b, 53) also reports that he had previously recommended Pirara to the bishop of Barbados (who was the Church of England bishop overseeing Anglican churches in British Guiana at the time) as a possible site for a future mission. This recommendation was probably made after Armstrong's visit to Pirara in 1833. Schomburgk's interests in this matter involved both antislavery goals and apparently British colonization (Rivière 1998, 7; see also Whitaker 2016b, 164). He reported encountering a slaving party from Brazil, consisting of Brazilians aided by a Makushi captain and some of his group (see also Lane's chapter in this volume), which had attacked and enslaved Atorai and Wapisiana people; he recommended that Britain take control of much of the disputed Makushi territory to end such slaving raids (Schomburgk 1839b, 53–54). The timing for this is important, since his recommendation was published a year after Britain ended slavery in its Caribbean colonies (including in British Guiana).

16. There is also some evidence of Brazilian Makushi groups seeking allied relations with Catholic priests (see Santilli 2014, 47–48; and Whitaker 2025).

References
Primary Sources

British Guiana Boundary (BGB) Arbitration Documents
    BGB. 1898a. *Appendix to the Case on Behalf of the Government of Her Britan-nic Majesty.* Vol. 3. London: Harrison and Sons.
    BGB. 1898b. *Appendix to the Case on Behalf of the Government of Her Britan-nic Majesty.* Vol. 4. London: Harrison and Sons.
    BGB. 1898c. *Appendix to the Case on Behalf of the Government of Her Britan-nic Majesty.* Vol. 6. London: Harrison and Sons.
    BGB. 1898d. *Counter-Case on Behalf of the Government of Her Britannic Maj-esty.* London. Harrison and Sons.
    QF. 1903a. *Question de la Frontière entre la Guyane Britannique et le Brésil: Annexe au mémoire présenté par le gouvernement de Sa Majesté britan-nique.* Vol. 1. London: Harrison and Sons.
    QF. 1903b. *Question de la Frontière entre la Guyane Britannique et le Brésil: Annexe au mémoire présenté par le gouvernement de Sa Majesté britan-nique.* Vol. 2. London: Harrison and Sons.
Cadbury Research Library (CRL), Special Collections, University of Birmingham
    Papers of John Armstrong (CMS/C/W/O14)
    Papers of John James Lohrer (CMS/C/W/O55)
    Papers of Thomas Youd (CMS/C/W/O100)
The National Archives of the UK (TNA)
    Colonial Office (CO) and predecessors: British Guiana, formerly Berbice, De-merara and Essiquibo, Miscellanea including Papers of the Dutch West India Company; Dutch association papers
        CO 116/31
        CO 116/34

Secondary Sources

Abbott, Miriam. 2009. *Makushi Dictionary.* Guyana: Makushi Research Unit/North Rupununi District Development Board.
APS (Aborigines' Protection Society). 1840. *The Third Annual Report of the Aborig-ines' Protection Society.* Presented at the Meeting in Exeter Hall, June 23, 1840. London: P. White and Son.
Alston, David. 2023. "The Guyana Maroons, 1796–1834: Persistent and Resilient until the End of Slavery." *Slavery and Abolition,* online preview, January 18, 1–24.
Barrington Brown, Charles. 1876. *Canoe and Camp Life in British Guiana.* London: Edward Stanford.
Brown, Charles Barrington, and James G. Sawkins. 1875. *Reports on the Physical, Descriptive, and Economic Geology of British Guiana.* London: Longmans, Green.

Benjamin, Anna. 1992. "A Preliminary Look at the Free Amerindians and the Dutch Plantation System in Guyana During the 17th and 18th Centuries." *Guyana Historical Journal* 4–5:1–21.

Bolingbroke, Henry. 1813. *A Voyage to the Demerary.* Philadelphia: M. Carey.

Bonilla, Oiara. 2016. "Parasitism and Subjection: Modes of Paumari Predation." In *Ownership and Nurture: Studies in Native Amazonian Property Relations*, edited by Marc Brightman, Carlos Fausto, and Vanessa Grotti, 110–32. Oxford: Berghahn.

Brightman, Marc. 2016. *The Imbalance of Power: Leadership, Masculinity and Wealth in the Amazon.* Oxford: Berghahn.

Burnett, D. Graham. 2000. *Masters of All They Surveyed: Exploration, Geography, and a British El Dorado.* Chicago: University of Chicago Press.

Capredon, Élise, César Ceriani Cernadas, and Minna Opas, eds. 2023. *Indigenous Churches: Anthropology of Christianity in Lowland South America.* New York: Springer.

Costa, Luiz. 2017. *The Owners of Kinship: Asymmetrical Relations in Indigenous Amazonia.* Chicago: University of Chicago Press.

Costa, Luiz, and Carlos Fausto. 2010. "The Return of the Animists: Recent Studies of Amazonian Ontologies." *Religion and Society* 1 (1): 89–109.

Descola, Philippe. 2013. *Beyond Nature and Culture.* Chicago: University of Chicago Press.

Drummond, Lee. 1977. "On Being Carib." In *Carib-Speaking Indians: Culture, Society and Language*, edited by Ellen B. Basso, 76–88. Tucson: University of Arizona Press.

Farage, Nádia. 1991. *As muralhas dos sertões: Os povos indígenas no rio Branco e a colonização.* São Paulo: Paz e Terra.

Fausto, Carlos. 2008. "Donos demais: Maestria e domínio na Amazônia." *Mana* 14 (2): 329–66.

Fausto, Carlos. 2012. "Too Many Owners: Mastery and Ownership in Amazonia." In *Animism in Rainforest and Tundra: Personhood, Animals, Plants and Things in Contemporary Amazonia and Siberia*, edited by Marc Brightman, Vanessa Grotti, and Olga Ulturgasheva, 29–47. Oxford: Berghahn Books.

Grotti, Vanessa. 2022. *Nurturing the Other: First Contacts and the Making of Christian Bodies in Amazonia.* London: Berghahn.

Grotti, Vanessa, and Marc Brightman. 2016. "First Contacts, Slavery and Kinship in North-Eastern Amazonia." In *Ownership and Nurture: Studies in Native Amazonian Property Relations*, edited by Marc Brightman, Carlos Fausto, and Vanessa Grotti, 63–80. London: Berghahn.

Halbmayer, Ernst. 2013. "Mission, Food, and Commensality among the Yukpa: Indigenous Creolization and Emerging Complexities in Indigenous Modernities." *Tipití* 11 (1): 65–86.

Hancock, John. 1835. *Observations on the Climate, Soil, and Productions of British Guiana.* London: Richard Taylor.

Harris, Mark. 2010. *Rebellion on the Amazon: The Cabanagem, Race, and Popular Culture in the North of Brazil, 1798–1840*. Cambridge: Cambridge University Press.

Harris, C. Alexander, and John A. J. De Villiers. 1911. *Storm van's Gravesande: The Rise of British Guiana*. London: Hakluyt Society.

Hemming, John. 1978. *Red Gold: The Conquest of the Brazilian Indians*. London: Macmillan.

Hemming, John. 1987. *Amazon Frontier: The Defeat of the Brazilian Indians*. Cambridge: Harvard University Press.

Hilhouse, William. 1825. *Indian Notices*. London: Printed for the author.

Humboldt, Alexander von, and Aimé Bonpland. 1881. *Personal Narrative of Travels to the Equinoctial Regions of America, during the Years 1799–1804*. Translated and edited by Thomasina Ross. London: George Bell and Sons.

Im Thurn, Everard F. 1883. *Among the Indians of Guiana: Being Sketches Chiefly Anthropologic from the Interior of British Guiana*. London: Kegan Paul, Trench.

Killick, Evan. 2009. "Ashéninka Amity: A Study of Social Relations in an Amazonian Society." *Journal of the Royal Anthropological Institute* 15 (4): 701–18.

Lévi-Strauss, Claude. 1949. *The Elementary Structures of Kinship*. Boston: Beacon.

Menezes, Mary Noel. 1973. "The Dutch and British Policy of Indian Subsidy: A System of Annual and Triennial Presents." *Caribbean Studies* 13 (3): 64–88.

Menezes, Mary Noel. 1977. *British Policy towards the Amerindians in British Guiana, 1803–1873*. Oxford: Clarendon.

Overing, Joanna. 1989. "The Aesthetics of Production: The Sense of Community among the Cubeo and Piaroa." *Dialectical Anthropology* 14, no. 3: 159–75.

Overing Kaplan, Joanna. 1981. "Review Article: Amazonian Anthropology." *Journal of Latin American Studies* 13 (1): 151–64.

Penfield, Amy. 2017. "Dodged Debts and the Submissive Predator: Perspectives on Amazonian Relations of Dependence." *Journal of the Royal Anthropological Institute* 23 (2): 320–37.

Raleigh, Sir Walter. 1848. *The Discovery of the Large, Rich, and Beautiful Empire of Guiana*. Edited by Sir Robert H. Schomburgk. London: Hakluyt Society.

Rival, Laura. 1998. "Prey at the Center: Resistance and Marginality in Amazonia." In *Lilies of the Field: Marginal People Who Live for the Moment*, edited by Sophie Day, Evthymios Papataxiarchis, and Michael Stewart, 61–79. Boulder, Colo.: Westview Press.

Rivière, Peter. 1984. *Individual and Society in Guiana: A Comparative Study of Amerindian Social Organisation*. Cambridge: Cambridge University Press.

Rivière, Peter. 1995. *Absent-Minded Imperialism: Britain and the Expansion of Empire in Nineteenth-Century Brazil*. New York: Tauris Academic Studies.

Rivière, Peter. 1998. "From Science to Imperialism: Robert Schomburgk's Humanitarianism." *Archives of Natural History* 25:1–8.

Rivière, Peter. 2006. *The Guiana Travels of Robert Schomburgk, 1835–1844*. Vol. 1. London: Hakluyt Society.

Roller, Heather F. 2021. *Contact Strategies: Histories of Native Autonomy in Brazil.* Stanford, Calif.: Stanford University Press.

Salomon, Frank, and Stuart B. Schwartz. 1999. *The Cambridge History of the Native Peoples of the Americas,* vol. 3, parts 1–2, *South America.* Cambridge: Cambridge University Press.

Santilli, Paulo. 1994. *Fronteiras da República: História e política entre os Macuxi no vale do rio Branco.* São Paulo: NHII/USP and FAPESP.

Santilli, Paulo. 2014. Política e ritual: A faina missionária beneditina entre os Makuxi no Vale do Rio Branco. *Patrimônio e Memória* 10 (2): 35–61.

Santos-Granero, Fernando. 2007. "Of Fear and Friendship: Amazonian Sociality beyond Kinship and Affinity." *Journal of the Royal Anthropological Institute* 13 (1): 1–18.

Schomburgk, Robert. 1839a. "Indians of British Guiana." Extracts from the Papers and Proceedings of the Aborigines' Protection Society, no. 4, December. London: William Ball, Arnold.

Schomburgk, Robert. 1839b. "Kidnapping Indians on the Borders of British Guiana." Extracts from the Papers and Proceedings of the Aborigines' Protection Society, no. 2, June. London: William Ball, Arnold.

Schomburgk, Richard. (1847) 1922. *Richard Schomburgk's Travels in British Guiana, 1840–1844.* Vol. 1. Translated and edited by Walter E. Roth from *Travels in British Guiana during the Years 1840–1844.* Georgetown [British Guiana]: Daily Chronicle Office.

Schwartz, Stuart B. 2002. "Denounced by Lévi-Strauss." CLAH Luncheon Address. *Americas* 59 (1): 1–8.

Sommer, Barbara A. 2005. "Colony of the Sertão: Amazonian Expeditions and the Indian Slave Trade." *Americas* 61 (3): 401–28.

Stone, Erin. 2017. "Chasing 'Caribs': Defining Zones of Legal Indigenous Enslavement in the Circum-Caribbean." In *Slaving Zones: Cultural Identities, Ideologies, and Institutions in the Evolution of Global Slavery,* edited by Jeff Fynn-Paul and Damian Alan Pargas, 118–47. Leiden: Brill.

Sweet, David. 1981. "Francisca: Indian Slave." In *Struggle and Survival in Colonial America,* edited by David G. Sweet and Gary B. Nash, 274–91. Berkeley: University of California Press.

Taussig, Michael. 1987. *Shamanism, Colonialism, and the Wild Man: A Study in Terror and Healing.* Chicago: University of Chicago Press.

Van Valen, Gary. 2013. *Indigenous Agency in the Amazon: The Mojos in Liberal and Rubber-Boom Bolivia, 1842–1932.* Tucson: University of Arizona Press.

Vilaça, Aparecida. 2010. *Strange Enemies: Indigenous Agency and Scenes of Encounters in Amazonia.* Durham, N.C.: Duke University Press.

Vilaça, Aparecida. 2016. *Praying and Preying: Christianity in Indigenous Amazonia.* Berkeley: University of California Press.

Walker, Harry. 2012. "Demonic Trade: Debt, Materiality, and Agency in Amazonia." *Journal of the Royal Anthropological Institute* 18 (1): 140–59.

Whitaker, James Andrew. 2016a. "Amerindians in the Eighteenth Century Plantation System of the Guianas." *Tipití* 14 (1): 30–43.

Whitaker, James Andrew. 2016b. "Continuity and Perdurance among the Makushi in Guyana." PhD diss., Tulane University.

Whitaker, James Andrew. 2017. "Guns and Sorcery: Raiding, Trading, and Kanaima among the Makushi." *Tipití* 15 (2): 158–72.

Whitaker, James Andrew. 2018. "Imagination and the Poetics of Being and Becoming an Other in Amazonia." *Anthropology of Consciousness* 29 (1): 120–31.

Whitaker, James Andrew. 2020. "Strategic Alliance and the Plantationocene among the Makushi in Guyana." *Social Anthropology* 28 (4): 881–96.

Whitaker, James Andrew. 2021. "Sorcery and Well-Being: Bodily Transformation at Beckeranta." *Anthropology and Medicine* 28 (1): 78–93.

Whitaker, James Andrew. 2024. "Shamanic Alliance in the Touristic Borderzone: Strategic Hospitality and Ontology at Surama Eco-Lodge in Guyana." *Journal of Latin American and Caribbean Anthropology* 29 (1): 38–49.

Whitaker, James Andrew. 2025. *The Shamanism of Eco-Tourism: History and Ontology among the Makushi in Guyana.* Cambridge: Cambridge University Press.

Whitehead, Neil L. 1988. *Lords of the Tiger Spirit: A History of the Caribs in Colonial Venezuela and Guyana, 1498–1820.* Dordrecht: Foris.

Williams, James. 1932. *Grammar, Notes, and Vocabulary of the Language of the Makuchi Indians of Guiana.* St. Gabriel-Modling, Austria: Verlag der Internationalen Zeitschrift.

Afterword

Alliances and Partnerships Today

APARECIDA VILAÇA

TRANSLATED BY CAMILA FERREIRA MARINELLI

To what extent, and in what ways, did the Indigenous peoples of South America act as active agents in their encounters with European invaders during colonial times? This is the central question that this edited volume seeks to address, challenging historiographical accounts that often obscure Indigenous agency by focusing predominantly on the colonizers' perspective.

Drawing on original letters, historical documents, and ethnographic research with contemporary Indigenous peoples who preserve the history of their ancestors, the authors of the chapters in this book reveal the diverse strategies developed by Indigenous peoples for their survival. These strategies range from direct partnerships with Europeans—facilitating, for example, the slave trade in exchange for material benefits—to alliances with neighboring Indigenous groups aimed at either opposing or collaborating with the Europeans. In other words, the European invasion required significant changes in local politics, involving various Indigenous peoples who reconfigured their relationships to confront these strange and powerful beings who had entered their territories.

The fact that Indigenous peoples developed strategies to manage their interactions with Europeans did not diminish the severity of the massacres perpetrated by the invaders. Although fewer in number, the Europeans possessed powerful weapons—not only guns but also unfamiliar viruses and bacteria, which were perhaps even more lethal—that caused devastating epidemics and decimated entire populations. Estimates suggest that in the first centuries of the invasion, precisely the period primarily addressed in the chapters of this book, the Indigenous population was reduced to approximately 10 percent of its original size.

Unfortunately, these armed and epidemiological massacres continued during the following centuries and persist to this day, as uncontacted Indigenous peoples (or those in voluntary isolation) find themselves under increasing pressure from land grabbers, loggers, and miners encroaching on their territories. Moreover, these threats are compounded by supposed benefactors, such as evangelical missionaries who now reside in or near many Indigenous villages. These missionaries engage in what could be described as cultural predation, harshly criticizing Indigenous ways of life, myths, and rituals, which often leads to the abandonment of these traditions in favor of Christian practices and morality.

Missionaries and Christianity

Relations between Indigenous peoples and missionaries is a central theme in several chapters of this book, particularly in the chapters by Loureiro Dias, Van Valen, and Whitaker, coincidentally aligning with many years of my research conducted among the Wari' people. The Wari' speak a language from the Txpakura family and inhabit the western region of Rondônia, Brazil, near the Bolivian border. This area is not far from the Mojos region, where relations between local Indigenous people and Jesuit missionaries is analyzed by Van Valen. Until the mid-twentieth century, the Wari' lived without any peaceful contact with the white (the Portuguese word Wari' use for non-Indigenous people) settlers who had arrived in the region at the beginning of that century to extract rubber. Indigenous people were perceived as obstacles to this extractivism, which led to organized and armed massacres aimed at exterminating entire villages. This in turn provoked retaliatory attacks by the Indigenous population against the settlers. Given the tense local situation, the Brazilian government collaborated with Catholic and evangelical missionaries to undertake what they termed "pacification."

As discussed in several chapters of this book, Europeans exploited Indigenous peoples' interests in unfamiliar material objects, such as knives, metal tools, mirrors, and beads, to entice them into settling near their newly established homes and camps. Once these Europeans had acquired a basic knowledge of the local Indigenous language, they initiated the process of religious catechism, which was based on an explicit critique of traditional Indigenous knowledge. Amid epidemics that ravaged Indigenous villages, the missionaries, armed with antibiotics (by the 1960s), came to be perceived as powerful beings, and the God they introduced was seen as the source of all power.

Can it be said, as Father Anchieta claimed in his sixteenth-century letters, and as evangelical missionaries continue to assert today, that religious conversion and partnership with missionaries was a choice solely made by the Indigenous peoples? This interpretation seems overly simplistic. In the immediate aftermath of European (and white in general) invasions—regardless of the century—Indigenous populations found themselves disoriented and afflicted by diseases that their shamans were unable to cure. The missionaries arrived offering protection from further massacres, as well as (in more recent times) effective medicines, which seemed to confirm their alliance with an apparently all-powerful divine being. In these circumstances, the Indigenous people had little choice but to attempt to establish some form of partnership with these invaders.

This does not imply, however, that Indigenous people passively accepted these partnerships. Rather, they often took advantage of them to achieve their own objectives, engaging in strategic actions that frequently went unnoticed by the Europeans, whose accounts express surprise at seeing shamans, not long after the invasion, mimicking the gestures and words of the priests during Mass. This mimicry was not merely imitative but a deliberate attempt to capture European techniques of communication with spiritual beings, and to extend the universe of allied spirits to include the Christian Trinity. In the case of the Wari', as I have analyzed in my monograph on the subject (Vilaça 2016), the Christian God—particularly through the creation mythology narrated in Genesis, the first book translated by the missionaries—became an important ally in the process of dissociating animals believed to be responsible for diseases and deaths. In this mythology, God emerges as the universal creator, who (in this foundational act) separates humans from animals and other beings of nature, thus inaugurating the very concept of nature. By positioning humans as predators and transforming animals into mere prey, the Wari' found themselves freed from dietary taboos related to the risks of counter-predation by animals (who had previously been considered subjects). From this perspective, and without ignoring the extreme conditions in which they found themselves, conversion can be seen as a strategic act aimed at achieving objectives consistent with Indigenous interests, although these were unknown to the missionaries.

As with the peoples of the Mojos in Bolivia, analyzed by Van Valen, these partnerships with missionaries were arguably also a means of becoming human. The missionaries and their God served as mediators in a relationship with spirits that had nothing to do with Christianity but in their attacks transformed Indigenous people into prey. In other words, the alliances and partnerships encouraged by the arrival of the Europeans involved not only those we (urban Euro-Americans) consider human but also other beings, spirits, and animals. To fully understand agency within the Indigenous worldview, one must consider the extended and inclusive concept of humanity that Indigenous peoples hold.

Misunderstandings

This brings us to the issue of misunderstandings, a topic particularly explored by Lane. Misunderstandings arise from actions taken by each side involved in the encounter, driven by entirely different motives and often grounded in divergent ontological principles. The outcomes of these simultaneous actions can vary. They might lead to harmonious relationships and shared objectives. Or they might result in disruptive conflicts that cause the relationship to break down. In some cases, the outcome could be a mix of both, considering the different contexts and times. An example of this is the inconstancy often reported in Indigenous conversion, as observed by various missionaries in both historical and contemporary contexts. For a time, the converted Indigenous people might behave as exemplary believers only to later revert to what the missionaries refer to as "worldly practices," such as polygamy and beliefs in spirits and shamans (Viveiros de Castro 2004, 2011). The positive reception of Captain Cook by the Hawaiians, as analyzed by Marshall Sahlins (1981), is another emblematic example. It illustrates an apparent convergence of perspectives that ultimately revealed themselves to be divergent, leading, in this case, to the European's murder.

Another example of this can be seen in the great interest shown by Wari' people of the OroNao' subgroup, who had lived in isolation for approximately fifty years, in participating in an expedition organized to pacify other subgroups. From the perspective of the non-Indigenous pacification agents, the eagerness of OroNao' to join the boat heading upriver was interpreted as an indication of Wari' understanding— that specific subgroup having been in peaceful contact with whites for around five years—of the importance of reuniting their relatives and ending the violent acts occurring in the region. For the Wari' people involved, however, the boat represented merely a means to reconnect with long-separated kin and to resume intragroup rituals and marriages. In this instance, the divergence of objectives did not obstruct the action. Both sides ultimately achieved their desired outcomes. I suspect, however, that the Indigenous people, accustomed to navigating differing perspectives and viewing misunderstandings as a relational possibility, strategically channeled the interests of the whites to their advantage, while the latter believed they were in control of the situation. It appears that these strategic actions by the Wari', which were subtle and grounded in principles unfamiliar to those who recorded the history, often went unnoticed (Vilaça 2010; see also Whitaker 2025).

Education and Contemporary Partnerships

I conclude by addressing some contemporary alliances and partnerships, both among Indigenous peoples themselves and between them and whites. Despite ongoing intense pressure on their territories and bodies, with invasions and massacres still occurring daily, Indigenous communities in South America and beyond have learned to resist with new tools. They have formed strategic alliances with environmentalists, anthropologists, and educators, from whom they have learned to engage in what they term "white politics" (Moura and Estellita-Lins 2021). Indigenous peoples have become councilors, deputies, ministers, mayors, and even presidents, as exemplified by Evo Morales in Bolivia.

Paradoxically, in some South American countries, this movement for Indigenous self-determination began during the turbulent period of national dictatorships, under the auspices of the Catholic Church, which was revitalized after the Second Vatican Council (1962–64) and the subsequent Medellín Conference (1968). In Brazil, the ecclesiastic base communities (*comunidades eclesiais de base*), organized around local parishes, became the birthplace of significant activism, whose efforts in favor of Indigenous people and other minorities often served as a platform for opposing the dictatorial regime (see Orta 2004). The focus on Indigenous societies was not limited to paternalistic protection but extended to the political mobilization of Indigenous people, enabling them to become protagonists in the fight for their rights. Numerous Indigenous associations emerged under the Catholic Church's guidance. Simultaneously, literacy schools were introduced in villages, equipping Indigenous people with the skills to read, produce documents, and, through mathematics education, engage in commercial relations with neighboring whites on more equitable terms.

Following the significant milestone of recognizing Indigenous rights in the Brazilian Constitution of 1988, the Law of Guidelines and Bases for Education (Lei de Diretrizes e Bases da Educação) was enacted in 1996, guaranteeing Indigenous people the right to an education aligned with their cultural principles. Consequently, programs for training Indigenous teachers were established at both the secondary and university levels. In parallel, various public universities in Brazil have opened, through affirmative action, places for Indigenous students in their regular and postgraduate courses. Today, as a result of these training programs, various Indigenous peoples in Brazil, as well as in neighboring countries, have their own Native anthropologists, lawyers, doctors, and other professionals.

This lengthy digression on Indigenous rights and the participation of Indigenous people in formal education highlights what I believe to be one of the primary contemporary arenas for the formation of alliances and partnerships, both among Indigenous peoples and between them and non-Indigenous groups. Multiethnic schools and universities have enabled the establishment of alliances between Indigenous peoples who previously had little contact with each other and who now unite in their common struggle. Regarding whites, they now find themselves working alongside Indigenous people who are well versed in the same disciplines they studied and capable of bringing arguments in tune with the highly valued Western sciences. As one might expect, however, this does not mean that the Indigenous perspective is absent from these arguments or that miscommunication has disappeared.

In nearly a decade of research concerning Indigenous schools and university courses, I have observed what could be called a properly Indigenous way of forming partnerships in the educational field. Generally, non-Indigenous teachers, even those well intentioned and well trained in so-called intercultural education, which presupposes an equal relationship between Indigenous knowledge and Western science, establish a marked hierarchy between these forms of knowledge. They often begin lessons by writing or drawing on the board about principles of their own science, only then asking Indigenous students what their culture thinks about it. Indigenous perspectives are treated as culturally situated interpretations of the scientific perspective, which is naturally seen as representing reality. For example, the heliocentric solar system is drawn on the board, after which Indigenous students are asked to share their myths that say the sun is a person or to explain their culture's perspective on the sun revolving around the Earth. Similarly, the initial numbers of the arabic numeral system are displayed on the board with their respective names in Portuguese, followed by questions about how they are named in the different Indigenous cultures represented in the classroom. It does not occur to the teachers that many cultures in South America do not have a numerical system beyond 2 or 3 (see Vilaça 2019, 2020, 2021). Faced with the teachers' insistence that Indigenous students find traditional names for the numbers, even if it requires what they call research with the elders, Indigenous students often feel compelled to invent names for numbers with which they were previously unfamiliar. Thus, a hierarchy is established within an otherwise friendly environment that ostensibly promotes the equivalence of knowledges.

What is most intriguing, however, is that I have never seen an Indigenous student contest the validity of academic knowledge. From the teachers' perspective, this is viewed as recognition of the truth that they present, a realization not unlike that of missionaries who understood (and often still understand) conversion as Indigenous peoples' acknowledgment of the existence of their God. From my perspective, this is not the case, nor is it due to fear of whites or reluctance to speak up in class. The Indigenous student's primary objective in attending school is to learn about the world of whites and their sciences, as well as to open up new opportunities for work as teachers in village schools. They are not there to challenge whites with their own knowledge or science. Instead, they quietly participate in the theater presented to them about the value of their culture. It is the same type of strategy employed in many other situations involving encounters with whites, including missionaries. Silently and discreetly, they guide the actions toward their own objectives.

This is not to suggest that such interactions do not have consequences. School and university life have the effect of producing an objectification of cultures that members never thought of as such. Through the eyes of whites, Indigenous people have become "conscious" of their culture, which has a positive political effect, as it allows them to select cultural aspects that most affect whites who are in political decision-making spheres concerning their territories and future. They create what Carneiro da Cunha (2009) calls "culture with quotes," which is a concept that exists within the context of interethnic relations, both with whites and between different Indigenous people. On the other hand, however, as Carneiro da Cunha demonstrates, this "culture with quotes" ultimately affects the culture itself, leading sometimes to the potential impoverishment of traditional practices and notions.

In conclusion, as the chapters of this book demonstrate, although Indigenous agency in interethnic encounters is evident, regardless of the period considered, Indigenous peoples invariably end up losing—whether in terms of population through armed or epidemiological massacres, or culturally, as they undergo radical transformations in their ways of life. The new external allies, especially teachers and contemporary Catholic missionaries, are weaker versions of the old agents who once imposed their thoughts and behaviors on them. These allies are essential today, however, enabling Indigenous peoples to navigate this unfamiliar world that has been imposed on them, protecting themselves as best as possible from more severe harm.

References

Carneiro da Cunha, Manuela, ed. 2009. *Cultura com aspas e outros ensaios*. São Paulo: Cosac Naify.

Orta, Andrew. 2004. *Catechizing Culture: Missionaries, Aymara, and the "New Evangelization"*. New York: Columbia University Press.

Sahlins, Marshall. 1981. *Historical Metaphors and Mythical Realities: Structure in the Early History of the Sandwich Islands Kingdom*. Ann Arbor: University of Michigan Press.

Silva, Marcelo Moura, and Carlos Estellita-Lins. 2021. "A *xawara* e os mortos: Os Yanomami, luto e luta na pandemia da Covid-19." *Horizontes Antropológicos* 27 (59): 267–85.

Vilaça, Aparecida. 2010. *Strange Enemies: Indigenous Agency and Scenes of Encounters in Amazonia*. Durham, N.C.: Duke University Press.

Vilaça, Aparecida. 2016. *Praying and Preying: Christianity in Indigenous Amazonia*. Berkeley: University of California Press.

Vilaça, Aparecida. 2019. "Christianity + Schooling on Nature versus Culture in Amazonia." *Tipití* 16 (2): 215–34.

Vilaça, Aparecida. 2020. "Inventing Nature: Christianity and Science in Indigenous Amazonia." In *Science in the Forest, Science in the Past*, edited by Geoffrey E. R. Lloyd and Aparecida Vilaça, 15–41. Chicago: HAU Books.

Vilaça, Aparecida. 2021. "A Pagan Arithmetic: Unstable Sets in Indigenous Amazonia." *Interdisciplinary Science Reviews* 46 (3): 304–24.

Viveiros de Castro, Eduardo. 2004. "Perspectival Anthropology and the Method of Controlled Equivocation." *Tipití* 2 (1): 3–22.

Viveiros de Castro, Eduardo. 2011. *The Inconstancy of the Indian Soul: The Encounter of Catholics and Cannibals in 16th-Century Brazil*. Chicago: Prickly Paradigm.

Whitaker, James Andrew. 2025. *The Shamanism of Eco-Tourism: History and Ontology among the Makushi in Guyana*. Cambridge: Cambridge University Press.

Contributors

Marta Amoroso is a professor of anthropology at the University of São Paulo and a founding researcher at the Center for the History of Indigenous Peoples and Indigenism and at the Center for Amerindian Studies at the University of São Paulo. Her research focuses on anthropological theory and Amerindian ethnology with an emphasis on the history of Indigenous peoples in South America, Amerindian territories, and interspecific relations in Amazonia. She works with Mura groups in the central Amazon. She is the author of *Terra de índio: Imagens em aldeamentos do Império* (Editora Terceiro Nome, 2019), *Paisagens ameríndias: Lugares, circuitos e modos de vida na Amazônia*, with Gilton Mendes dos Santos (Editora Terceiro Nome, 2013), and *Vozes vegetais: Diversidade, resistências e histórias da floresta*, with Cabral de Oliveira et al. (Ubu Editora, 2020).

Elisa Frühauf Garcia is a professor of Latin American colonial history at the Fluminense Federal University, a research productivity fellow at the Brazilian National Council for Scientific and Technological Development (CNPq), and a researcher at the Carlos Chagas Filho Foundation for Research Support of the State of Rio de Janeiro. Her research focuses on Indigenous peoples in the early modern period. In particular, she uses a long-term approach, which articulates history, heritage, and uses of the past, to examine the relationships between Indigenous women and

European men in Brazil during the sixteenth and early seventeenth centuries. She is the author of *As diversas formas de ser índio: Políticas indígenas e políticas indigenistas no extremo sul da América portuguesa* (Arquivo Nacional, 2009). She is co-editor of *Mulheres do Mundo Atlântico: Gênero e condição feminina da época moderna à contemporaneidade*, with Georgina Santos (Fino Traço, 2021).

Mark Harris is a professor of historical anthropology and head of the School of Philosophical, Historical, and Indigenous Studies at Monash University and an honorary professorial research fellow at the University of St Andrews. His research focuses on the Brazilian Amazon and what makes it a place of global historical and anthropological significance. His wider interests include ethnohistory, environmental anthropology, and knowledge and methodology of the social sciences. He is the author of *Life on the Amazon: An Anthropology of a Brazilian Peasant Village* (Oxford, 2000), *Rebellion on the Amazon: The Cabanagem, Race, and Popular Culture in the North of Brazil, 1798–1840* (Cambridge, 2010), and *The Making of Some Brazilian Amazonian Societies* (forthcoming from Cambridge). He is the editor of *Ways of Knowing: New Approaches in the Anthropology of Knowledge and Learning* (Berghahn, 2007). He is the co-editor of *Reflections on Imagination: Human Capacity and Ethnographic Method*, with Nigel Rapport (Routledge, 2015), and *Delta Life: New Approaches to More-than-Human Dynamics at Water's Edge*, with Franz Krause (Berghahn, 2021).

Kris Lane holds the France V. Scholes Chair in Colonial Latin American History at Tulane University. His research focuses on the history of the Andes region in South America, lately in global perspective. Lane's work treats mineral extraction and mineral-related conflicts, along with the history of piracy. He is the author of *Basques and Vicuñas at the Mouth of Hell* (University of Nevada Press, 2024), *Pandemic in Potosí* (Penn State Press, 2021), *Potosí: The Silver City that Changed the World* (University of California Press, 2019), *Pillaging the Empire: Piracy in the Americas, 1500–1750* (Routledge, 2015), *Colour of Paradise: The Emerald in the Age of Gunpowder Empires* (Yale, 2010), and *Quito 1599: City and Colony in Transition* (University of New Mexico Press, 2002). He is the co-author of *Latin America in Colonial Times*, with Matthew Restall (Cambridge

University Press, 2015), and *Piracy in the Early Modern Era*, with Arne Bialuschewski (Hackett, 2019).

Camila Loureiro Dias is a professor of history at the University of Campinas, a collaborating researcher at the Center for Amerindian Studies at the University of São Paulo, and a member of the Center for Research in Indigenous Ethnology at the University of Campinas. Her research focuses on relationships between Indigenous peoples and the state during the colonial period and in contemporary Brazil with a particular emphasis on the Amazon region. She is co-editor of *Os Índios na Constitution*, with Artionka Capiberibe (Ateliê, 2019).

Cecilia McCallum is a professor of anthropology at the Federal University of Bahia and a professorial fellow at the University of St Andrews. Her research focuses on Amerindian studies and on Brazil in urban and rural contexts with an emphasis on the anthropology of gender, kinship, personhood, sociality, race, health, and reproduction. She is the author of *Gender and Sociality in Amazonia* (Routledge, 2003). She is co-editor of *The Cambridge Handbook for the Anthropology of Gender and Sexuality*, with Silvia Posocco and Martin Fotta (Cambridge University Press, 2023).

Gary Van Valen is a professor of history at the University of West Georgia. His research centers on ethnohistory and cultural contact in Bolivia and New Mexico. He is the author of *Indigenous Agency in the Amazon: The Mojos in Liberal and Rubber-Boom Bolivia, 1842–1932* (University of Arizona Press, 2013), which won the American Society for Ethnohistory's Erminie Wheeler-Voegelin Book Award.

Aparecida Vilaça is a professor of social anthropology at the Museu Nacional at the Federal University of Rio de Janeiro. Her research focuses on sociocultural changes among Indigenous peoples in Brazil with an emphasis on conversion to Christianity, schooling, and science. She has carried out ethnographic research among the Wari' people in southwestern Amazonia for over three decades. She is the author of *Strange Enemies: Indigenous Agency and Scenes of Encounters in Amazonia* (Duke University Press, 2010), *Praying and Preying: Christianity in Indigenous*

Amazonia (University of California Press, 2016), and *Paletó and Me: Memories of my Indigenous Father* (Stanford University Press, 2021). She is the co-author of *Of Jaguars and Butterflies: Metalogues on Issues of Anthropology and Philosophy*, with Geoffrey Lloyd (Berghahn, 2023). She is the co-editor of *Science in the Forest, Science in the Past*, with Geoffrey Lloyd (HAU Books, 2020), and *Science in the Forest, Science in the Past: Further Interdisciplinary Explorations*, with Willard McCarty and Geoffrey Lloyd (Routledge, 2022).

James Andrew Whitaker is an assistant professor of anthropology at the University of Southern Mississippi and an honorary research fellow at the University of St Andrews. His research focuses on historical anthropology, historical ecology, and ontologies in lowland South America. He has worked with Makushi and Akawaio people in Guyana. He is the author of *The Shamanism of Eco-Tourism: History and Ontology among the Makushi in Guyana* (Cambridge University Press, 2025). He is co-editor of *Climatic and Ecological Change in the Americas: A Perspective from Historical Ecology*, with Chelsea Geralda Armstrong and Guillaume Odonne (Routledge, 2023), and *Sorcery in Amazonia: A Comparative Exploration of Magical Assault*, with Matthias Lewy and Tarryl Janik (Ibero-Amerikanisches Institut, 2025).

Index

Note: Page numbers in *italics* refer to illustrative matter.